GET YOUR JUMBO JET OUT OF MY AiRPORT

Random Notes For AC/DC Obsessives

by

Howard Johnson

First published 1999 by The Black Book Company Ltd, Box 2030, Pewsey, SN9 5QZ, United Kingdom

ISBN 1-902799-01-1

A CIP catalogue for this book is available from the British Library

Design by Keith Drummond
Reprographics by Rival Colour
Cover by David Black

Black Book Company Ltd
"Cos it ain't no fun waiting round to be a millionaire"

About The Author

Howard Johnson works as Managing Editor of Football365, the only online football newspaper and website (you can find it at www.football365.co.uk). His taste in football clubs is as 'eclectic' as his preferred music, having been an avid supporter of Manchester City since getting a letter printed in the club programme, aged 11 (prize, two tickets). When not discussing the finer details of City's greatest ever side, he also contributes to a variety of magazines, including *Q, Sky TV Guide, ZM* and *New Woman*.

During his 20 years as a journalist Howard has worked for countless magazines, including *Kerrang!*, *MoJo, Total Sport, FHM, 442, Select, Sounds* and *GQ Active*. He has also written for the *Daily Telegraph*. Over the years he has heard John Lydon lie about loving Van Halen, Black Sabbath's Tony Iommi recommend apricot crumble as a dessert classic and countless footballers saying nothing much at all. He has met all of the Spice Girls and helped write their book "for the money". He liked Sporty best. His finest experience to date has been writing British Lions rugby captain Martin Johnson's diary of the successful 1997 tour to South Africa. The rugby player is not an AC/DC fan.

These days he lives in the suburban haven of Bushey, Herts with his wife, child and cat. His wife and cat leave the room whenever AC/DC is played.

His child (age nine months) seems only marginally more impressed.

FOREWORD

Most books about music are either full of chin-scratching, navel-contemplating, ever-so-worthy prose or bash-it-out-for-the-money scribble. I know about the former, because I've given up trying to wade through their like too many times to mention. I know about the latter because, strapped for cash and knowing that principles don't pay the bills, I foolishly did one once. Never again. Anything's better than the torture of churning out stuff you don't care about. If nothing else, now that this book's finished I know that it falls into neither of these soulless categories.

I once saw a TV interview with Black Sabbath's Tony Iommi where, in answer to a question about why they'd got Ronnie Dio back in the band again, the moustachioed Brummie very reasonably asserted "Because we wanted to." It seemed to me the most logical reason in the world for doing something. And it still seems so now. So… I wrote this book because I wanted to.

I'm not the world's biggest AC/DC fan. I don't know the band personally. And they've written too many rotten songs to be considered my favourite ever group. But they have a hold over me – and many millions of others – that I've found impossible to shake in 20 years. At their best – that's anything up to 'Back In Black' – they're the most powerful, infectious, straight-from-the-heart rock'n'roll band there ever was. And the funniest. At their worst they're utterly clueless, but let's not dwell on that just now, eh? This book acknowledges the group's faults, but plays to their many strengths; their single-mindedness, their desire not to be part of the crowd, their purity of spirit, their humour… and yes, their punctuality. Bon Scott was as charismatic a rock frontman as there has ever been, Malcolm Young still is the greatest rhythm player in rock. Reasons enough to want to listen to them for ever, yes. But to write a book about them? Not so sure. So why *have* I written one, exactly?

Because I wanted to, of course. But maybe there's something more tangible that I can put my finger on as well. Maybe this is the answer. AC/DC do publicity under duress. They do it with the same enthusiasm with which I go to the dentist. So if you're expecting a (cue TV voice-over) "behind the scenes look, up close and personal, at one of the world's greatest rock bands", then forget it. I never even contacted the band to see if they were interested in the project. Truthfully, I didn't really want them involved, because no matter how nice they would've been, they would eventually have wanted control over what went in. And that couldn't be allowed to happen. Why? Because at the end of the day this book is about me, I'm afraid. Not just me, though, but also the millions around the world like me. It's a book about how we see AC/DC. A book about people who have locked into something in AC/DC that touches a raw nerve, that sets off some unexpected devotion.

So while this book is full of interesting, quirky, detailed stuff about the band themselves – you even get numerous interviews with the members for your money – it's really *for* and *about* the fans. There's some rhyme or reason for what's gone in it, and where and also why. But not that much. Like the title says, this book is random notes for AC/DC obsessives. If you don't have a love for the band, no matter what crooked form it may take, then this book is not for you. And as a sticker on a certain album once said, you might as well 'f**k off and listen to something in the new age section.' There will be mistakes in it, but you'll have to forgive me them. For what is such an intensely private band I've amazed myself about what it was possible to dig up. To that end my heartfelt thanks go to a huge number of people who have helped with stories, information and anecdotes. I couldn't have done this without Thomas Schade in particular, and his mine of info, *The Daily Dirt*, which he kindly let me plunder. But there were many others who have helped in large or small ways. My sincere thanks go to Rod Vincent, Enrique Diaz Galvez, Andrew Shal, Glenn Robertson, Gary Campbell, Phil Alexander, Diamond Dave, Pete Vukovic, Sean Kilkenney, Bill Voccia, Smari Josepsson, Nikki Goff, Clayton

Lovell, Paul Cadden, Marco Weber, Michael Jones, Steve Colwill and Kaz Helagan. They are at the heart of this effort.

Needless to say many of my personal friends were also invaluable, both with their time and with their enthusiasm for the project. I am deeply indebted to Paul 'Gooner' Elliott for constant 'eavy metal banter, to Jim 'John' Parsons for the VH1 gubbins and to Dante Bonutto for his insight into the band. Thanks mates.

You will be bored of my thanks list by now, but they're really not for the readers, are they? So at the risk of sounding selfish, thanks are also due to the following people:

Dave Henderson, whose enthusiasm and brilliance means there's a book publishing company to publish this effort in the first place; Gary Perry and Nick Clode, the best Rivals in the business; Keith Drummond 'Bass'. The King of Designers.

Emma, Lewis and Maia; Emma and Alice; My mate and mentor Danny Kelly; Steve 'Am I Alone In Thinking This Is Shit?' Anglesey; Johno and Kay; Andrew, Julie, Chili and Pepper; John Aizlewood; Mark, Carolyn, Magali and Adam Johnson; Stan and Moirya Brett; Ravy Wavy Gravy Davey and Jill Alder; Kevin Cummins; John and Eileen; Philip Cornwall; Maggie, Keith, Helen and Beth Crockett; Paul Meredith 'Meredew'; Warren, Claire, Ruby and Lewis Hawke; Martin Sharrocks; Robert and Nicola Swift; Colin, Sue, Hannah and Connor Smith; 'Handsome' Eddie Taylor.

And last but not least, I dedicate this book to Louise and Elliott Johnson. They know I love them more than anything... even Australian rock bands!

I enjoyed writing this.
Hope you enjoy reading it.

Howard Johnson, Bushey, 1999

GET YOUR JUMBO JET OUT OF MY AIRPORT
THE RUNNiNG ORDER

continued over...

CHAPTER SiX

FOR THOSE ABOUT TO WRITE
A career in journalism

Plus!
Thomas Schade Interview – On the brilliant *Daily Dirt* fanzine
Mike Jones on his DC tour of Oz
Paul Elliott Interview – The *Kerrang!* journalist on why DC are best
Black Sabbath and the flick knife incident
Al Narvaez on why DC beats working at Taco Bell
DC Rarities – Some you may not know

CHAPTER SEVEN

VIDEO NASTIES
University Dope Smokers' Club

Plus!
The Fans' Forum On DC
AC/DC line-ups
Andrew J. Shal on his expensive hobby
Jack Bonny's Collector's Corner
VH1 producer Jim Parsons on an amazing live performance
Kerrang! editor Phil Alexander Interview – Why DC are so important

CHAPTER EiGHT

DAWN TO DUSK
Joining a band

Plus!
Bill Vocchia Interview – On tribute band Ballbreaker
DC Superfan Gary Campbell
Brian Johnson Interview
Undercover – Tribute albums, bands and cover versions
'Diamond Dave' Interview – "My Beano obsession!"

CHAPTER NiNE

A MEETING OF (TINY) MINDS
Interviewing the group

Plus!
Chris Slade – the man who was 'too good'.
Dante Bonutto Interview – On working with the band
Angus Young Interview – *Kerrang!* 1990
Paul Cadden on appearing in a DC video
Reviews

CHAPTER TEN

THE MORE THINGS CHANGE
It was 20 years ago today

Plus!
Phil Rudd Interview – the life of Riley
Fan Meets Band – what *you* would ask Angus
In Praise Of Brian
Madrid Rocks!
Smarri Josepsson on a shared SG obsession
AC/DC Quiz

Chapter One

iN THE BEGiNNiNG

My mum, bless her, was not one to strike the fear of God into you. She was a big woman, but she didn't throw her weight around. She was much more subtle than that. She got me and my brother to do what she wanted by one of two methods. Either she would make us feel sorry for her, which looking back on it displayed extraordinary powers of manipulation considering Mark and I were 16 and 14 respectively and had yet to really wrestle with the meaning of the word 'sensitivity'. Or alternatively she would threaten us with telling our dad about all of our full-of-ourselves teenage stroppiness when he got home. That was usually at the end of the week, because dad was a rep at the time and he was away a lot. And if you think that threatening two teenage boys with telling tales on them to their old man was hardly going to put the wind up us, well let's just say that's most likely because you don't know my dad.

I can't really remember which tactic she employed on this particular occasion when she and I locked horns, whether she'd appealed to my better nature or sworn to wreak great and terrible vengeance if I didn't toe the line, but I'd decided long before the night in question that this time she would be ignored. I was prepared to deal with either the hurt look on her face or the more general hurt I'd feel when my dad got hold of me. Whichever way it panned out I was going to do it, whether she liked it or not. Do what? I was going to go out wearing my schoolboy uniform, that's what.

Bizarre, isn't it? Most kids spend half their lives trying any excuse not to put the dreaded gear on and there I was having to defy my mother on this daft issue. I actually *wanted* to be wearing my uniform for once. Couldn't wait, in fact. You'd have thought the old dear would have been delighted. Until you know exactly why I wanted to put on the crisp cotton shirt with the too-stiff neck, the blazer with those odd leather patches on the elbows to stop its over-zealous occupant from wearing the material away and the cap that was

always, always too small. The reason was simple. AC/DC were in town.

I'D FIRST HEARD ABOUT this rock group called AC/DC through my brother Mark. Two years older and always two years ahead of my musical game, that was him. When I was 10 and nicking hooped socks off Altrincham market to show my affection for the Bay City Rollers, he was listening to Strawbs' 'Part Of The Union'. When I was 12 and thinking Queen was the most radical rock thing anyone had ever heard (even though I never quite associated the band name with Freddie Mercury's flamboyant antics) he was bringing home 'Tarkus' by ELP and 'Wish You Were Here' by Pink Floyd. I couldn't understand any of that stuff at all, too fiddly and intricate and boring. When I was 14, though – in 1978 – something must have happened to my 16-year-old brother. Instead of thinking it was cool to treat music like an intelligence test, one day he pitched up with an album that was the complete antithesis of the music all those student wanker bands he'd been listening to were making. He'd bought 'If You Want Blood…' by a band called AC/DC, though for the life of me I can't remember why. But once the needle of our portable mono record player had hit the groove of the first track, I was transfixed.

Well that's not quite true. I think I'd actually developed a liking for the band from the minute I'd clapped my teenage eyes on that album cover. On the front was an image which made up in memorability what it lacked in finesse. A guitarist dressed in school uniform was mugging furiously as the neck of his guitar poked straight out of his chest, spewing rivers of 'blood' all over his white school shirt. The singer, meanwhile, leered over the guitarist's shoulder, apparently oblivious to his mate's distress and far more interested in giving good face to camera to prove that he was both mad as a hatter and horny as hell. If I saw the cover for the first time today, no doubt I'd scoff at it using every ounce of my 34-year-old maturity and dismiss the band as nothing more than a bunch of brain-dead gumbies. At the time I'm pleased to announce I thought it was cool as fuck.

The music contained on the vinyl inside was, truthfully, like nothing I'd ever heard, which in retrospect had a lot more to do with the fact that I hadn't had much of a musical education to speak of than any genius the band had for innovation. "Listen to this," my brother said excitedly as he slid the vinyl out of the white inner sleeve, blew on the shiny black plastic to dislodge any stray bits of fluff and peered at the label to work out which side was which. With side two facing upwards he slipped the record over the small cylinder sticking up in the middle of the player, then moved one hand underneath to release the catch that let records slip down one at a time if you were going for that multiple disc-spinning thing. *We* never did that. It wasn't cool. The latest hi-fis didn't even have that facility – you could only play one LP at a time – so we were damned if we were going to stoop that low. Mark picked the arm of the record player up in his hand and gently placed it at the outer ring of the album, then we both watched as the needle quickly caught the groove and we heard that familiar crackling sound, the hint that music was on its way.

It didn't take long. First the whistling and hollering and stomping and shouting of what sounded like an unruly but good-natured mob, then the clearly audible chant of 'Angus… Angus', then the introduction of a huge guitar riff, then the syncopation of the two elements of crowd and band together. "Wanna tell you a story, 'bout a woman I know"…

I THINK IT WAS AC/DC's energy, their relentless, driving force and their easy-to-understand don't-give-a-fuckery that made them so appealing to me. The other rock bands I'd discovered were fine and dandy, but when I thought about it, that's exactly what many of them were – dandyish. Airy-fairy and dealing in the currency of fantasy. That was OK in small doses, but AC/DC absolutely reeked of something those other bands did not. They reeked of authenticity. Something in their records made you believe absolutely that this group was for real. They were coarse and bombastic if you wanted to see it that way, but they were also as pure as you please in terms of their intent. I learnt a phrase later in life that absolutely summed up AC/DC at that time. They weren't making music because they wanted to. At that point in time they were doing it because they *had* to. 'If You Want Blood...' was full of music which was absolutely joyous in its simplicity, like it had mainlined its way straight into your soul. The album connected instantly and while my intellect was aware that the riffs were somewhat repetitive and the song structures were pretty basic, my emotions responded in a second. I loved this music.

No matter how much you don't want it to happen, eventually you end up forgetting just how exciting those first musical discoveries can be. As you get older it's as if your eyes don't see colours as vividly, your nose doesn't smell with quite the same strength and your ears

That's me, aged 15, trying hard to grow my hair. Nice fringe!

"Within twelve months of buying 'Highway To Hell' i'd be half-starving myself, saving the school dinner money my mum had given me to buy other releases."

don't hook the sounds you hear so directly to your emotions any more. That's why people will always say 'Well, it was better in my day.' When you're young your antennae, your receptors, are switched to stun and they dull as you get older. But those first records, even more than first loves, stay as packed with emotional power as ever they did. Records can almost unlock the door and transport you straight back to the time when there was so much to discover, when everything was an adventure and your own future stretched out before you like an endless plain.

HOW DO I KNOW THIS? Because whenever I look at the cover of 'Highway To Hell' I can instantly think myself back to the record shop in Altrincham where I first saw it. Tucked away around the back of the main drag of shops, hanging on to the edge of an insignificant hill, this was the kind of shop – not store – that has been all but driven out of business by the advent of the music supermarket. Of course you didn't have anywhere near the choice of music in those places that you can get now in your HMV or your Virgin, but somehow what they did have for sale in their racks seemed more exciting, more worth spending your money on somehow. It's probably just the way your memory tints everything sepia and gives your long-past experiences a warm glow, but even the way the 12" album sleeves sat in their racks, peering out at you through gloomy plastic covers that seemed somehow to have clouded through overuse, seems simply magical to me now.

It was August of 1979 and my allegiance to 'If You Want Blood...' was total. From 'Whole Lotta Rosie' – the first song I'd ever heard by the group and, as I delighted in finding out, a tune about singer Bon Scott's one night stand with a dodgy old boiler – to 'Problem Child' and 'Bad Boy Boogie' I loved every single minute of AC/DC's raw, energised live performance. But in the strange workings of my 14-year-old mind there was still something missing from the magic of that record – and I knew exactly what that something was. It wasn't *mine*. I didn't own it. It belonged to my ➤

11

brother. Oh sure. I could *look* at the cover artwork whenever I wanted. I could *listen* to the tracks whenever I wanted. I could even check out the credits of the songwriters, Young-Young-Scott, on the record label as often as I wanted. But the record itself wasn't mine and would never be mine. It belonged to my brother, Mark, and that was an undeniable fact. As sure as night follows day or whatever other rank bad cliché you'd like to mention.

I'D STARTED READING *Sounds* of late. Now defunct, in its pomp it was the only weekly music magazine that could stand up to the might of the *New Musical Express*. And it was the only magazine that would give heavy metal, hard rock, whatever, a fair crack of the whip. Everywhere else, rock was the great pariah as punk and post-punk swept all before them, but I devoured the three or four pages a week in *Sounds* that you were guaranteed would focus on the hairier bands with indescribable pleasure. Imagine my delight when I read a review of the new AC/DC album, 'Highway To Hell'. A good one, too, if I remember rightly. This was my big chance.

Brian on sexism...
"Of course we're sexist, but life is sex. That's why we're here. Sexism, mixed with humour, is a wonderfully funny thing. We say things with a big tongue in the cheek. And it's not supposed to be just for men, it's for women as well. Women are horny buggers – there's a lot of them about who want to tie you up and use your little body, ya know."

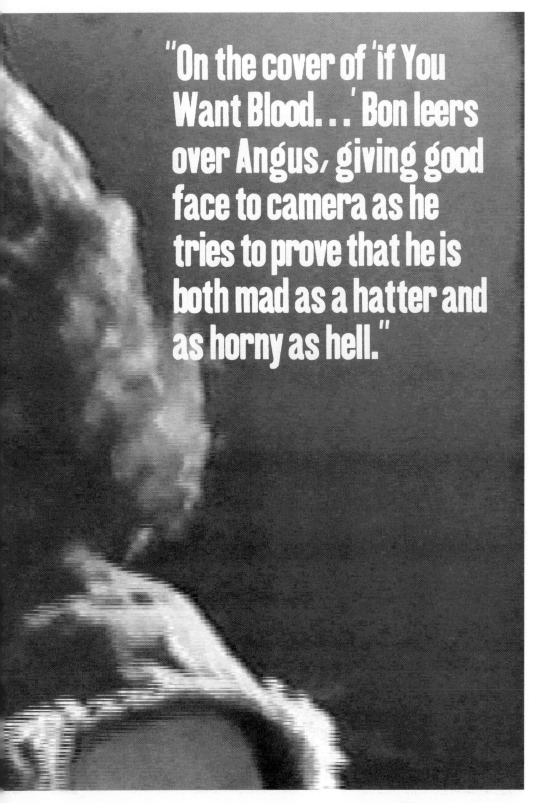

"On the cover of 'if You Want Blood...' Bon leers over Angus, giving good face to camera as he tries to prove that he is both mad as a hatter and as horny as hell."

I've no idea how I got the money for the album together. I know that within twelve months of buying this particular record I'd be half-starving myself saving the school dinner money my mum had given me to buy other releases. But how I got that first £3.99 or whatever it was isn't important. What was important was that when I saw the album sleeve in that shop in Altrincham, I knew that, like the guy in *Wayne's World* who gets the girl of his dreams through sheer force of will, that very album would soon be mine. Oh yes, it would be mine.

In retrospect 'Highway To Hell', like 'If You Want Blood...' before it, was another mind-bendingly cretinous sleeve. I've just picked it up to have another look as I write this. There are the five band members, stuck together in a way that I can only assume was supposed to signify casual loafing rather than the messy feel they ended up with. Some manipulation of the shot to give it an eerie red glow – 'hell', geddit? – and Angus Young standing there with a fake pair of devil's horns drawn on and holding a satanic tail in his right hand. Painting a rosy picture here, am I? At the time, though, I thought that sleeve was the work of genius.

The album's 10 tracks have worn considerably better than the sleeve. What would turn out to be Bon Scott's last ever album with the band proved that AC/DC could take the uninhibited rawness of their live sound and put a studio gloss on it without losing any of their edge or integrity. 'Highway To Hell' was a magnificent release and the news that the band would be playing at the Manchester Apollo on their forthcoming tour wasn't just exciting news for me, it was seismic. Which is where the schoolboy uniform comes in. And, of course, the arguments with my mum. And that determination to ignore her and enjoy my first ever live experience of AC/DC dressed, to bend a phrase from *Spinal Tap* a little out of shape, like an Australian's nightmare. ∎

Red Rocks

British rock band 3 Colours Red are confirmed AC/DC obsessives and no tour is complete without 'Back In Black' blaring out of the tour bus stereo. Vocalist and bassist Pete Vuckovic explains his fanaticism.

How did you first get into the DC then, Pete?
It was through my dad, actually. He was well into most rock and went from Free to Whitesnake to AC/DC to Rainbow, so I grew up with that kind of music. But the only group that had any lasting effect on me was AC/DC.

Why? What was so different about them?
Just the dirtiness of it all, the 'four on the floor' rock and roll element. I still think to this day there's no other band like them. Nobody else even comes close. They're really special and, incredibly, they're still around. I remember getting home from school having narrowly avoided a right kicking one time and sticking a video of AC/DC at the Joe Louis Arena in Washington on and just thinking 'Bollocks to everybody.' While people like Dio were singing about wizards and dragons, AC/DC were just so totally real. They gave me a reason to live.

How did your obsession go down at school, then?
You'd get an hour at dinner time where you could go into the common room and play records and I'd always bring 'If You Want Blood' in and stick it on. I didn't give a fuck who liked it or who didn't. Nobody I knew at school liked rock music, but I didn't care. I had a V-neck school jumper with about 11 badges all around the V-neck, pictures of Angus and what have you. I'd play the band's music really loud to make sure everyone got the point. People didn't understand it, but I didn't give a shit. It was the gospel to me.

And that passion for the band has stayed with you?
Oh yeah. If me and the missus have a good night

A young and mulleted Vuckovic showing his allegiance with a crap 'Fly On The Wall' T-shirt.

in and knock back a good few drinks then we always end up with AC/DC on the stereo.

So she likes them too?
Well, she's got no choice, has she? Actually, we had a massive row just before the band came on at Wembley on the last tour, but they sorted us

right out. As soon as they came on it was "Wow, they're going to do 'Back In Black'. Put life on hold for a second."

What do you think of Bon?
Bon Scott was a genius, full stop. The longevity AC/DC have comes from Bon; his attitude and the lyrics he wrote. "You got the lips to make a strong man weak and a heathen pray," that's brilliant. 'Highway To Hell' has amazing lyrics. That song is just everything that a kid stands for... still.

So do you think the band aren't as clever with Brian as they used to be?
By the time Brian joined they'd already had a big hit album, were using bigger producers and the whole thing was pretty polished. The grit and the reality of AC/DC had already gone when he joined the band. Bon had the most influence on AC/DC of the two singers, that's general opinion even amongst much younger people who weren't around when he was alive. I mean, the first album of theirs I got was 'Back In Black' when I was 10 or 11 and it sounded massive. Still does, it's a rock milestone. But the next thing I got was a 'Dirty Deeds' single and it seemed bizarre to me. It was like listening to Slade or something. I just didn't get it. I fell in love with 'Rock'n'Roll Ain't Noise Pollution' and then got into the 'buying eight of the old albums in a row' vibe and everything was weird, a bit more glammy. The first thing I got into was 'Back In Black' and the first song of AC/DC's that I ever heard was 'Hells Bells', all this dark shit. I was into the power of it at first, but as I went back, ➤

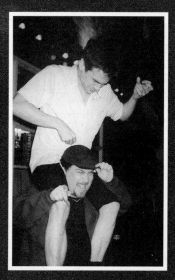

Taken on the night of the interview outside a pub in London's Belsize Park area after strong drink was taken. Pete does his best Angus, while pal Diamond Dave *(see page 118)* goes all Beano. The flat cap was rented from an old regular for a fiver.

"The real reason why i love AC/DC is because they appeal to your primal side."

Pete Vuckovic

"Our tour bus is packed with AC/DC – and it's all Bon-era stuff that we listen to, except for 'Back in Black'."

Pete Vuckovic

then I got into the cleverness of what Bon did.

Brian's voice is fucked these days, but wouldn't yours be? He comes over more like Chubby Brown now, with his flat cap. Did you see them when they did a live set for VH1 around the time of the 'Ballbreaker' tour? The band was kicking up great and, while I don't want to come down on Brian, he just wasn't cutting it there. Still, Angus once said that Brian sings like a truck's rolling over his foot, which I suppose is the best tribute anyone could pay him!

A lot of people have tried to copy the DC sound...
Definitely. There was this band called Dirty Looks that I remember, but like everyone else who's had a go at it none of those groups have ever got it.

So have you met the band?
Yeah, met them on the 'Ballbreaker' tour. I went up to Phil Rudd, but what do you say to the guy? I had all these questions buzzing around my head and all I could come out with was 'What have you been doing for the last 12 years?' He just looked at me and said 'Nothing', all deadpan. I told Angus 'I failed my school exams because of you' and he said 'Me too cobber.' I was in heaven. I was made-up. It was weird meeting them, though. They're very odd creatures, aren't they? Creatures from another planet.

Some people say that's because they're too cut off from everyone else, even their own fans. They're too secretive...
Ah, but the beauty of DC is the fact that they're shut off. I read a book on the band by a guy called Clinton Walker, and in it Angus and Malcolm come across like the Mafia. It claims that they treated Bon like shit, but I have to say I find that hard to believe.

Tell us about 3 Colours Red and the band's collective obsession.
Well, there are three of us in this band who are really hardcore DC fans. You know how you get those CD changers in a tour bus? That's absolutely packed with AC/DC, it's pretty much all we listen to. It's like *Groundhog Day* on our bus – and it's all Bon-era stuff that we listen to, except for 'Back In Black'. I'll stretch to 'For

Those About To Rock...' sometimes, which I think is great. From a musical point of view it's legendary, even.

Didn't you think it was just too 'metal'-sounding?
Not really. I read an interview somewhere when Malcolm admitted that they started using more power chords around that time, but I still thought it was fantastic.

Do you ever worry that your own band might not be able to match up?
Every day. You ask yourself what the hell you're trying for. I went through a period when I lost faith

in being in bands for that very reason, because AC/DC have everything. Even their gimmick is a good gimmick. Angus's schoolboy uniform thing will last forever, it wouldn't be AC/DC otherwise. I actually heard that the band were pissed off with it themselves and that they wanted to stop doing it maybe five or six years ago. But the kids all love it – and there's just no arguing with that, is there?

So how many times have you seen the band live?
Ten or twelve times. I go religiously whenever they tour. My first ever gig was on the 'Fly On The Wall' tour. I didn't really get the irony or the lyrical content when I first saw them, but I've made the transition from being a kid to an adult and really understanding the nuances of the band now. Even so, the real reason why I love them, why everyone loves them, is because they appeal to your primal side.

How about cover versions? Ever had a go at AC/DC songs yourself?
I've done loads of them, especially when I was young. The first song I ever played live was 'Live Wire'. I was 12 or 13 and had drunk four of those little cans of Special Brew just before I went on stage. I sobered up straight away when I got up there, though. It's strange to think that I'm still just as inspired by AC/DC today as I was back then. I've stuck with The Who and The Stones since I was a kid, but none of the heavier bands besides AC/DC. Twisted Sister? I don't think so. But I reckon I've stuck with DC because of the groove they have and the formula. No-one else can touch them. You can go and see them now and they're 50 years old, but as soon as they start playing 'Back In Black' you nearly come. And that's it, for me. ■

RATZ explains why he loves AC/DC, but not why he's called Ratz, sadly...

At the age of 10 in 1978 I was never interested in any kind of music at all. Then I heard a song called 'T.N.T.'. It was a bad quality recording on a friend's tape recorder, but my life was changed forever.

I discovered that the band who had recorded the track was AC/DC and from that moment on I bought every AC/DC record I could get my hands on. I wore a band T-shirt all the time and dreamt about seeing them live – a dream I finally realised in September '84 at the Monsters Of Rock Festival in Nuremberg. I just couldn't believe how great the band was, and made a real effort to go see them as often as possible after

that. I got to three shows on the 'Fly On The Wall' tour in '86, four on the 'Blow Up Your Video' tour of '88, seven in 1991 on 'The Razors Edge' tour and 36 (!!) on the 'Ballbreaker' tour in 1996, including seven gigs in the United States and seven in Australia!

I got to meet the band for the first time in Kiel in 1988 and have met them plenty of times since. They're always very friendly, especially Brian who is definitely one of the nicest people I've ever met; always laughing, always funny.

My favourite AC/DC experience has to be when I was used as an extra in the video for 'Hard As A Rock' in London back in 1995. I'm not kidding when I say it was one of the greatest days of my life.

The breaks between albums and tours are always too long for me, but next time the band are out on the road then I'll be there with them to see some great rock'n'roll – and to party around the world! Rock on AC/DC!

Angus Young

Playing since he was a little kid, Angus' introduction to the rock business came via his older brother George in the Easybeats. Despite his parents worrying about whether he should be hanging around the rock business at such a tender age, Angus was determined to play in bands and got his first break when he was offered the chance to play on a project his brother was working on, 'Tales Of Old Granddaddy'. The album appeared as performed by The Marcus Hook Roll Band. Angus had already been playing in working bands by this stage, including Kantuckee, which later mutated into Tantrum. But it was really only when he joined Malcolm's band AC/DC that his career really began. Their dad was amazed that the band lasted at all. He'd given it a week, knowing how the two brothers fought like cat and dog.

AC/BB

...That's 'Before Bon', by the way. AC/DC's first singer, Dave Evans, joined in November of 1973 and lasted for about nine months, recording the band's ultra-rare first single 'Can I Sit Next To You Girl'/'Rockin' In The Parlour'. Here's his take on what went on in those early, early DC days...

°How did you end up in Australia?
I was born in Wales and came to Australia when I was five. My family settled in North Queensland, but by the time I was 17 I was living in a place called Charters Towers where I started a band called In Session. It was just lead guitar, rhythm and drums, no bass. That was around 1969, but the band didn't last long and I moved to Sydney, hooking up with a band called Django. Then I ended up in the Velvet Underground – the

> **Angus On Groupies...**
> *"Mine were good, Bon's weren't. I wouldn't touch 'em with a bloody pole"*

Sydney version, not the New York one of course. The band was one of the biggest in Sydney at the time, but hadn't actually recorded anything. They'd just been about to go in the studio when the singer who was called Steve Phillips left with the guitar player. It turned out that that guitar player was Malcolm Young, who they all called "the little fella", so that was the first time I'd really heard of him, though I knew he was George Young's brother.

Velvet Underground split in the end and so I found myself living at Bondi Beach without a band. One day there was a knock at the door and in came Angus Young. I didn't know who he was and had hardly heard of him. He was this little bloke, five foot high, long curly hair down to

his shoulders and green teeth. I really remember thinking to myself "Fuck, he should clean those teeth." He was with this big, fat bass player which made them look like a comedy double act. Angus told me he was Malcolm's brother and asked if I'd join his band which was called Kantuckee. They were playing hard guitar rock. I listened to some of their songs, but they didn't do anything for me, so I didn't join. I was still on the lookout for another band to join and one day when I was flicking through the classifieds I saw an ad in the *Sydney Herald* looking for a singer. It sounded good so I phoned up.

And did you know who'd placed the ad?
No idea. I phoned and said "This is Dave Evans.

18

Dave Evans on stage with AC/DC before either Bon Scott or decent dress sense came along.

HOW TO BUY AC/DC

Want to own everything the band has issued in the last 20 years? Here's what you need to get hold of...

The band's first release was the issue in Australia and New Zealand of the single 'Can I Sit Next To You Girl?'/'Rockin' In The Parlour' (AP10551 on Albert's in Australia, New Zealand release on Polydor, catalogue number unavailable) This version of 'Can I Sit Next To You Girl?', a song which eventually appeared on the 'High Voltage' album in the UK, features Angus, Malcolm, and original vocalist Dave Evans and also appears alongside 'Rockin' In The Parlour' and a tune called 'Carry Me Home' on the bootleg album 'AC/DC Rip Off' as well as on an American bootleg 7". 'Rockin' In The Parlour' was also released on the 1979 compilation album 'Albert Archives' (APLP 037) This once rare compilation has now been released on CD (465395 2) where the only change is that the song has now been faded. Bootleg video tape is available of the original band miming to 'Can I Sit Next To You Girl' on an Aussie TV show, *The Last Picture Show*, and has been subsequently shown on an ABC Network show in Australia called *Countdown*.

"We hit the stage in these bizarre clothes and the crowd went: 'What the hell is that?' Then they went mad!"

Who's that?" and the voice said "Fuck, this is Malcolm Young. I've heard a lot about you." They asked me to come down for a jam, so I went to Wilson Street on the corner of Urskinville Road in the Newton district. It was a kind of office that wasn't being used any more and that was where we had our first session. There was Malcolm, a drummer called Colin Burgess who I knew from a band called The Masters Apprentices who'd been big in the '60s. I was impressed that he was there! The bass player was a guy called Larry something... Larry van Knedt. So we jammed a bit, a load of 12-bar stuff, a bit of Free, things like that. It sounded good, so afterwards we shook hands and that was it, we were a band.

Angus wasn't involved, then?
No. We had a few rehearsals and then Malcolm told me that Angus had split his band because he couldn't find a singer. He said maybe we should get him in, so Angus came down and that was it. Malcolm had told us that his brother George was interested in producing the band so we were all well pleased, even though we still didn't have a name. In November and December of '73 we rehearsed a lot and racked our brains thinking of a name. It was decided that at the next rehearsal everyone should bring three suggestions, we'd stick them in a hat and pull one out. I had a few in mind when I got there for the rehearsal, but Angus and Malcolm said their sister had suggested AC/DC. It sounded powerful. We all thought it was great and that was it.

The next thing I remember is a guy called Allan Kissick. He was a businessman in his fifties who knew all the bands and used to help the ones he liked. He knew the people at the Chequers Club in town and he got us the New Year's Eve gig there. We only had 10 songs, so we decided we'd just make more up as we went along, 12 bar things. Malcolm would start a riff and we'd just join in. Malcolm was a better player than Angus back then, because he was a lot more experienced. He'd played lead until Angus joined, and then we practically had two lead players, duels on stage and all the rest of it. It was good. These two little guys in jeans and this huge sound. People started talking about us and we started doing the Sydney circuit.

What songs were you doing then? Can you remember?
We played loads of Chuck Berry, one or two Free songs. I think we did 'All Right Now' and some of our own numbers. There was a song called 'The Old Bay Road' which Malcolm wrote, which never got released. It was a great song and I always thought it would be on the first album. Things were going well and George Young was impressed too, saying he'd record us, so that's how we started recording for Albert's, even though we physically recorded in the EMI studios in Sydney. Albert's own studios didn't exist back then. We recorded 'Can I Sit Next To You Girl', a new song that Malcolm had written which we'd hardly done live. We also recorded 'Rockin' In The Parlour' for the B-side which was new as well and hadn't really been in the live set. Richard Lush engineered and George Young and Harry Vanda produced.

You recorded three tunes, one of which was never released, right?
Yeah, we also recorded 'Rock'n'Roll Singer' which we thought we'd use on our first album. Colin played drums and Larry was on bass, but Malcolm told me that George went in and re-did the bass lines, so it's actually George on that first single.

The single came very early in your career, didn't it?
Yeah, it was only about six weeks after our first gig. We recorded in the middle of February. It became obvious that we had trouble with the rhythm section pretty quickly, though. Malcolm didn't rate Larry, and Colin was losing interest, so Malcolm got together with a couple of guys he knew from one of his previous bands and brought Neil Smith in on bass and Noel Taylor on drums. We had a gig in Victoria Park in Sydney, right by the University – an open air show with another band called Flake. It was just before the single was due to come out and we said "Well, every band in the state wears jeans and T-shirts," so we thought we should do something different. We decided we'd get some bizarre stage clothes so we'd be remembered. Angus' sister had the idea that he should wear his school uniform with his satchel on his back and short trousers. The bassist chose a biker's outfit with helmet and shades, the drummer wore a clown's costume with a harlequin hat. Malcolm looked like a parachutist with blue platforms. I wore red platforms and trousers cut off at the knee. Nobody knew how we'd go down. We'd only ever worn jeans and T-shirts on stage before. They would be expecting to see the same thing and we had this whole new image. We went on-stage and the public went 'What the hell is that?', but everything went well and the crowd went mad. Malcolm and Angus weren't happy with Noel and Neil, though, and they were kicked out straight away. They were only with us for about six weeks, but they were in the band the first time Angus wore his schoolboy uniform, a historic moment.

Bon On Requirements For Joining The Band...
"It's a pretty rare type of bloke who'll fit into our band. He has to be under five foot six."

The band's first album, the Australian version of '**High Voltage**', featured the line-up of Bon, Malcolm and Angus with sessions from George Young on bass and Tony Kerrante on drums. In 1984 the mini-LP '**74 Jailbreak**' was issued in the US, Canada, Japan and Brazil, and the versions of the songs taken from 'High Voltage' differ slightly from the recordings on the original album.

'**High Voltage**' (AP10829) was issued as a single on 23rd June 1975 and was the first recording to feature bassist Mark Evans and drummer Phil Rudd, to many the classic AC/DC line-up. B-side '**Soul Stripper**' is taken from the '**High Voltage**' album. The song is faded and features on the worldwide release of the '**High Voltage**' album. The same track is featured on the Australian '**T.N.T.**' album along with 'School Days', unavailable worldwide prior to the release of the 'Bonfire' box set.

The worldwide release of '**High Voltage**' features both '**She's Got Balls**' and '**Little Lover**' off the Australian version, although it seems unlikely that the bass and drum tracks were recorded especially for this release, even though Evans and Rudd are credited on the sleeve. The band next released the single '**Jailbreak**'/'**Fling Thing**' (Aus AP11135, UK K10805)

AC/DC's third album, '**Dirty Deeds Done Dirt Cheap**' features different UK and

There are rumours that Angus also had a Zorro outfit and a Superman one too...
He had two costumes that his sister had made for him, the school uniform and the Zorro outfit. He used to change between the two of them. The Zorro outfit consisted of short trousers, a mask, hat and coat. Angus even had a plastic sword that he used on his guitar like he was playing a violin with a bow. We used to have fights on stage. He'd go for the microphone with the sword and I'd fight back with the mic stand. We'd have a fight, then I'd put him on my shoulders like Bon would do later. I was the first to do that.

Malcolm nicked the bassist and drummer from Flake, the band that we'd played with that day in Victoria Park. Rob Bailey played bass and Peter Clack was on drums. They joined just as we were doing a TV clip for 'Can I Sit Next To You Girl'. We shot it in Cronulla on the south coast for a set called *The Last Picture Show*, so Rob and Peter appeared on the clip even though they weren't on the record. It got on a ten-minute rock show called *Got To Know*, or *GTK*. It was brilliant being on TV and really unusual for a rock band in

those days. The single shot up the charts because of it – it made the Top Five, and we couldn't believe it. I mean, 'Can I Sit Next To You Girl' was a good song, but we had better ones in the live set. At the time we were managed by a guy called Dennis Laughlin who used to be in the Australian band Sherbet. He arranged a tour in Australia and we started at the Sydney Opera House opening for Stevie Wright, who had a massive hit in Australia at the time with a song called 'Evie'. In our set we had the A and B side of the single, then 'The Old Bay Road' and a few others, including 'Rock'n'Roll Singer'.

Which was credited to Young-Young-Scott on the 'T.N.T.' album...
Well, there were two other songs that they changed the lyrics to. 'Show Business' was originally called 'Sunset Strip' and there was a slower one called 'Love Song' that we'd worked up together and which was originally called 'Fell In Love'. We played that one at the Opera House gig.

I was enjoying myself in the band. As the lead singer I was doing most of the interviews and it

Phil Rudd

Born on 19th May, 1954, Phil Rudzevecuis (aka Rudd) came to AC/DC via Buster Brown, a Melbourne boogie band which featured Angry Anderson, eventually frontman of Rose Tattoo. He recorded an album, 'Something To Say', with Buster Brown in 1974 and the album featured a cover of Chuck Berry's 'Roll Over Beethoven', but the LP didn't make an impact and the band disintegrated. Rudd claimed that he was also a member of a band called Mad Moll for a time, but never recorded anything with them. Known as 'Left Hook', owing to his propensity to use it when the need arose, Rudd's straightforward style immediately put the developing sound of Malcolm and Angus into context and helped to define exactly what AC/DC should become. Although Rudd joined the band in time to appear on some low rent promo shots for their first album, 'High Voltage', he didn't actually appear on the record and only made his recording debut with AC/DC on a single version of 'High Voltage' in Australia, released upfront of the band's second album, 'T.N.T.'.

was a lot of fun. Sometimes me and Angus didn't see eye to eye, but not that often. He thought I looked like a wop, as he called it, and sometimes he told me so, but I think some of that was down to jealousy because I was the singer and I was getting the most chicks. But the tour went well and we played at the Festival Hall in Melbourne with Stevie Wright and Lou Reed. We were still dressing up then, while Lou Reed played in black jeans and T-shirt. He bored the public to death, so we capitalised on that. We were new and exciting and blew everyone off stage. We worked really hard and played tons of gigs; evenings, late nights, whatever we were offered, but I started to fall out with Dennis Laughlin. He was swanning around like a pop star while we didn't have two cents to rub together. We argued and I think we even had to be pulled apart one night. Tensions were mounting. Angus hadn't had a shag all tour and I don't think that helped either. I had the feeling that things were going wrong, but I couldn't quite put my finger on exactly how or why. As the tour moved on, we got to Adelaide where Bon Scott was living at the time. I knew of him from the '60s in a band called The Valentines and in Adelaide he came to all our gigs, standing in the front row screaming. He knew our whole set inside out.

One day we had a day off and when I got back from doing whatever it was I was doing they said they'd been jamming with Bon. I wasn't overly happy about it and said to Rob and Peter that if the atmosphere didn't improve and if we didn't start getting paid some money, then I'd be off anyway. I was fed up with it all and so when we were in Melbourne they made the decision for me and told me I was out. "Fucking great," I said. "Give me my money and a flight out of here and I'm gone." So I flew back to Sydney and phoned them up a week later to ask where my money was. Of course I was told there wasn't any. In retrospect I guess I was pretty naive to get upset about it, because I reckon they were telling the truth and there probably really wasn't any money, but I felt I'd earned it.

The band then scheduled a gig in Victoria Park

Dave didn't escape the Eighties unscathed.

again and I turned up out of curiosity to check out the new singer. When the band came on stage I couldn't believe it was with Bon. That was a real shock, this guy from the '60s who seemed way too old for them. I was really pissed off about it, but when I was in Albert Studios with my band Rabbit making the 'Too Much Rock'n'Roll' album I met Bon. AC/DC were recording there as well. He knew all about my history with the band, but I told him I had no hard feelings towards him and he said the same to me. I never met him again because the band moved to London shortly afterwards.

And you never spoke with any of the other band members again?
Yes, I did. I met them one time in Melbourne. I was playing at this big open air festival with 30 or 40 bands on over three days. I met Malcolm and

Why Malcolm didn't put some jam on his shoes and invite his trousers down for tea was never fully explained.

asked him how he was doing. The atmosphere wasn't poisonous and there was no big scene, but it was frosty. I didn't have a problem with Malcolm. In fact, I respected him because he

we'd only been together six weeks and we'd already recorded a single. Of course the band was good, but being in the studio after just six weeks is unbelievable. That only happened

"We'd only been together six weeks and we'd already recorded a single."

Dave Evans

was the sound of AC/DC. He always had a vision, he always said that we'd go to America just like his brother George had in The Easybeats. I always wondered why he didn't just think about being big in Australia, but he always said "I don't give a shit about Australia. We're going to be really big!" Hardly any Aussie bands had made it big in America, but Malcolm had the vision of being huge and he was young enough to be able to work at it.

How much did George Young help the band, then?
George was the band's mentor. He produced the recordings, helped with the songwriting, helped arrange them. Without George and Harry... well

because George was their brother. And he was the Albert Productions A&R man. You can't underestimate his value to the band. He was very, very important. He could advise Angus and Malcolm because he knew the business inside out. You couldn't buy that kind of help.

After leaving AC/DC Dave Evans formed Rabbit in 1975 and released an eponymous album. A second release, 'Too Much Rock'n'Roll' appeared and did well in Australia, but Rabbit split in 1976 and Evans drifted between various club bands. He formed Hot Cockerel in 1984 and appeared with the band in a film called Coming Of Age, *writing a few songs for the soundtrack. Evans recorded an album, 'Thunder From Down Under' in the late '80s which failed to set the world alight and Evans finally gave up the music business for good. He now works for a PR agency in Australia.*

Australian versions. The two albums together will give you all the recordings from the sessions, including the two bars shorter single cut of the title track for the UK release alongside '**Love At First Feel**', recorded in mid-'76 at London's Vineyard Studio (which also produced '**Carry Me Home**' and probably '**Fling Thing**')

The single '**Dog Eat Dog**'/'**Carry Me Home**' (AP11403) was released ahead of the '**Let There Be Rock**' album on 23rd March 1977 and is the only official release of the B-side. '**Let There Be Rock**' was released at different times worldwide during 1977 and the US and Canadian editions replaced '**Crabsody In Blue**' with '**Problem Child**'. The Australian CD release features the original tracks.

The band's next album, '**Powerage**', was also released in various different formats. The band left Australia for a spring tour of the UK in 1978 and the album was released in Britain and Germany with a track listing and mixes that weren't finalised. By June the band had moved on to the US and the completed version of the album was released in Australia, the US, Canada and France. It is this version of the album that has tended to dominate the market ever since. The CD release features the finished album, of course.

'**Highway To Hell**', '**Back In Black**', '**For Those About To Rock**', '**Flick Of The Switch**', '**Fly On The Wall**' and '**Ballbreaker**' all contain identical and complete tracks worldwide.

The '**Who Made Who**' album provides the re-mixed single version of '**Shake Your**

Problem Child

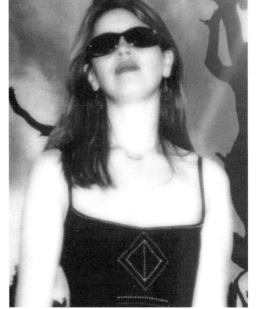

Kaz Helagan was 15 when Angus Young first took a shine to her and helped shape her life. She tells her own story here...

Monday, 14th March, 1977. St. Albans Civic Centre, Hertfordshire. Vibrating sound travels under your feet and up through your body like an electrical charge, lighting you up like the Empire State at Christmas. Something in the lyrics touches a chord of the 15-year-old mind fighting the chains of parental control – you are that 'Problem Child'.

You decide you just *have* to meet the band after the gig, no two ways about it, and manage to blag your way in at the back door as the roadies begin the job of shifting the equipment

Malcolm gives Kaz a hand with her biology homework. What a guy!

"Maths, now. One and one makes two, see?"

out of the venue. You find yourself in the dressing room and ask for the autograph of the guy who makes his Gibson talk your language. He gives you his address in London and asks to see you again. After that your life is totally consumed by the band and their music – you're evangelical about their talents and tell everyone you know from your granny to your best friend to go out and buy their records.

Angus sends you a long letter from their tour in America and later phones you on his return to the UK to set up a rendezvous in Leeds. You attend the gig in the Polytechnic dressed up as a schoolgirl. You strut around like a peacock on stilts and figure you will get used to the stilettos eventually.

You move to London and Angus comes over to your flat for a visit – everyone wants to meet him. He asks you to join him on the 'If You Want Blood You've Got It' tour. You take time off work and get to know the band really well. You watch them rehearse, you get invited to parties, you

Foundations', but you'll need the 12" of 'Who Made Who' for a longer collector's mix of the title track.

With the release of the 'Blow Up Your Video' album and the advent of CD, things can get a wee bit confusing.

The 12" and CD singles of 'Heatseeker' feature non-album track 'Snake Eye' while the 12" of 'That's The Way I Wanna Rock'n'Roll' also features 'Borrowed Time', another non-album number.

The 1990 album, 'The Razor's Edge' saw the 12" and CD versions of 'Moneytalks' featuring 'Borrowed Time'. Australian 7", 12" and CD singles of 'Moneytalks' all feature 'Down On The Borderline', another out-take from the 'Blow Up...' sessions featuring Simon Wright on drums.

The single 'Big Gun' was released to coincide with the Arnold Schwarzeneggar film *The Last Action Hero*.

The 'Bonfire' box set features many out-takes and rarities. 'Dirty Eyes' is an original working of 'Whole Lotta Rosie', 'Touch Too Much' is a completely different song from the one which ended up on 'Highway To Hell', 'If You Want Blood You've Got It' is different again, as is 'Get It Hot', while 'Back Seat Confidential' is an original attempt at 'Beatin' Around The Bush'.

LIVE RECORDINGS

The 'Bonfire' box set features the double live 'Let There Be Rock – The Movie' soundtrack, plus previously unreleased live recordings of 'Sin City' from a show called

The DC rock St. Albans. Note Angus' home address in London's Lancaster Gate scribbled down for Kaz.

"Anytime i want to revisit my past i only have to play 'Dirty Deeds Done Dirt Cheap' and i'm 15 again."

Kaz Helagan

even get to appear on stage with Angus in Sheffield. All in all you're having the time of your life and wishing deep down that you too could be a rock star, if only you'd learnt the guitar instead of the recorder!

Your parents don't seem too pleased at your increased notoriety, especially after they see a photograph of their 'little girl' published in *Sounds*. You tell them not to believe everything they read in newspapers and, besides, if you

want to spend the rest of your life on the road with the best rock group in the world, then that's surely your decision. Your mother rolls her eyes up like a duck in thunder as you show her what a great headbanger you've become – after all you've just won first prize in a contest in London and you'd think that would make her proud of you. Didn't she make a special effort to see you when AC/DC were on *Top Of The Pops* and wasn't she chuffed when you told all the

reporters that she ironed your shirt before the start of each gig?

You get to spend a lot of time with the roadies who look after you like their kid sister. You watch them as they perform miracles setting up the equipment night after night in a different venue. You hear all their stories of life on the road with other famous bands and begin to wonder if your life will ever be as interesting.

Eventually though all good things come to an▶

That infamous *Sounds* cutting, complete with cheeky text.

SPOT THE SCHOOLGIRL: *This enticing young girl, almost certainly the victim of exploitation, comes to us courtesy of Brian Duddington of Doncaster, snapped at AC/DC's Sheffield Poly show. Excitable Brian writes "In a mad frenzy Angus Young gets on his knees in the middle of the act and rubs his face in her crotch!" Soon come.*

Midnight Special and '**She's Got Balls**' from a gig at Bondi Lifesaver.

'**Dirty Deeds Done Dirt Cheap**' was recorded at the Festival Of Sydney concert on 30th January 1977 and was released by Aussie radio station 2JJ as part of a compilation album, '**Long Live The Evolution**' (AA9042) in 1977. The track later appeared on a Raven Records compilation '**Boogie Balls And Blues, Vol. 1**' (RVLP 30) released in 1987.

The official live album, '**If You Want Blood You've Got It**', saw a single of '**Whole Lotta Rosie**' backed by a live version of '**Dog Eat Dog**'. The only other live releases of the period, versions of '**Live Wire**' and '**Shot Down In Flames**', appeared on the UK single of '**Touch Too Much**', a studio track from '**Highway To Hell**'.

'**Let's Get It Up**' from 1982 featured live versions of '**Back In Black**' and '**T.N.T.**', while '**For Those About To Rock**' featured a live take of '**Let There Be Rock**'.

1984's 12" single of '**Nervous Shakedown**' was backed with live takes of '**Rock'n'Roll Ain't Noise Pollution**', '**Sin City**' and '**This House Is On Fire**'. The German 7" features '**Rock'n'Roll Ain't Noise Pollution**' with a slightly longer intro.

The 1986 12" of '**Shake Your Foundations**' also included a 13 minute version of '**Jailbreak**', while the 7" and 12" versions of '**Who Made Who**' featured a live '**Guns For Hire**'. The same year's re-issue of '**You Shook Me All Night Long**' featured the only Bon Scott track issued after his death, a 77 live version of '**She's Got Balls**'. The 7" features an edited version and the 12" adds a live version of '**You Shook Me**' from 1983.

end – I guess when Bon sadly died in 1980 I felt a part of my life had gone too. I couldn't believe he'd gone in such a tragic way and so alone. I felt that no-one could ever replace him and I hung up the old school uniform and closed a chapter of my life that had without doubt shaped the person that I've become today.

Anytime I want to revisit my past I only have to play 'Dirty Deeds Done Dirt Cheap' and I'm 15 again, and telling everyone who has pissed me off to 'get their fucking jumbo jet outta my airport'. Not bad for someone who owns a strip of grass the size of a hamster's cage – but then we must all have our dreams and the band gave me mine. ∎

Angus' 'Man At C&A' stage gear never caught on.

Phil tries his hand at the bass (above), while a boyish Angus plays it straight for the camera.

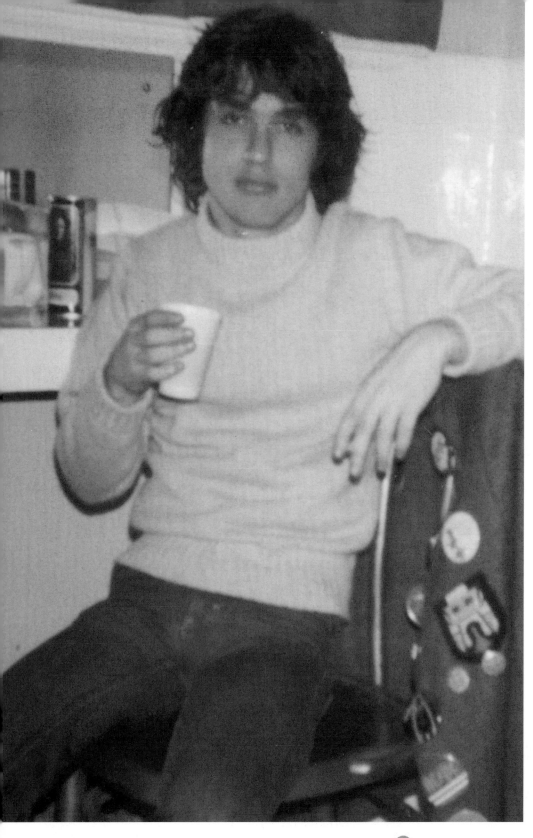

The official live album, cunningly-titled '**Live**' contains 23 tracks, while the double vinyl LP features only 20 songs (omitting '**Moneytalks**', '**Are You Ready**' and '**Bonny**')

The first single from the live album, '**Highway To Hell**', featured four non-album versions of songs on the CD singles. The first featured '**Hell's Bells**' and '**The Jack**', while disc two included '**Hell Ain't A Bad Place To Be**' and '**High Voltage**'. The second single taken from the live album, '**Dirty Deeds Done Dirt Cheap**', also featured different versions of live tracks. Both the 12" and CD single feature '**Shoot To Thrill**' and an alternative version of '**Dirty Deeds...**'.

'**Big Gun**' featured two live numbers on the 12", '**Back In Black**' and '**For Those About To Rock**'.

The '**Hail Caesar**' single featured a live '**Whole Lotta Rosie**' from 1991, although nobody seems sure whether this is the version which made the 1992 '**Live**' album.

There's still debate about a French five-track live CD (CA820) which features a version of '**Whole Lotta Rosie**' from Moscow, and which may be the version on the live album.

For the definitive, story on every AC/DC release check out AC/DC – An Illustrated Record Collector's Guide *by Chris Tesch. It's an exhaustive study of recordings that's available in a two-volume set documenting over 700 releases. Contact him at, 415 S 38th Street, Apt 8, Omaha, NE 68131-3847, USA.*

So who the hell is that geezer top left?

AC-DC

THE STRANGE CASE OF THE MISSING BASS PLAYER

AC/DC's early personnel history is a tangled web of intrigue. The line-up which recorded the band's first single, 'Can I Sit Next To You Girl?' / 'Rockin' In The Parlour' featured Angus, Malcolm, vocalist Dave Evans, drummer Colin Burgess and bassist Larry van Knedt. However, by the time the band had their first Australian album, 'High Voltage', AC/DC had already been through another rhythm section of Rob Bailey and Peter Clack, though it later emerged that neither of these played on the tracks which appeared on the album either. It's been confirmed that producer George Young removed Bailey's bass lines, which he believed weren't up to scratch, and replaced them with his own. The drums, meanwhile, were laid down by one Tony Kerrante, a session player who'd played

in a group called The 69ers and who turned up again playing in a band named Winter in 1976.

Phil Rudd and Mark Evans first appeared with AC/DC on a new single recording of 'High Voltage' in 1975 and eventually made their full recording débuts on the Aussie-only 'T.N.T.' album that same year.

However, a photo session exists from 1975 which clearly shows Rudd in the band alongside an unidentified bass player who is definitely not Mark Evans. The photo appeared in the most popular Australian pop magazine at the time, *Spunky*, but there are no line-up details. When asked about the mystery man recently Rudd would only say: "He wasn't with us for very long. I could play better bass than him!"

30

Chapter Two

YOUR MOTHER KNOWS BEST

Towards the tail end of 1978 I had broken my rock gig duck, much to my utter relief. Until I saw Motörhead at Manchester's Free Trade Hall, swiftly followed by those preposterous Germans The Scorpions, I had just one gig under my belt. The story of how I made my concert-going debut at a Boney M show in 1977 while the white heat of punk raged all around me is a salutary lesson for all would-be hip parents. God knows what had got into them, because my mum and dad had never shown the remotest interest in any form of pop or rock before, but suddenly they decided that Mark and I should venture into the outside world and discover the joys of contemporary music. And who better to break our popular culture cherries than... Boney M, the German disco troupe guided by producer Frank Farian and fronted by the 100% under-dressed Bobby Farrell and his towering afro? As a first ever gig I've later decided that Boney M was actually a pretty daring experience. The three black girls who made up the quartet wore about as much as their male mentor and I can still distinctly remember looking at the programme before the show started and thinking that those girls looked pretty rude. But just how raunchy this Eurodisco experience actually turned out to be has somehow failed to find storage space in my memory banks, which does tend to suggest that the performance may have been more tame than the pictures implied. It doesn't matter anyway, because by the following year and my meeting with Motörhead I'd decided that heavy rock was my music of choice and I wasn't going to be admitting to anyone that I'd last been seen dancing with the mix of enthusiasm and two left feet that the good people from Manchester seem endlessly capable of generating at a Boney M Concert!

AND YET WHILE Motörhead's wall of noise had excited me and my school-pal, Alan Mushing, who I'd ventured out with, and while I chuntered on incessantly about how great the gig had been, the truth was that deep down I wasn't really that fussed about Motörhead. Their sound was too slushy, too loose, too noisy for me. They couldn't hold a candle to AC/DC and their 4/4, straight-down-the-line, body-built boogie. The Scorpions were fine and their gig was exciting, but when the AC/DC tickets went on sale and I headed down to Piccadilly Records in the centre of town to shell out for my third 'proper' gig, in my own infatuated mind I'd already built this up to be the big one. It was going to be the night of all nights, especially when I decided that out of homage to guitarist Angus Young I would simply have to attend the gig in schoolboy uniform the better to show my allegiance. My mum was mortified.

She had indulged me in the build-up to the gig, I suppose. I'd cut up an old pair of grey school flannels to make shorts, was intending to wear the last school blazer I'd had, that had been put to the back of the wardrobe because my mum thought it was too much of what she called 'a sight', and had taken one of my cricket caps and crudely sewn an A in green felt that I'd nicked out of the sewing tin. But all along she'd insisted, like a million mums before her, that I wasn't going out dressed like that. I'd thought she was bluffing, that she was simply registering her displeasure before relenting and letting me make an arse of myself in front of the general public. But maybe she figured that the shame of her 15-year-old son wandering around Altrincham as an overaged Primary School goody-goody really was too much to bear. The realisation suddenly dawned on me that, yes, she actually was serious. She wasn't going to let me out of the house like that.

A PLAN WAS HATCHED. I was going to meet a couple of my schoolmates at Piccadilly Station in Manchester, a shortish walk away from Ardwick Green and the Apollo, where the gig was happening. My brother wasn't going for some reason, so I was to travel alone; local bus to Altrincham, train to Manchester. I knew that I had to wear the outfit. The whole idea of dressing up had taken on an importance beyond all reason by the day of the gig and I was obsessed with carrying my scheme through. It was a matter of principal. But the idea I came up with to dupe my mum was about as amateurish as you would expect from a 15 year old with precious little time for fine detail and meticulous planning. As soon as I got home from school on the afternoon of the gig I stuffed the shorts, blazer and cap into one of the hundreds of plastic carrier bags that all families stock-pile as if rationing of the damn things is about to be introduced any minute. Then I went ➤

Cheesy sandwich, cheesy grin.

This man in particular is responsible for the author's mis-spent youth.

"it suddenly dawned on me that, yes, she was serious. She wasn't going to let me out of the house like that."

semi. She couldn't stop me now and I was ready to... well, ready to rock.

AC/DC HAD CHOSEN the perfect place in Manchester to stop off at on the 'Highway To Hell' tour. The Apollo was situated in Ardwick and if it didn't exactly seem like hell to me, then it certainly had the feel of Beirut or one of those far-flung, war-torn places they showed on the news. Broken bottles littered the streets, competing for space on the pavement with the dog shit and chip paper wrappers. Kebabs were as yet way too exotic for

"The Apollo was situated in Ardwick and if it didn't exactly seem like hell to me, then it certainly had the feel of Beirut."

to the outhouse, a low-rent term for a tiny sliver of a prefab which had been slung up against our back door for no earthly reason that I could fathom – until now. I took the bag, scrunched it up as tightly as I could and tucked it behind an enormous pile of shoes that had gathered, almost of its own volition, under the plastic corrugated roof. You would hardly have needed a team of crack police sniffer dogs to root out my alternative dress, but I figured it would be good enough to fox my mum at least.

I was right. I sauntered into the kitchen at around six, dressed in jeans and the Motörhead T-shirt I'd bought a few months previously. Coats, of course, were for the birds. The orange gig ticket was stuffed in the back pocket of my trousers. "See ya later" I chirruped with all the false nonchalance I could muster. "Enjoy yourself," mum responded. I opened the back door and entered the outhouse, making sure that I shut the door tight behind me. With my

heart beating at what felt to me like three times its normal volume, I gingerly made my way to the back of the shoe pile and located the plastic bag. To my mind the rustle as I slowly raised it in the air sounded at that moment about as loud as the band I was going to see. I was sure my mum would fling open the kitchen door to see what I was up to. Nothing happened. I gingerly pulled out the gear and proceeded to swap the clothes I was in for the clothes I really wanted to wear. The whole operation can't have taken more than a couple of minutes, but you won't be surprised to hear that it felt like an eternity to me. Still, the luck of the gods was with me and eventually there I was in full regalia. Even at the grand old age of 15 I felt just a wee bit foolish as I dived out of the outhouse and legged it away around the corner to catch the bus. But I'd decided it was part of the AC/DC ritual and that was that. I wasn't worried if my mum saw me sprint past the front bay windows of our suburban

the northern palate. To a boy brought up in the leafy, suburban idyll of Altrincham this was another world. As I walked up from Piccadilly station with Alan and my other pal Nick Gibbon (Mushing and Gibbon? You couldn't have made those surnames

There's an AC/DC comic available. Produced by Revolutionary Comics of San Diego in 1991, it's a visual documentary of how the band rose from the bottom of the heap – with some fanciful guesswork on top. It's exploitative crap, but if you have to get hold of it, then contact Revolutionary at 519 University Ave, Suite 103, San Diego, CA 92103

up), I tried to exude false confidence. Not as easy as it sounds when you're wearing shorts, the most emasculating piece of clothing ever invented.

When we reached the Apollo, however, I was both enraptured by the place and at the same time mildly terrified. The hall looked like an identikit Seventies concert venue, an austere, imposing building that threatened rather than welcomed. I didn't really wonder about what its history was at the time, but I do now. Was it a decaying relic of the old music hall days? Had it survived the war, hosting variety shows in defiance of the bombs that Hitler would have been hurling down on the North's industrial heartland? It'd be fascinating to know today. At the time I didn't give a toss about that though, because to my mind in its not-quite-decrepit-but-getting-there state, it was still both endlessly fascinating and curiously alluring.

The slight arc of the neon advertising board that clung to the facia of the building threw out a brilliant glow which had disintegrated to an almost eerie echo of its former brilliance by the time it had filtered down to the eyes on the street below. The letters AC and DC, with no slash in-between of course, stood out in vibrant red.

On the steps of the hall the ticket touts were already hard at work. These were a motley crew of folk, ranging in age from 16 to 60 and in size from scrawny to slobbish. I assessed that they had two things in common. Firstly, by the look of their clothes, none of them were turning any big bucks with this scam. And secondly, I knew that while they were all operating on the wrong side of the law, clearly none of them had the stomach for anything really and truly nasty. Even I'd worked out that if they were any good at being criminals, they wouldn't be wasting their time standing outside an AC/DC gig trying to make a couple of quid here and there. The scene was still a bit too scary for me though and I felt more comfortable once I'd made my way through the glass doors and into the reception area of the grand old building. ➤

Malcolm Young

Born on 6th January 1953, the second-youngest of seven, Mal was given his first guitar as a present aged 10. This only fostered his hatred of school; the only reason he ever turned up there was to play in his first band aged 12. Leaving the dreaded institution aged 15 in 1968, Malcolm took any piecemeal work to keep his head above water and eventually settled on a job in a bra factory to get money together to buy gear for a band.

In 1972 he formed Newcastle Velvet Underground, which went nowhere fast. A year later he had another try with a band that at first had no name, but featured the first AC/DC line-up of Mal, Dave Evans on vocals, Colin Burgess on drums and Larry Van Knedt on bass. Quickly realising that he needed another guitarist to realise the sound he had in his head, younger brother Angus was brought in to play lead. After numerous personnel changes Mal and Angus moved to Melbourne to hook up with their producer brother George and try to put a new band together. They eventually settled on a line-up of Mal, Angus, Bon Scott, Mark Evans and Phil Rudd, the first classic DC team.

I HEADED FOR the merchandising stall at once. It was a ritual I was to follow for many years to come, staring up at a range of items, many of which I would immediately dismiss as tacky. AC/DC's range though, like Motörhead's before them, seemed to pride itself on its no-frills approach. The T-shirts were basic; logo on the front, 'Highway To Hell Tour' lettering on the back. I couldn't afford the T-shirt, so I plumped for a tour programme, a thin and weedy affair most memorable for some typically lecherous shots of Bon sporting a particularly lairy Hawaiian shirt. It was so far removed from the typical metal apparatus of black leather and blue denim that I chuckled to myself. Irony, I would soon find, was in short supply in the world of rock.

The support band's name escapes me. Was it Def Leppard on their first ever big name tour? Thinking about it now it might well have been, but if it was I have no recollection whatsoever of their attempts to warm up this partisan crowd. If it really was Leppard, I wasn't that bothered then and even if I'd known they were on their way to becoming one of the world's biggest rock bands, I wouldn't have been any more impressed. I was both too underage and too scared to try and get away with drinking in The Cottage, the pub next door to the venue. That would come later. So truthfully, I haven't got a clue what I did between setting foot in the Apollo and feeling an almost sickening sense of excitement when the house lights finally went down. By this time I'd heard those pansticked American rockers Kiss' 'Alive II' album and was familiar with the kind of chest-beating that pre-empted most self-important rock bands' arrival on stage. But tonight there was no disembodied voice screaming at the audience in a ludicrously baroque style, there was no exhortation to 'rock'. Simply a steady bass riff, the gentlest of guitar fills and a roar from the crowd that sounded every bit as earthy, every bit as thrilling as the roar on 'If You Want Blood...' that I constantly heard at home. Then came the most basic of rhythms drilled out on the hi-hat and the full-throated roar of a stupidly simple, massively engaging riff. And then came the voice...

"Well if you're looking for trouble / I'm the man to see / If you're looking for satisfaction / Well satisfaction guaranteed / I'm as cool as a body on ice / Hotter than the rolling dice / Send you to heaven take you to hell / I ain't fooling can't you tell." At the age of 15 it would have taken an awful lot of imagination for anyone to have looked at me and thought that I was in any way like the guy in the song, cooler than cool and ready to do violence at the drop of a hat. No matter, when I stared at the Apollo's stage under the full glare of the band's lights, I honestly saw myself right up there where Bon Scott stood, cocky and confident, belting out the words to 'Live Wire' in a whisky-coarsened voice, showing off my tattoos and leching at the few game girls who were brave enough to have risked this predominantly male audience.

IT WAS EASY TO SEE what Bon's appeal was. You didn't have to be a brain surgeon to work it out. He was cocky, confident and macho; all the things that I certainly wasn't, but secretly aspired to be. That doesn't sound very pleasant in retrospect, but my instant affection for Bon really wasn't as single-mindedly bone-headed as that. Even from twenty rows back, Bon exuded a raw charm that was instantly appealing. He had the common touch, all right. Even in a room of two thousand odd people he let you know right away that he was one of the boys, rather than some untouchable fanny merchant doing you a favour by deigning to perform for you. Big deal, you might say. And yes, that might not sound like much in these post-grunge,

Producer Harry Vanda on Bon...
"What can you say? He could sum up in two sentences what would take me two books."

back-to-basics rock days. But back in 1979, when Led Zeppelin's flowery frontman Robert Plant was the benchmark for hard rock singers, Scott's no-frills frontman-work was utterly unique.

At the Manchester Apollo AC/DC relied on sheer bloody-minded rock power for their effect. The stage was nothing but bare boards and amps, the lights functional rather than flashy, and if the whole point of heavy rock was supposed to be the marrying of music with the theatrical, then these five Aussies certainly hadn't been tapped on the shoulder and told about it.

While Scott concentrated on the basics of rock howling, the band's rhythm section locked into the groove and played things totally, commitedly straight. Drummer Phil Rudd's Sonor kit was a nothing of a set-up. One bass drum, floor tom, one hanging tom, snare, hi-hat and ride. These tools were not there for effect. They were there for work.

"i became dimly aware in my as-yet-underdeveloped mind that something as seemingly stupid as a rock gig was most likely going to be a life-altering experience."

If, like me, you've always admired drummers who know their place in a band, then Phil Rudd was the guvnor; a no-frills and no bullshit metronome.

Flanking Rudd, bassist Cliff Williams and rhythm guitarist Malcolm Young were equally inconspicuous. They hugged the backline at the rear of the stage with what I interpreted as a need to feel the rumble of their instruments throbbing back at them. They ventured to the front to sing backing vocals like a couple of sulky schoolkids

being asked to come to the front of the class to read, then scuttled back into the shadows as soon as the chores were completed. They looked mean and hard and stupid. I'd read somewhere that Malcolm was the brains of the operation. Even then I knew this spoke little for the intelligence of the rest of the band. But idiocy certainly didn't seem to hinder their ability to play so tight they almost squeaked. And anyway, I was in the audience dressed in a schoolboy uniform. So who was the fool, eh?

THE OBJECT OF MY teenage hero-worship, Angus Young, is quite a sight when you witness him in the flesh for the first time. I obviously had some clue about his performances on stage from what I'd read in the music press. I knew he liked to duck walk like Chuck Berry, I knew he had a distinctive-looking Gibson SG guitar and, of course, I knew he wore the schoolkid's uniform. But knowing all that didn't prepare me for that night in Manchester. Because what impressed me most of all was the guy's sheer energy. From the minute he came on stage to the minute I left the building, chords ringing in my ears with that dull buzz that I soon came to know well, this preposterous little man never stopped moving. It was as if it was him, not the guitar, that was plugged into the mains. His whole skinny body, unappealingly shiny under the lights, was itself a shuddering mass of electricity. It was as if every power chord and every solo juddered through his veins, turning him into a twitching, convulsing loon. Angus Young's performance was so, well, *real* that I was in awe.

The sheer human endeavour of his two hour show was what I loved most about the guitarist. I suppose, given that at 15 I was so poor that the phrase 'not having two ha'pennies to rub together' wasn't strictly accurate because I didn't even have one, he made me feel I was getting my money's worth. He even made me forget I was wearing a school uniform. For a while, anyway. But even as I stood shaking my not-very-hairy head in the Manchester Apollo, surrounded by a sea of patched denim interspersed with about a dozen other supposed schoolboys; even as I became dimly aware in my as-yet-underdeveloped mind that something as seemingly stupid as a rock gig was most likely going to be a life-altering experience; even as I wondered why something that was this good hadn't been banned by some crowd of repressed do-gooders or other; it suddenly dawned on me what an absolute complete and utter twat I looked. The fact that I wasn't put off AC/DC for life, I put down to a minor miracle. For no matter how much I worshipped Angus' guitar playing, no matter how much I thought this was an incredible rock and roll gig, I was also quickly coming to the conclusion that my mum had been right all along. The schoolboy uniform was a rotten idea. I even thought *he* looked stupid in it. But at least Angus was on stage – a place where you're supposed to act the goat. I, meanwhile, was merely a bit-part player in this spectacle, some hopeless extra trying to muscle in and shine ahead of the star actor. Ten minutes into the gig I slipped the cap off my head, rolled it up sheepishly, stuck it in my pocket and vowed never again to do anything as ludicrous. And while I never remotely managed to live up to that vow, of course, as on so many occasions in life, the whole event proved one simple thing to me. You should always listen to your mum. Of course I didn't though. I just kept listening to AC/DC. ∎

A CAUTIONARY TALE

Gero Probst, a student at the Academy of Media in Cologne, has this to say about his obsession...

I've been a huge AC/DC fan for about 12 years now. Since 1986, when I first heard 'Who Made Who', I've been absolutely obsessed with them – even to the extent that I always took a Walkman to school and never listened to anyone else. The band took over my whole life. In the evening, when most people were out at parties, I would sit on the floor in my room, grooving to the beats of Phil Rudd. It got even worse when I decided to start learning electric guitar in 1988 – then I simply lost contact with the outside world pretty much until now.

I've had to pay a pretty heavy price for my obsession – losing friends all the time over the years. There are now only really two mates who accept my addiction to the band. I know it sounds silly, but virtually no day goes by which doesn't contain a dose of AC/DC. Instead of drinking cups of coffee early in the morning, I simply put on 'Overdose' from 'Let There Be Rock' and turn up the volume in my little student shack. Wow, here come those power-chords and in a nanosecond I'm awake!

It's become a personal ritual to play along with the boys on my Gibson SG, everything from 'High Voltage' to 'Bonfire'. Each album has its own unique flavour and I rock around the clock, while the neighbours wonder what the hell is going on. They have to be pretty tolerant of my AC/DC obsession too. After all, you know you got to play it loud!

"IT GOT LODGED IN MY BRAIN"

German fan Erik Zimmer got in the frame with DC back in 1980. Now 31, he explains why the band got a hold of him...

I remember just how it started. There were some guys at school carrying a ghetto-blaster around, playing 'T.N.T.' all the time, and the song just got lodged in my brain so I could never shake it. To me the music was raw like meat; rough, hard and loud and it really kicked ass.

At Easter 1980 I got my first AC/DC record, 'Highway To Hell', and from then on all hell broke loose. I spent all the money I earned, stole or got as a gift on AC/DC records, posters, mags... anything I could find that I could afford at the time. One day I bought three great posters of the guys and I was really happy with them. Then, only a few days later, I went to Frankfurt with a friend. We ended up checking the record stores, like you do, and what did we find? The Australian release of 'Dirty Deeds...' with extra tracks. I should have been over the moon, but instead I was devastated. I didn't have enough money left to buy it because I'd spent it all on those damned posters. That should have taught me a lesson about not just buying everything I came across!

In November of '82 I saw AC/DC live for the first time in Frankfurt and it was amazing. It was my first "big" concert, and I really got a taste for it. I followed the band closely after that, looking forward to every record and tour, spending a shedload more money along the way. In the middle of '83 the band's German record company organised a competition in conjunction with a teen mag to coincide with the release of 'Flick Of The Switch'. We were asked to write a review of the new record and the best efforts were published in the mag and won special prizes. I got a runners-up prize of an interview record (which I couldn't understand!), an Angus full-size poster and some other bits and pieces. I traded the record and I think I've lost the other stuff. I must be a bloody idiot...

In the late Eighties I spent a day in Luxembourg and I discovered a record store selling a lot of bootlegs. I must admit I wasn't very experienced in buying bootlegs at the time, but I remember holding vintages like 'Jailbreak', 'Trip Wires', 'The Bad Boys On Stage' in white vinyl and 'Monsters Of Rock '84' in my hands... but once again I had the slight problem of too little cash. I could only afford the cheapest of them. Life can be tough...

1990 came, and with it the fabulous 'The Razors Edge' album. I got tickets for the show six months before it happened, but exactly a week before the gig I had to spend 14 miserable days in hospital. Remember the video for 'That's The Way I Wanna Rock 'n' Roll' where the guy's lying in bed? That might as well have been me... I felt truly sorry for myself. It's the only DC gig I've missed in the Frankfurt area in the past 15 years

Now it's 1999 and I'm looking forward to a new album and tour. I expect I'll hear all the old rumours again like "It's the last album and tour," but I've heard that one since 1987. I don't worry about it too much, though, because I'm sure there will be a load more fun to be had with AC/DC's pure high voltage rock'n'roll in the future.

THE FIRST TIME

Tony Dixon first saw DC on the 1979 'Highway To Hell' tour. This is his story of the Liverpool Empire Theatre gig on 5th November.

This was it, the day I'd waited for all summer. As soon as I got home from school, the uniform was changed and tea was eaten in about 10 seconds. I made my way to the train station and met my mates, Andy, Brian and Andrew. We'd been looking forward to this gig for ages as it was our first ever concert and to us AC/DC were *the* band.

Something had to go wrong, of course, and on the train Andrew's face suddenly went white: "I've forgotten my ticket," he said. He got off at the next stop to phone home, while the rest of us carried on into Liverpool, hoping we'd meet him later.

As we got to the Empire there were lots of people surrounding the doors, pushing and shoving, trying to get to the bar. We went straight to our seats and it wasn't long before the support band came on. As we sat and watched we agreed that the band were good, especially as they were only a group of teenagers. As it happened they were to become one of the world's biggest rock bands, Def Leppard. As soon as they left the stage, though, the chants of 'Angus! Angus!' rang out around the theatre. There was still no sign of Andrew, though!

The lights went down and you could hear the speakers and amps start to rumble as though they were getting ready for the musical onslaught. The drums and rhythm guitars started, then the spotlight moved across to the back of the drum kit. There was Angus, head nodding slightly to and fro and moving along the wall of speakers. Then he jumped down and roared into 'Live Wire', hurtling across the stage like a madman. I couldn't believe my eyes!

While Angus did his stuff, Bon coolly walked across the stage, tore off his sleeveless denim jacket, threw it to the side and began to sing his stories. Next came 'Shot Down In Flames' and Andrew suddenly appeared. He'd managed to phone his dad, who'd picked him up and brought his ticket with him. 'Sin City' and 'Hell Ain't A Bad Place To Be' soon went by before Bon asked the crowd if we were alright. A large cheer confirmed that we were. Then we got it between the eyes again. 'Girl's Got Rhythm', 'Highway To Hell', 'Bad Boy Boogie', 'If You Want Blood', 'High Voltage', 'The Jack', 'Whole Lotta Rosie' and 'Rocker'... Angus never stopped for a minute and Bon jigged his way through all the songs, before the encore of 'Let There Be Rock'.

As the house lights came on I felt like I'd been hit by a steam train, but it left a huge grin on my face. This was my first AC/DC concert and since then I've watched them every time they play the UK. To me they're the *only* band worth their salt.

THE DC FILES

Bon Scott

Born on 9th July 1946, Bon Scott's first ventures into rock'n'roll began as a 16 year old while in Perth's Riverbank boys' home. Riverbank was a remand centre where the young Scott spent nine months for nicking 12 gallons of petrol. While inside, he played drums in a band he'd formed with two other inmates and gained a real taste for rock'n'roll, so when he found himself at liberty again in 1965, he formed a band called The Spektors, playing Beatles and Stones songs in the local youth clubs. Occasionally Bon would venture from behind the kit to have a crack at singing, and when he joined a more professional outfit, The Valentines, he packed in the drums and shared vocal duties with Vince Lovegrove. The Valentines played syrupy pop, perfectly displayed on their first single, a cover of Arthur Alexander's 'Every Day I Have To Cry', released in May 1967 on the Clarion label. The band became friendly with George Young and Harry Vanda of The Easybeats, even releasing a cover of their 'Peculiar Hole In The Sky' as well as a

Vanda/Young composition, 'My Old Man's A Groovy Old Man'. The band's clean-cut image – Bon even covered his tattoos with make-up – was at odds with their offstage partying, though. When the band were busted for possession of pot the writing was on the wall. The Valentines split on 1st August 1970.

In a dramatic turnaround, Bon next hooked up with Fraternity, a group that was attempting to be Australia's answer to The Band. Two albums, 'Livestock' and 'Flaming Galah', didn't do much to endear their hippyish rock to music fans and the band eventually upped sticks and moved to Finchley in London to have a go on the other side of the world. This neither helped the band's career, nor Bon's recent marriage to Irene. Changing the band name to Fang in April 1973 saw no upturn in fortunes either, the band finally split and Bon and Irene were back in Australia by the end of the year.

The marriage was looking distinctly rocky. Irene wanted Bon to give up bands and settle down, but he still hankered for the rock'n'roll life. He picked up casual work in Adelaide, mostly labouring, before winding up as an assistant to promoter Vince

Lovegrove, his old singing partner from his first group, The Valentines. Various members of Fraternity ended up forming the Mount Lofty Rangers and Bon joined for a time. Things didn't seem to be going anywhere, though, and Bon was getting more and more frustrated.

After one particularly heavy argument with Irene, Bon went on an all-day drinking spree, then turned up at the studio and argued with the rest of the band. Swigging on a whisky bottle he rode off on his motorbike at speed and collided with a car, ending up in a coma for three days and nearly dying. Months later Bon finally came out of hospital, recorded two songs (eventually released on Head Office Records in 1997!) in July of 1974, and went back to his job with Vince. Vince told him he'd hired a band called AC/DC to play a local venue and that they were looking for a singer. Bon thought it might be interesting...

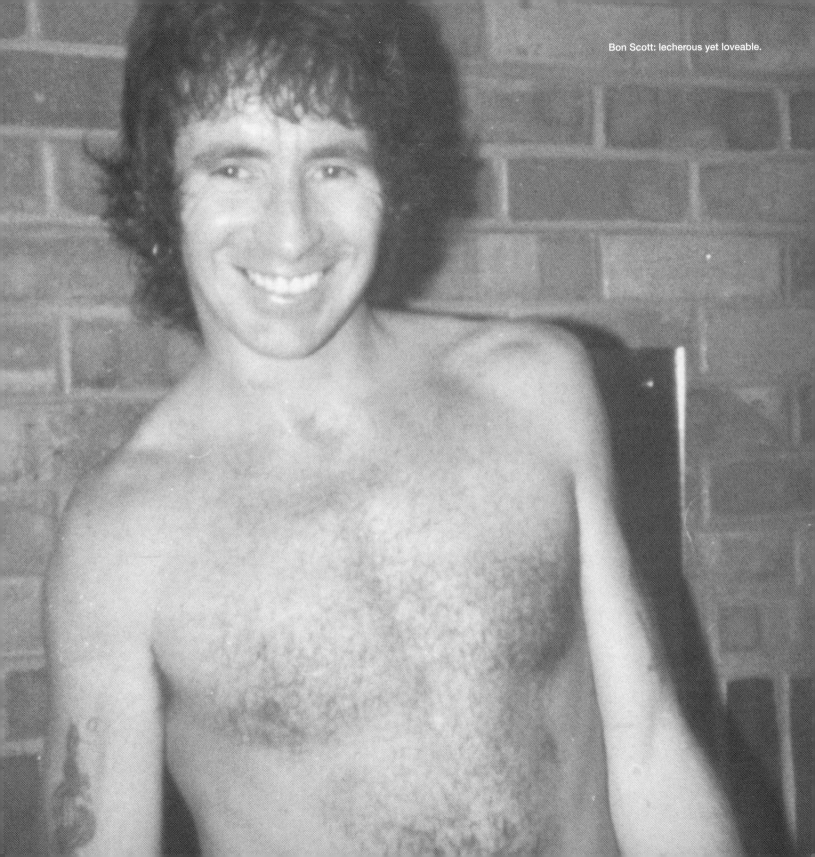

Bon Scott: lecherous yet loveable.

Chapter Three

SCOTT iS DEAD

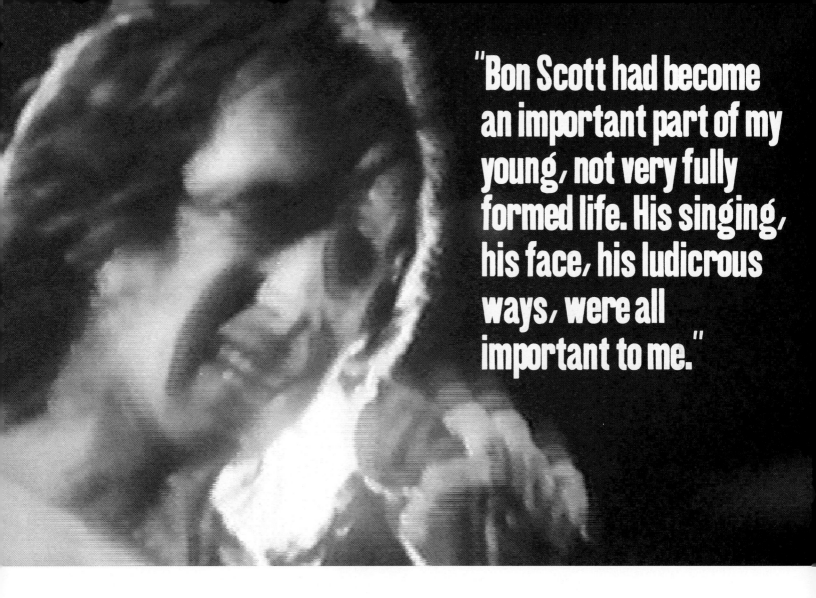

"Bon Scott had become an important part of my young, not very fully formed life. His singing, his face, his ludicrous ways, were all important to me."

When they want to be, kids can be cruel. Systematically. Mercilessly. Endlessly. Ever thought you've been the butt of the jokes at work? Then cast your mind back to your old schooldays and chances are you'll find instances of mental cruelty that would even make seasoned torturers in obscure South American states agree that things had simply gone too far.

There was always somebody getting picked on at my school. The victim would change from time to time as important matters such as new haircuts or new trousers led the mob to change their target. But as often as not the baiters would religiously taunt one sorry individual, out of continuing spite or, more likely, just out of simple laziness. Some people seem born to be victims and often I've wondered about the debilitating effects of such systematic and relentless bullying on these people in their later lives. Once in a while I really worry about Andrew Hill, an unassuming and ugly kid with crooked teeth and greasy hair. Andrew Hill was the victim I remember most when I look back at my days at The Manchester Grammar School.

I'd passed the entrance exam to this respected and revered educational institution and at age 11 had started to make the hour-long journey from suburban Altrincham to the centre of Manchester, then out again to Burnage, home, unbeknownst to me at the time, of the Gallagher family, soon to produce the seedlings of Oasis. MGS was always recognised as a school for clever kids, often mis-interpreted by those with an axe to grind against the direct grant system as a school for posh and privileged lads. And while some of its intake undoubtedly did come from well-heeled families, the school's egalitarian traditions ensured that gifted boys from average to poor backgrounds still found a way in through various bursaries and scholarships.

It was a pretty happy place to be. Racism and violence were not only unheard of, but were simply not tolerated by a schoolboy population from many different backgrounds and many different creeds. Fair play, and a feather in our school caps, then. But whereas intelligent boys might have found racism pathetic and revolting, the idea of bullying and picking on the weaker members of the clan was not only tolerated, but as near as dammit encouraged. Poor Andrew Hill has probably never recovered and I'm ashamed to admit that I played my part in his misery. Hill was hardly a sight for sore eyes, his crooked teeth bursting through the front of his mouth with the same vigour that the acne was forcing its way out from under his skin. A greasy swathe of hair topped off his overall unfavourable appearance and the combination of these three visual sins was enough for the rest of us to deem Hill fair game for anything.

Our jibes were pathetic and childish and featured all the usual nonsense. If someone farted the whole class would look at Hill and start chanting his name. If some chore needed doing – the blackboard cleaning or the waste

paper basket emptying – there was no doubt that Hill would be forced into it by the sheer will of his peers. Hill was never threatened or physically beaten, and maybe you'll think that those silly little mind games we played don't sound particularly damaging to a 15-year-old boy. But I still remember looking in his eyes all those years back, seeing Hill trying to force out a foolish grin that was somehow trying to tell us that he too was in on the joke. I still remember somehow knowing even then

that this young lad was probably lying on his bed at night sobbing his heart out with the shame and hurt of it all, not even cursing his wretched class mates, but simply wishing that it would all somehow, miraculously, stop. I knew that Andrew Hill felt like that, but of course I didn't stop. Because schoolboys are cruel. Systematically. Mercilessly. Endlessly. As I found out for myself soon enough.

THERE IT WAS. On the board. Scrawled out in big, bold chalk letters. 'SCOTT IS DEAD'. I'd just swanned into the classroom, amazed as always by the amount of dust particles swirling in the air. You could see them in all their glory whenever you walked into our particular classroom, because whatever aspect it was facing meant that the harsh winter sunlight would flood in through the window. That day, though, my attention was soon diverted from such trivia by the smirking faces of about 20 lads. 'SCOTT IS DEAD'. At first the message didn't really register. I didn't know anyone called Scott. 'Scott who?' I thought. Then it suddenly hit me. Bon Scott. I looked back at the blackboard. 'SCOTT IS DEAD'. And then I noticed something else, written in tiny letters in one corner, a real afterthought. 'Sorry Howard'.

I don't know why, but I suddenly felt extremely foolish. My love of AC/DC was obviously well known amongst my classmates. They would have had to have been pretty moronic not to have cottoned on, what with my frankly pathetic attempts at drawing that distinctive logo on various copy books. But above all they would have known of my love of the band because of The Badge. I can't remember where I got it from, but I remember it as if it were yesterday. An enormous sideplate of a badge it was, featuring a live shot of the band with Angus going through his usual paces

"There it was. On the board. Scrawled out in big, bold chalk letters. 'SCOTT iS DEAD'."

Fremantle Cemetery, Australia.

IN LOVING MEMORY OF
BON SCOTT
LEAD SINGER OF
THE ROCK GROUP AC/DC
THIS SEAT WAS DONATED
BY HIS FAMILY

and the logo slapped across the dead black space at the top which was the roof of some concert hall or other. The style of the day was for tiny button badges depicting all the punk and new wave bands that dominated the British music scene; Joy Division was a particular favourite, local boys and all that. Not for me, though. I'd decided that my allegiances lay with the rockers, and as such good taste wasn't something I possessed in bucketloads. That huge bloody badge, though, was both an admission of a lack of street savvy and also a confirmation of a desire not to be like everybody else in the school.

The Badge, which was so big it actually pulled the lapel of my school blazer out of shape, seemed particularly foolish now that I'd been greeted with the news of Bon Scott's unfortunate demise. Someone gave me a copy of *The Sun*, where there was a short snippet which gave only the most basic information. Apparently Bon had choked on his own vomit and died while sleeping off the effects of one big night out too many in his mate's car down in London. This just made things all the more embarrassing for me, though. "What a pathetic, pointless and avoidable way to die," I thought. "Alone. Drowning in your own puke." Christ. What a stupid, ugly, ridiculous waste. I was shocked and saddened, but above all I was suddenly angry. Yes, that feeling of foolishness suddenly gave way to anger. Anger at the stupidity of it all. And anger at

the chattering, laughing and joking that continued all around me at the start of another day of school. I was upset. Bon Scott had become an important part of my young, not very fully formed life. His singing, his face, his ludicrous ways, were all important to me. AC/DC were very important to me. I loved their music and I loved the band as an entity, the way you do when you're 15 and nailing your colours to some cultural mast or other. Bon was dead and while the rest of the world thought it was just an excuse for a cheap gag to be forgotten in seconds, drowned out by the general hubbub of existence, to me it was a matter of great national importance. The rest of that day just went by in a blur. ■

Getting Court On Camera

Nikki Goff, Editor of the AC/DC fanzine *Electric Outlaws*, wrote this account of a visit to Bon's home at the time of his death, Ashley Court in London.

'Why did I let myself in for this?' I think, as I try to curl up into a comfortable position on the seat. The temperature is dropping rapidly. I manage to tuck myself up like a large cat trying to sleep on a small cushion, but my back and neck ache. At last someone shouts "Turn the bloody heating on" and as the coach driver obliges and pumps warm air through the bus I can finally get some sleep. I eventually wake up to see the rising sun reflected on the glass walls of London skyscrapers.

We reach Victoria coach station at six o'clock in the morning and it's three hours before anywhere opens. I have to clear the carbon monoxide from my brain, so go down to the river and walk along the embankment, past Battersea Power Station and on to the Tate Gallery. It's still way too early, though, so it's off to find some breakfast. The café is quite rough and ready, filled with a mixture of builders and office workers. A typical yuppie wanders in with slicked hair, white shirt and braces, giving it some 'OK, ya' on his mobile phone. Time to go...

Back at Victoria things are very different. It's nearly nine o'clock and there are loads of people about. I study the map and realise I'll have to head down Victoria Street. It's the rush hour and you have to walk fast and avoid colliding with anyone. Escaping the human tidal wave I see a gap in the wall of glass and steel, which turns out to be a small square. You can see Westminster Cathedral. It's a huge and ornate building, with red and white stripes, a tower and a mosaic of angels above the door. I get my camera out of my rucksack and go to examine the buildings immediately around the cathedral. I know I'll find what I'm looking for. A newspaper cutting I have states that Bon lived in a block of flats called Morpeth Terrace. I've also discovered that he lived in a building called Ashley Court, so all I have to do is walk round the cathedral, starting with Ambrosden Avenue. I see a block of flats called Ashley Gardens, but that's not what I'm looking for. I move on to Francis Street, more flats

and buildings being refurbished which are covered with plastic sheets. There's no chance of seeing any nameplates. I turn into Morpeth Terrace, where I notice that there's a building standing alone at the end of the row. This must be the place. A small group of trees casts dappled shadows over the stonework, but I can still see a carved nameplate over the double glass doors. It reads 'Ashley Court'. This is it, the site of one of the most intriguing of AC/DC legends, the case of the missing writings.

According to various sources, shortly after Bon died somebody went to his flat and collected most of his property, including most of what he'd written for the next AC/DC album. We know the band had a lot of his notes, but they probably only had copies they were working with anyway. Tour manager Ian Jeffrey has also claimed he has some lyrics, though to date he's not been willing

to share them with the rest of the world. Whoever has them must realise their value, so it will only be a matter of time before they surface.

Whatever intrigues and dramas were played out here, though, I'm standing on the pavement, feeling uneasier by the second. I know no famous people live in Ashley Court, but I still feel like a stalker as I swing my camera up and drop to one knee to get a good shot of the name plate. Someone opens the door. I fire off a shot quickly and walk away swiftly. I bet they think 'Bloody tourists!'. I realise I can get a good view of the building from the plaza in front of the cathedral, so I get out my sketch pad and a drawing pen and get to work. The building appears to be a mixture of Georgian and Gothic styles, though it's not particularly eye-catching. I move on, happy in the knowledge that I've visited an important place in the life of one of my heroes.

BON'S LAST HOURS

The French AC/DC fanzine *Let There Be Light* described Bon's final days in this fascinating article...

After a gig in Birmingham on 20th December 1979 Bon left the UK for Fremantle in Australia to spend Christmas with his parents Isa and Chuck. At the start of the following year he attended Angus' wedding where the little man got married to Helen, and that turned out to be the last time he ever saw Angus' new bride.

On 16th January the band began the second half of a French tour, which was made up of extra gigs that had been added when the demand for tickets proved to be higher than first expected. The band were fast becoming the fans' favourite all over the world and at the Midem music industry convention in Cannes they were given two gold discs for 'If You Want Blood...' (for France and the UK) and a UK silver disc for 'Highway To Hell'. Two days later the band played an incredible gig in Brest with French rockers Trust as support, then on the following day (23rd January) they finished their French dates at Le Mans, where they also filmed a couple of sequences for what turned out to be the *Let There Be Rock* film. On the 24th the band headed back to England for two more shows that had been cancelled the previous year. They played in Newcastle on the 25th and Southampton on the 27th, a show which turned out to be Bon's last ever gig.

At the end of the month of January the band camped out in London. Bon had found himself a place in Victoria, while Phil, Cliff, Malcolm and

Bon's personal 'Highway To Hell' tour jacket, now owned by a fan.

Angus got themselves some temporary accommodation. They started rehearsals for the follow-up to 'Highway To Hell' at the start of February and recording was pencilled in for March. Things were going pretty well – Bon began work on lyrics and around 10th February Malcolm and Angus tried out a few ideas with Bon on drums (not such a mad idea as back in

Australia between 1959 and 1963 he'd won six awards on the instrument).

During this rehearsal period Bon spent a lot of time hanging out with Trust, the French band he'd become friendly with and who were recording their second album, 'Repression', in London's Scorpio studios. They were getting on so well that the band's lead singer Bernie asked Bon if he would like to translate the original French lyrics into English – a job which eventually fell to Sham 69 vocalist Jimmy Pursey. On the afternoon of 17th February Bon recorded a superb version of 'Ride On' with Trust during a jam session, as well as advising the French band about some potential changes to their songs. That same evening he invited Trust to dinner at his new place in Victoria.

The following night at about 10 o'clock, Bon phoned Bernie up at the White House Hotel where the band were staying to see if he wanted to meet up at the Music Machine, a venue in North London's Camden Town area. Trust, however, had flown out to Paris in the afternoon to pick up gold discs for their eponymous first album and were out on the town celebrating their achievements. Nobody went back to the hotel to pick up messages and so Bon's call remained unanswered. Bon decided instead to go out with Allistair Kinnear, a singer and former flatmate, and they headed for the Music Machine. A band called Lonesome No More were playing there, but Bon wasn't interested in them and stayed propping up the bar. Faithful to the nickname that he'd picked up from the rest of the band in 1978, 'Over The Top' drank at least seven

The seat in Fremantle Cemetery donated by Bon's family.

double whiskeys and was pretty tanked up when they left the venue at three in the morning. He laid down in the back seat of his mate's Renault 5 and fell asleep.

ALLISTAIR DROVE TO Bon's place and tried to get him out of the car, but couldn't manage it. He was hardly sober himself and it wasn't easy to lift Bon's dead-weight body. He decided to take Bon back to his own place at 67 Overhill Road in East Dulwich, South London. When he got there he realised that he wouldn't be able to get Bon in the house there either, so decided it would be best to let him sleep in the car. He covered Bon up and locked the doors of the car for safety. It was four in the morning.

Allistair woke 15 hours later and immediately went out to check on Bon, but the singer wasn't moving. He realised at once that something was wrong and in a panic he headed straight for King's College Hospital, which wasn't far from his house. It was about seven in the evening of 19th February. When he arrived at the hospital Bon was pronounced dead. He'd been sick in his sleep, his windpipe had blocked and he'd

choked. Informed about the events by a friend of Allistair's, Angus was the first band member to hear what had happened. He phoned Malcolm straight away with the news, but tour manager Ian Jeffrey was convinced that this wasn't Bon they were talking about, because as far as he was aware Bon had gone to bed early the night before. Even so, Angus wanted to know for certain. He spoke with the hospital after getting the number from Allistair's girlfriend. They confirmed the news that it *was* Bon after all, which left Malcolm with the unenviable task of phoning Chuck and Isa Scott so that they wouldn't first learn of the death of their son on the television news.

The band's manager Peter Mensch got down to the hospital as quickly as he could to find out

> **Bon's mum turned up at the first gig of the 'Ballbreaker' tour in 1996. 78-year-old Isa Scott knows all the words to all the band's songs.**

what had happened and to identify the body, because nobody wanted to believe that Bon really was gone. He was the last person from the band's organisation to see Bon – the band members were told that they weren't authorised to view the body. Bernie from Trust tells how he reacted to the news:

"I had to lean on a wall and it felt as if I'd been hit by an iron bar. I stood up straight again, but I couldn't believe what I'd heard. I went back into the dining room and began to eat again, automatically, not really thinking about it at all. Then I drove to the studio, still not really believing it. I got to Scorpio and realised when I looked at the rest of the people in the studio – they were all pale – that it was in the papers. They said nothing. I went in, sat down and started to cry."

ON FRIDAY 22ND FEBRUARY the group went before the magistrates to give their account of events and to hear what the autopsy had discovered. The doctor in charge concluded that Bon had about a half a litre of whiskey in his stomach at the time of death. Aside from that, his body was in perfect condition and in the

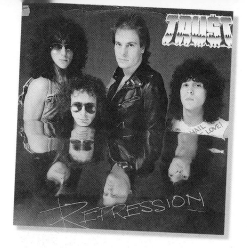

The dedication to Bon from the inside of Trust's 'Repression' album. Note the differing dates on the French and English versions.

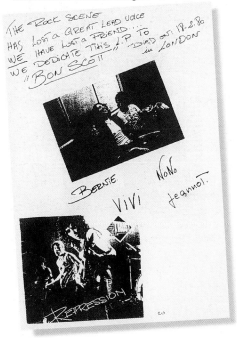

doctor's opinion this was a case of death by misadventure. He concluded that Bon was responsible for his own demise. The group defended his reputation, claiming he was no alcoholic and confirmed that he hadn't missed even one of 250 concerts. Allistair Kinnear was cleared of any wrongdoing.

BON WAS BURIED in Fremantle, Australia on 1st March. Several fans went to pay their last respects to Bon in the chapel where the funeral service took place, but the actual burial was attended only by a small family gathering.

It was Bon's parents who told the rest of the group that they should continue the band, saying it was what Bon would have wanted. Malcolm spoke with Angus two days later and they went back to work.

Over the next few months several bands paid tribute to Bon. During their 1980 tour Trust played 'Ride On', 'Live Wire' and 'Problem Child' and Bernie wrote 'Ton Dernier Acte' ('Your Final Act') as a tribute to the great man – a song which appeared on the 'Marche Ou Creve' ('March Or Die') album. But Angus has the final word on Bon:

"He was our trump card. He was our big brother, the person we'd turn to for advice and the guy who plotted out our career. No way would AC/DC have been where they are without him. We miss him and we'll always miss him. But we believe that as long as we're together, then Bon's spirit is still alive."

The Highway To Hell

When DC fan Solveig Schuster visited London, he just had to visit the place in East Dulwich where Bon lost his life...

O n 10 November 1991 I had the opportunity to go to London for the first time and decided that above all else there was one thing that I had to do... visit the house in Underhill Road outside which Bon met his maker. I made the pilgrimage there on the 12th. After visiting the London Dungeons horror museum with my friend, we decided we were too lazy to go all the way back to Victoria Station, even though that was where my directions to the house in East Dulwich started. We tried another route, heading for Brixton in the hope that we'd be able to pick up a bus from there. Things didn't go too badly and we managed to get a bus that was heading for Dulwich, but soon realised that none of the bus stops had any signs written on them explaining exactly where we were. We got off after about 15 minutes in Crystal Palace and to our

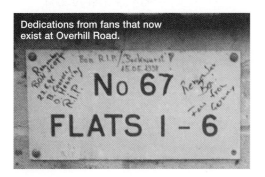

Dedications from fans that now exist at Overhill Road.

horror found that we were still about seven kilometres away. We started walking.

After about two hours we came to the first road that we knew by name, Lordship Lane. According to the map it was only about 200 metres, up to the second crossroads on the right and we should be there at Underhill Road. We couldn't be sure about it, though, because the street sign was missing. Then I remembered reading somewhere that it had been 'liberated' by another AC/DC fan. Still, I thought it was time for my first photo and noticed that at least the sign was still in place on the other side of the road. Someone had scribbled 'In memory of Bon Scott' on it.

We headed up the street and soon discovered that it was a really steep hill, but when we finally made it to the top at least we were rewarded with a decent view. In contrast to the other houses in the street, number 67 seems simple and dark. Dulwich isn't a poor area, so that in itself was quite weird. Next to the house there's an entrance to a garage and in the driveway stood a blue Renault 5. I thought back to that fateful night and wondered whether it could be the same car that had been parked there on the night of the 18th February 1980. Even though I don't like Walkmans I stuck one on to hear the song which I believed best summed up this place, 'Carry Me Home'. I looked around and found something very surprising. There were no spots where fans had written their tributes. They'd probably been cleared by the people doing road-works nearby. Shame.

We decided to go back again the next day and take more photos and also discovered some more important AC/DC landmarks on the way. During our bus journey this time we went past King's College Hospital where Bon was taken, and also the Red Lion pub where the band first started playing in London. So that was it. It may not have been a very exciting journey for a non-Bon fan, but for me it was a truly great experience.

Bon was rushed to King's College Hospital, but was dead on arrival.

One Step Closer To Bon...

Thomas Krogh thought he'd hook up with plenty more DC fans when he visited Bon's grave on the anniversary of his death. But things didn't quite work out that way.

On 10th January 1994 I finally set off on the Australian holiday that I'd been planning for two years. After a few weeks on the East Coast I headed west towards Perth, arriving there on 15th February which gave me enough time to work out the route to Fremantle and Bon Scott's grave. And what better day to pay my respects to Bon than 19th February, the anniversary of his death?

I knew that I had to make my way to the Fremantle Cemetery and so on the day in question I left my hotel on foot heading for Perth's main train station. I took a local service and after a journey of about 25 minutes arrived at Fremantle. I then had what turned out to be a pretty long walk to the cemetery. I wasn't bothered about taking a cab, though, because I had my Walkman and just the right kind of music to set the mood. It took about an hour to get to the cemetery, and in a 30 degree heat, even in the shade, the cans of beer in my rucksack were getting heavier by the minute. Why was I carrying so many cans of beer, you might ask? Well I had them with me because I wanted to toast Bon with other AC/DC fans.

I arrived at about 11 o'clock. Someone had told me where the grave was, but try as I might, I just couldn't find it. I went up to the caretaker and asked for the grave of Ronald Belford Scott and he just stared blankly at me, so I put the question another way. "Where's Bon Scott's grave? The singer from AC/DC." Then it dawned on him what I was looking for and quickly pointed out exactly where it was. I set off for the grave hoping to see some other AC/DC fans in the distance, but there was nobody there. I was the first one to arrive, but at least I'd made it there.

It was a strange feeling to be standing at the grave of one of the greatest rock singers ever – in my opinion *the* best. I'd been listening to AC/DC for 14 years, knew all the songs, had seen the band live countless times, but had still missed seeing Bon perform by a year. And now here I was. A few tears welled up in my eyes. I suppose I should have known that I would cry. I was a bit shocked that there was no real gravestone and no real grave, only a remembrance plate tucked away amongst a few others and I actually started to wonder whether Bon really was buried here at all. Surely there must be a real gravestone somewhere. Whatever, I was happy enough with what I'd seen. The paved footpath in front of the remembrance stones is covered with tributes and greetings from all over the world. About two metres from Bon's plaque you can find a bench with an inscription. I took a few photos and sat down in the shade under a tree a few metres away to wait for the other fans. To make the wait more enjoyable I stuck on my Walkman and listened to my favourite group again, rounding the moment off by cracking open my first can of beer. It was a little bit early, but on a day like today...

After two hours of endless waiting and a few more cans the first Australian fans arrived. 'Now it'll all start happening,' I thought and I started chatting with some of them. There were five fans, aged about 15 or 16, who had been listening to the band for about a year and were big fans of Bon's stuff. But after about an hour they left again. And that was it. No crowd around the grave. No more fans. Not one.

I thought I'd meet so many AC/DC obsessives here that it would be like visiting Elvis' grave. OK, maybe not quite that big, but I was expecting 50 or so people. At the very least I'd hoped to meet some fans who's actually seen Bon live. But nothing. Just one solitary German spent his day there thinking about Bon. I was both astonished and disappointed. There must be hundreds of AC/DC fans in Perth and the surrounding area, people who know the day of his death and who visit his grave on the anniversary. And it was a Saturday, so there was no excuse for people not to make it. I stayed in the cemetery until about five in the evening enjoying the beer, then I took a taxi back to Fremantle train station. As far as I was concerned the day trip had been well worth it… even if I was the only person who'd really been bothered to pay his respects.

Chapter Four

BLACK MAGIC

Everyone knows about the notion of strength through adversity. That's what 'Back In Black' seemed to sum up to me. The effect on the band of losing Bon Scott must have been enormous, but the impression that the first album following his death left on the world was simply staggering. 'Back In Black' is an album whose impact was both immediate and enduring.

It seemed to me back then as if AC/DC had put the album together in double quick time. Bon Scott had died on 18th February 1980 and yet by July of that same year they'd found a new singer and recorded a new album. I'd remembered reading a piece in *Sounds* when former Geordie singer Brian Johnson was announced as Bon's replacement. Three things struck me. One: I'd never heard of Geordie and I certainly didn't know any of their music. Two: This fella looked like a right old codger. Three: I didn't like the stupid flat cap he was always being photographed in. Still, I was willing to give him a chance, especially since the rest of the band seemed so enthusiastic about him. It was either Angus or Malcolm who said something at the time about how there'd been loads of guys auditioning for the band who'd done nothing but ape Bon's singing style and approach. They liked Brian because he didn't seem that familiar with what AC/DC had been doing and because he had his own distinctive vocal style. Well, we'd just have to see about that, wouldn't we?

I'd just discovered a new record shop in Manchester when 'Back In Black' came out; Yanks.

Anyone who was an avid music purchaser in the North West 18 years back will remember Yanks. I don't know if it's still open, but at the time I thought it was the coolest place on earth. Yanks didn't seem to advertise anywhere. You just somehow 'found out' about the place. I can't remember who first introduced me to its delights, but I could never thank them enough for all the pleasure they gave me. The shop was located in a tiny cobbled alley, Charlotte Street, just off the main drag of Oxford Road. I had to go to Oxford Road station every day to get the train back home to Altrincham after school. The biggest thrill of the day was trying to catch the four o'clock diesel to Chester. It made just one stop before Altrincham, at Sale, but finishing school at quarter to four gave you the thinnest of margins to make it by jumping on a special bus outside the school gates and hoping that the traffic wouldn't be too slow on the way into town. If you missed that train you were condemned to the tedious electric chugger that stopped at every station between town and home. Pure torture, and enough of an incentive for hordes of bedraggled lads to jump out of moving buses, dash across roads with only the most cursory of glances for traffic and risk life and limb trying to fling themselves through the doors of moving locomotives. It seemed only a matter of time before our shared obsession with catching the four o'clock would end up with someone getting killed, so maybe rock music really did save my life. Why? Because once I'd discovered Yanks, I didn't give a toss about the four o'clock – I was going to spend my after-school hours checking out vinyl.

THE PLACE EVEN smelled great. It was nothing to look at, that was for sure. It was just a big old dilapidated warehouse building that summed up the Manchester I grew up in, from the days before clever developers worked out that you could turn these hoary old buildings into designer desirables.

You entered through a heavy door that, as I recall, didn't have any kind of logo or advert on it. Once inside you walked down a steep set of stairs to face another, even more sturdy-looking set of double doors. These did have a logo of sorts on, though; a shockingly bad cartoon figure who was an amalgam of Abraham Lincoln and Superman, wearing some kind of stars and stripes tunic. You couldn't have come up with a corporate image less likely to wow the punters, but once you'd opened those doors it simply didn't matter.

Beyond the two shutters lay a room whose every inch I can still remember. Fanning out on both sides were row after row of albums. Black gold. But this place was nothing like the mainstream shops you could find in any town centre. It smelled musty, which made me think for some strange reason that there was something faintly illegal about the place. There was hardly any daylight which could penetrate, so no matter what time of day you slipped into Yanks you were always shrouded in gloom, which only added to the place's mystique. And the records themselves were... different. They smelled different, they looked different to the albums in the HMV. And I soon worked out why. They were all imports.

I don't know what the legalities of importing thousands and thousands of albums from America are, but whichever way Yanks were doing it, it meant that everything in the store was cheaper than you could buy anywhere else. Which was doubly thrilling for me. Hard rock was still a minority sport in Britain. A huge cult, but a cult nonetheless. America had a much more buoyant market and so Yanks had a whole load of albums that hadn't been released in Britain just waiting for me to discover them. I didn't need asking twice either.

'Back In Black', released in Britain of course but an American pressing in Yanks, cost me about £3.99 and if you're talking pure value for money it has to be one of the steals of the century. Just looking at the cover had me intrigued. After the lairiness of 'Highway To Hell', where the five band members had been staring out at the record buyers with attitude to spare, this was a low-key, sombre affair that reflected the trauma that the group had just been through. A thin white keyline traced out the familiar logo, while the album title was embossed black on black so that you could barely pick it out. Bon's personality, his garishness, his pre-lad culture laddishness, had been such an integral part of the band's presentation. Now it seemed as if the intention was to strip every last vestige of it away – visually at least.

I wasn't disappointed by the change, though; it needed feeling of continuity, while adding enough individuality to kill off any suggestion that he was merely a Bon copyist. 'Back In Black' felt as dark as the title suggested and yet one of its quirks was that most of the titles and lyrics were still possessed of those lewd, funny innuendoes that had been so much a part of Bon's lyrical style.

'Whisky gin and brandy / With a glass I'm pretty handy / I'm trying to walk a straight line / On sour mash and cheap wine / So drink it pour it quick boys / We're gonna make a big noise / So don't worry about tomorrow / Live for today / Forget about the cheque we'll get hell to pay / Have a drink on me' It was just the kind of stuff Bon would have written, talking about the kind of devil-may-care really been offended by its stupidity. Even as a 16 year old who'd copped his first feel little more than a year before and whose hormones were raging out of control, I never saw AC/DC's lyrics as an invitation to behave like an asshole towards women. Besides, from the pictures I had by then seen of Bon it seemed to me that there were plenty of women in the world who didn't seem to have any problem with either Bon, Bon's lyrics or his ridiculously hairy chest. If these girls didn't seem particularly ruffled by AC/DC's daft sex fantasies, then I was damn sure that I wasn't going to get hung up on it either. To be honest I just thought it was funny.

I also thought 'Back In Black' was a masterpiece.

"This was a low-key, sombre affair that reflected the trauma that the group had just been through."

somehow seemed appropriate. I sat on the train on the way home after I'd bought the album, cursing the fact that there wasn't a later version of that four o'clock diesel. Through Deansgate, Old Trafford, Warwick Road, Sale, Brooklands, Timperley and Navigation Road. The stops seemed never-ending and while I devoured every last bit of information on the inner sleeve and checked the titles over and over, seeing if I could imagine how the choruses for songs like 'Shoot To Thrill' and 'Shake A Leg' actually went, all I really wanted to do was get home and listen for myself.

AND WHAT A REVELATION the album was. Robert John Lange's production added a meanness to the band's sound which reflected the anger they seemed to feel at Bon's death. Johnson's vocals were amazing, a lung-busting scream that echoed enough of his predecessor to give the band a much-hedonism that precipitated his boozed-up death. And while the writing credits ran Young-Young-Johnson, I can't be the only one who believes that more than a few of Bon's notebooks were rummaged through when the material for 'Back In Black' was being assembled. When you look at the lyrics the band have put on record since 1980, there's precious little of that roguish charm Bon was so easy with. Brian's lyrics have tended towards the bombastic, without capturing the cheekiness that Bon was so capable of pulling off. But make no mistake, all that cock-sure, tight-trousered lechery, that tongue-in-cheek naughtiness was still there on 'Back In Black', just daring you to be offended. I wasn't offended at all. In the days before the curse of PC took over in Britain I just thought it was a bit of a laugh. 'Give The Dog A Bone' was schoolboyish in its silly innuendo, but you'd really have to have been some kind of po-faced, hair-shirted Presbyterian to have Even on first hearing it had something about it that was different to all the AC/DC albums that had preceded it. It sounded bigger, for a start. Mutt Lange's production had moved the band's sound forward from a slightly hokey pub rock feel to something that I suspected could be appreciated on a much larger scale. I still play 'Back In Black' on a regular basis and it's always a Walkman favourite when I'm sunning myself on various holiday beaches. That damn tape's been with me way, way longer than even my wife. But looking back on the band's development 19 years later it's easy to see that in the triumph of 'Back In Black' also lay the seeds of AC/DC's demise. Lange's instinct to make the guitars somehow bigger, more suited to stadiums than sweaty clubs, made 'Back In Black' a landmark album for the band, taking them out of concert halls and into stadiums. Brian Johnson's more extreme vocal style, a more ➤

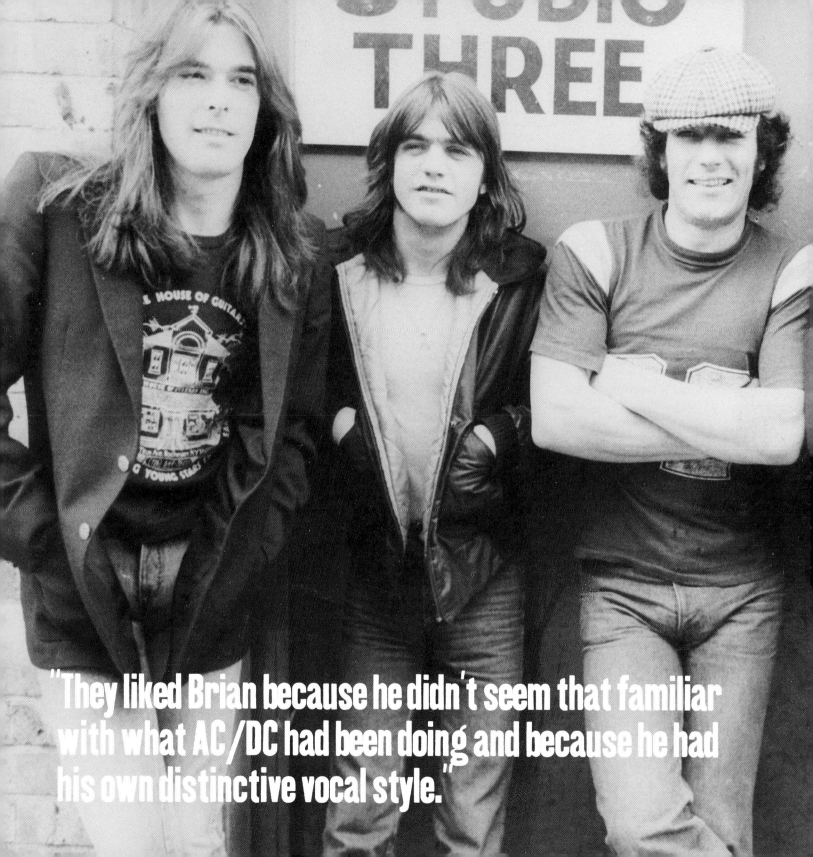

"They liked Brian because he didn't seem that familiar with what AC/DC had been doing and because he had his own distinctive vocal style."

theatrical, more 'rocktastic' version of Bon's singing, made the group seem like they somehow should be less matey, more like superstars. They were making big music, global rock now and the group's trajectory over the next few years saw them grow ever bigger, ever more bombastic, while as far as I was concerned their music slipped into decline, a big-budget parody of what it used to be, stripped of its humour and warmth and replaced with an unappealing chest-beating bravado that saw the group sleepwalking through most of the '80s as far as creativity was concerned.

'BACK IN BLACK' remains many fans' favourite ever DC album. It's not as good as 'Powerage' in my humble opinion. But then again it's a very different beast and has stood the test of time immaculately. I've been told by the wife to turn

> *"How a grown man like Brian Johnson could sing, far less write songs of such retarded adolescence as 'Hard As A Rock' ("Her hot potatoes will elevate you"), 'Cover You In Oil' ("Pull on the zip/She gave good lip service"), 'The Honey Roll' ("Baby bend over/Touch your toes/She take over/The bomb explodes") 'Caught With Your Pants Down' ("She rips off her stockings when the place starts rocking.") and 'Ballbreaker' ("Building steam/whippin' cream/You are a ballbreaker") defies belief."* – Review of 'Ballbreaker' by George Byrne in *The Irish Independent*, 3rd October 1995

'that bloody awful racket' down many a time, which has to be a good sign. And what 'Back In Black' does for me better than any other AC/DC album is to take me back to being 16 again, back to Yanks record store and the feeling that, even if it's just for 40 minutes, this music is the single most important thing in the world. The wife might not believe it, of course, but to me 'Back In Black' is conclusive proof that, as the song itself goes: "Rock'n'roll ain't noise pollution". ∎

THE PRODUCERS

AC/DC have only ever used five producers and have done their own production work on two albums. Here's a run-through of the guys behind the desks...

VANDA AND YOUNG

Producers of the classic early albums at Albert Studios in Sydney, Australia who again worked with the band in the late-'80s on the 'Who Made Who' and 'Blow Up Your Video' albums. Their importance in the AC/DC story is undeniable, not only for their production vision, but also for their business knowledge and contacts gained from their own band-playing days with The Easybeats. They helped the band develop their own identity and their own sound and while they didn't work on the band's most commercially successful albums, their influence is still obvious.

In 1993 Angus acknowledged his brother George Young and his partner Harry Vanda as the most influential and creative producers he had worked with. George taught Angus exactly how to work in the studio and gave both him and Malcolm their first taste of recording on a project called The Marcus Hook Roll Band.

Vanda and Young produced 'High Voltage', 'T.N.T.', 'Dirty Deeds Done Dirt Cheap', 'Let There Be Rock', 'Powerage', 'If You Want Blood', 'Who Made Who' (the majority of tracks) and 'Blow Up Your Video'

ROBERT JOHN 'MUTT' LANGE

Suggested by the band's US label Atlantic for production duties on 1979's 'Highway To Hell' after initial recordings with Eddie Kramer had proved a disaster, Lange went on to produce the following year's 'Back In Black' and the 1981 album 'For Those About To Rock' and was responsible for helping the band achieve supergroup status.

Although Malcolm and Angus have always acknowledged Lange's efforts, they have also been quick to criticise some of his production style. Lange is a perfectionist and enjoys spending a long time on the recording process. AC/DC have always preferred to work quickly to keep their spontaneity.

Atlantic brought Lange in specifically to make the band's sound more radio-friendly, especially for the USA, whereas the band themselves would have preferred to retain their own hard-edged style. Malcolm described the way around this dilemma, saying "we met somewhere in the middle" and Lange eventually managed to produce a sound that was both pleasing to the record company, yet which didn't stray too far from the band's established sound. He was particularly influential on Bon's singing and helped him realise his full potential. "He concentrated on the commercial side, while we looked after the riffs," explained Malcolm.

Later Angus was more inclined to play down Lange's contribution, even going so far as to say that Malcolm had really produced the best moments of 'Back In Black' and the band was very public in its dislike of the way certain tracks on 'Highway To Hell' had turned out, especially 'Love Hungry Man'. It also seems that the band feel 'For Those About To Rock' was their worst album, not least because it took so long to record.

Lange has also worked with the Boomtown Rats, City Boy, The Outlaws, Def Leppard and Graham Parker. He's now married to country crossover star Shania Twain.

Mutt Lange produced 'Highway To Hell', 'Back In Black' and 'For Those About To Rock'.

BRUCE FAIRBAIRN

Fairbairn was already a well-known production figure when he first worked with AC/DC in 1989. His credits included Aerosmith, Bon Jovi, Poison and INXS.

When he was first suggested to AC/DC, Angus in particular was unhappy with his polite Canadian sound. Malcolm, however, flew to Canada to talk to Fairbairn and was tremendously impressed. "Bruce is a real gentleman," he said. Fairbairn was given the producer's job for 'The Razor's Edge' and threw himself into the project, trying to capture a blend of influences as well as experimenting with such things as backing vocals. He himself said that he didn't want to change the band's sound and wanted to make the album sound like something Malcolm would have heard when he was a kid. In spite of this, he did have creative ideas and Angus remarked that it was good that he could bring something new to the process. He wasn't afraid to say when he thought something was wrong and so really performed the task of a proper producer: "We wanted to make it possible to

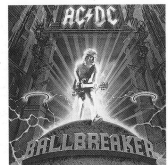

hear each instrument loud and clear and produce a sound that was right in your face," he said. The plan must have worked because the album was the band's most successful since 'Back In Black'.

Malcolm and Angus seemed more than happy with his work and Fairbairn was brought out on the road to record a live album during the 'Razor's Edge' tour. He also produced the soundtrack for the *Live At Donington* film and many of these tracks later appeared as B-sides. Maybe the band liked the fact that he was a musician himself, if only a trumpeter! Malcolm joked in 1993 that the band had to take his contributions off their records!

Bruce Fairbairn produced 'The Razor's Edge' and 'AC/DC Live'

RICK RUBIN

Rubin had been pestering the band's management for years for the chance to produce AC/DC. He'd been a fan since high school and had claimed he'd even had fights at school with friends who'd called the band unhip. Rubin made his name mixing AC/DC riffs together with rap songs, then moved on to produce artists such as Slayer, Johnny Cash, The Red Hot Chili Peppers and The Cult. He was the man responsible for turning the latter's 'Electric' album into something of a quasi-AC/DC tribute.

Rubin first worked with AC/DC on the 'Big Gun' single for the *Last Action Hero* film soundtrack and the band were delighted with the results. He had a big physical presence and, as Brian Johnson himself admitted, most of the time the band's answers were "Yes Rick".

Though Rubin had been

criticised in the past for being lazy in the control room, Malcolm defended his style, saying he worked just as hard as anyone. The Youngs were impressed by his technical knowledge of the studio, both in New York, where initial recordings were made for what became 'Ballbreaker', and at Ocean Way studios in Los Angeles where the album was finally nailed. "We ended up with a harder sound than before without all that technological brilliance," said Angus. Malcolm explained that Rubin was particularly attentive to the snare sound.

Rumours have circulated that Rubin was already out of the picture when the finishing touches were being put to the 'Ballbreaker' album and people have also said that his taste now leans towards much harder music, but there's no denying that he turned out the best AC/DC product in years.

Rick Rubin has produced just the one album, 'Ballbreaker'

SELF-PRODUCED ALBUMS

The band said "Mutt Lange couldn't work with us in 1983 for personal reasons and because there was no-one else in the frame we took on the job of recording 'Flick Of The Switch' ourselves." AC/DC then went on to self-produce 'Fly On The Wall' too. Many people see these as the band's two weakest efforts, though Cliff Williams said that they were both useful records, serving to get them away from "the wrong track". Both records were a reaction to the way 'For Those About To Rock' had been so painstakingly recorded and they felt more live than Mutt Lange's crafted sounds. The production, however, never matched the level of the songs, especially on 'Fly On The Wall'. Even though the band enjoyed being their own bosses, Brian Johnson admitted that it would have been better to have spent more time in the studio to really work out what was good and what was bad. This period was not a highpoint in the band's history.

Highway To Mal

The band's driving force is another one who doesn't like to talk so much. But this 1990 interview shows that he's always thinking...

What was the truth behind your problems with alcohol that we heard so much about in 1988?
It's gone something along the lines of 'too much', 'a lot', 'not much', 'now nothing'. It's only a cup of tea for me these days. I was drinking an awful lot before; I reckon you could have written a book about the things I got up to. But I had to give it up and get myself back together. I was bored of it, getting ripped all the time. It was always the same story and I couldn't leave it alone. I was a real Jekyll and Hyde character. I'd lost my self-control. I was still playing the songs OK, but I was always drunk. Things would get really bad after the gig though. I was the first one to start drinking and the last to leave any club. I always had to be dragged out. I've never been on tour without a drink inside me before and I never thought it would be a problem. So it's always difficult to stick with the tea when things get stressful.

You've always been the creative head of the band. Is the recording process more difficult now than it used to be?
A hell of a lot more. You do a lot of things with technology these days. Nowadays you could never just go in there, set up your gear and after a couple of hours have your tracks down like we did in the old days. You need two weeks of messing about before you're even ready to start. We used to work on about five or six tracks a

A young Malc locates frets, despite out-of-control fringe!

week after gigs and by, say, two in the morning we'd have something ready. Then we'd drive to the studio and work with George and Harry. They always had a few dozen cans and some whisky and we'd have a bit of a party. Then at some point we'd have a break and lay down some tracks: 'Let There Be Rock' or 'Whole Lotta Rosie'. That way we were looser, like we would be if we were on stage. Those are the best memories of the studio, because the whole idea behind it was just recreating a gig. That's just not the case any more.

Live performance always seems to have been the focus of the band, right?
We always used to have to fight to win people over and I guess from that point of view nothing much has changed. We used to play in all these crazy little clubs like The Red Lion in London or the 76 Club in Burton On Trent. They were great places and we learnt our trade there. We'd be playing some big gigs in Australia back then even, in front of 20,000 or whatever, but then the next time we were in England we'd be in a small club in Burton On Trent. I guess we still do the same kind of thing nowadays. The worst places we've ever played are the Australian bars ➤

"We always used to have to fight to win people over and i guess from that point of view nothing much has changed."

Brian Johnson

Born on 5th October 1947 in Dunston, Newcastle, Brian Johnson's pre-AC/DC career started with a band incredibly named Gobi Desert Canoe Club in his native North East, but his first serious outfit was called USA. The band changed its name to Geordie after about six months, and in 1972 found themselves with a minor hit single on their hands in their native Britain. That single, 'Don't Do That', reached No. 36 in the UK charts. The band then chalked up two more hits, 'All Because Of You' (No. 6 in 1973) and 'Can You Do It' (No. 13, again in 1973) and recorded five albums with Johnson on vocals. These are: 'Hope You Like It' (1973), 'Masters Of Rock' (1974), 'Don't Be Fooled By The Name' (1974), 'Save The World' (1976) and 'No Good Woman' (1977).

though. They were full of bush farmers. Some nights we'd be sitting there in a dressing room that had windows full of bullet holes, trying it on with the local girls. That's all part of the fun, though – or at least it used to be! It's pretty trouble-free these days, but most of us would still prefer to make our own way to the venue. Unfortunately we have to go with managers and security and all the rest of it, because of the financial implications if one of us didn't turn up. But it seems so stupid when you know you can think for yourself.

So how long do you think the band can keep going for?

Well, we haven't got our pensioners' bus passes just yet, which can't be bad. We're all proud that we're still quite fit. I think Bon taught us in a way not to end up like him. You know, even back in the drinking days we were pretty lively. We always did something – played tennis or whatever. I think we're as fit and full of energy as we've ever been.

What about sex on the road in the old days?

It was more bravado, really. It happened more when we were young and inexperienced, of course, but as far as lyrics are concerned we've always used sex for inspiration. We never have a problem with sex in the words. It doesn't embarrass us. The reality is that there were a few stories to tell back then, and now they're just good memories.

Who do you see as your competition?

It's weird. When we first started people told us the competition was the Sex Pistols and that we were a punk band. Later on we were competition for Black Sabbath and the heavy bands. I think you're in competition with everyone, but at the end of the day you're really in competition with yourself. We do what we want to and that's always been our recipe for success. I know quite a few guys from the younger bands and they seem good kids. They always say they were heavily influenced by us and that's nice. We can be proud of that.

What about the competition within your own band that people like to bring up – the one between your two singers?

Bon had a lot of talent that a lot of people only

seemed to discover after he died. Then people came up to us and told us how great he was. He was a great character, an original with a great voice, but we really feel that Brian's a great member of the band now. He's played a big role. He came to us and in a way he already was one of us. We knew that we couldn't get a Bon clone in, because Bon had his own, very distinct personality. It was really tough for Brian coming in to replace him, but it was the only way that was open to us to carry on. The one thing I can tell you, despite any line-up changes we've had, is that our attitude's never changed. We were more irresponsible and wilder in the early days, but when it comes down to it nothing much has really changed.

BOINNNGG!!!

What's the story behind the original Hell's Bell?

In the middle of Loughborough, Leicestershire, stands the Carillon, a memorial to the men of the town killed in both The Great War and the Second World War. At the top of the 200ft high tower sits a cradle which holds 47 bells. The largest in the tower is the Denison Bell, on which an inscription reads:

'In proud and loving memory of his three nephews, killed in action in France... John William Taylor, Courcelette, 1916 Gerald Bardsley Taylor, St Quentin, 1918 Arnold Bradley Taylor, Contalmaison, 1916 Sons of John William Taylor (1853-1919), Grandsons of John William Taylor (1827-1906). Edmund Denison Taylor, the founder of these bells, gives this the largest, 1923.'

This four tonne bell, made by J. Taylor and Sons (bellfounders) was the bell which was recorded in the summer of 1980 by Tony Platt on the Manor mobile for AC/DC's 'Back In Black' album. 24 microphones surrounded the bell to record its chime.

The bell taken on tour by the band is a one and a half tonne replica of the Denison. And just in case you're interested, The Denison Bell was also number 26 in a series of beer mats titled 'Other Famous Bells', which was issued by Bells whiskey.

Chapter Five

CYNiCAL CiTY

By 1981 I'd decided it was time to actually do something about my love of rock music. I was 16 and starting to build up an album collection that was impressive for nothing if not its consistency. Music's a different animal now, of course. Different for me, certainly. I'm 34 years old now and I've realised that, in music as in everything else in life, there are good things to be found everywhere if you know how to look properly. At the risk of sounding like one of those loathsome would-be trendy dads, I enjoy all kinds of music and though I'm probably too cynical in my thirty-fifth year to believe that music really can

in 1981? MTV hadn't been dreamed up, cable was nothing more than something on the end of your phone, satellite a big dish-type thingy that the Russians and the Americans were squabbling over up in space. Nobody had a video player and the only computer games available were those primitive *Space Invaders* machines that I was in the process of wasting all my dinner money on when I was supposed to be revising for A-levels in Manchester's Central Library. Nowadays there is no common cultural currency for young people in Britain. How can there be? When one person's watching the footy on Sky Sports, another one's watching *Mission:Impossible* on a movie channel. Or playing

Cheap Trick. None of them sounded like each other, exactly. Only a moron could honestly have argued that the smooth radio rock of Journey sounded anything like AC/DC's nasty pub-styled boogie. But all those groups somehow belonged together. They all had long hair and they all based their sound around the raw power of the guitar. It was, for all those little differences, still a club. There seemed to be loads of rock bands out there, but only a few places where you could read about them. The weekly music paper *Sounds* always devoted a couple of pages to metal bands each issue, but that seemed to me to be just the tip of the iceberg. There were other bands out there and judging by the

"AC/DC had misplaced their charm. And i just didn't know whether they'd lost it forever"

change the world, at least I can still recognise that back in 1981, music was certainly changing mine.

But music's different for kids in 1999 too. 18 years ago you were defined by the music that you liked. The bands you followed said everything about you; about the social group you wanted to identify yourself with, about the section of teen society you wanted to belong to. Don't ask me for the anthropological reasons as to how that state of affairs had come about, but trust me, we all believed it was important to be labelled as 'mod' or 'metal fan' or 'soul boy' or 'punk'. If you didn't make a stand for one type of music or another, you were dumb, you were boring and you were, worst of all, a stiff. Nowadays the very idea that you can be defined by what's on your turntable is just laughable. The cultural landscape's changed beyond all recognition. I mean, what else was there

Tomb Raider II. Or surfing the Net. Or something else that maybe I'm too old to know about yet, but which is surely going to invade my conscience before too long. The day of the gang is over. The day of the gang mentality even more so. The idea that someone could have a record collection that contained one style of music pretty much to the exclusion of everything else is utterly hair-brained now. If you haven't got an Oasis album, one by The Prodigy and a Sinatra classic, you're considered uneducated, closed-minded, unhip. Back in '81, though, the circles I moved in would definitely have thought that anything that wasn't metal was utter bollocks.

SO THAT COLLECTION, THEN. Well as far as I can remember I had records by Motörhead, Scorpions, AC/DC, UFO, Blackfoot, Journey and

Sounds letters page, there were plenty of teenagers like me scouring the pages of the music press trying to find out little snippets about them. I was interested in, soon to be obsessed with, discovering more and more about rock bands and in telling other people about the music that I loved. Maybe there was an opportunity here...

I'm not exactly sure when the idea for *Phoenix* came to me or whether it was purely for selfless motives that I decided I was going to start a fanzine. There was probably a lot more arrogance behind my decision than I'd like to think. I always reckoned that the reviews I was reading in *Sounds* didn't seem that hard to cobble together. Listen to an album, write down what you think of it while faithfully copying the stylistic conventions of the time and... and that was it, really. That's probably more like what I was thinking, rather than the idea I like to believe now that I was only motivated to offer a service to frustrated rock fans like myself. The truth, though, is that I wouldn't be surprised if I'd worked out that if I did a fanzine cheaply enough, then I might break even selling it – and be able to get all my records for free. Pure economics.

Whatever the reasons, *Phoenix* had first emerged in 1980. My dad had funded the printing costs of the first issue – I seem to remember a figure somewhere in the 120 quid region – after I'd dug out an address and phone number for The Rochdale Alternative Press, a printers' collective who seemed to be about five times cheaper than Prontaprint and the rest of the high street chains. I phoned them up and soon worked out that they were some kind of 'commune' who were intent on bringing the power of the press to those who wanted to have a voice, but just couldn't afford to be heard. I don't know what they thought of the idea of a heavy metal fanzine, but after being driven to what felt like the other side of the world by my dad for a preliminary meeting, the good vegetarian-looking folk at RAP didn't give me the impression that they were laughing at my meaty musical taste. For this I am still extremely grateful.

WITH THE HELP OF THREE schoolfriends. two of whom you'll remember from that first DC gig in Manchester – Alan Mushing (great name), Nick Gibbon (groovy name) and Tony Bailey (rather disappointing name) – we plotted out our little magazine, doing the minuscule sums that at the time felt like such a scary amount of money to risk losing. For our 120 quid we'd get 1000 copies of a magazine, though none of the pages would be stapled because that would have pushed the price up. It seemed like a goer. If we shifted all the copies at what we thought was a reasonable cover price of 25 pence, then we'd take £250, and would make £140. Easy. Easy sums, anyway. Have you ever wondered, though, what it takes to sell a thousand copies of a magazine for which you have no distribution and no publicity? We hadn't, but once we'd got the pristine first issue of Phoenix printed and spent three thankless nights stapling the bloody things together, we soon realised how much hard work it was going to be.

We put magazines in Yanks on a sale or return arrangement, I took an ad out in the *Sounds* small ads page, we all hawked them around at school and stood in the freezing cold outside any Manchester metal gig trying to flog the mag. I even arranged with my boss at the HMV store in Manchester where I had a Saturday job that I could stick them on the counter. I took his benevolence as a green light to try to force-feed *Phoenix* to anyone who looked like they might be vaguely interested in rock music. I can't count the number of times I asked some poor, unsuspecting person who had long hair or who was wearing denim: 'Would you like a copy of *Phoenix* heavy metal fanzine?' It was hard graft, but every time I sold a copy the sense of satisfaction was enormous. We were one sale nearer breaking even, one sale nearer moving into profit. ➤

Donington, 1981. That's me with Angry Anderson of Rose Tattoo. He is short. I am a geek.

THERE WERE FOUR ISSUES of *Phoenix* over the course of about a year, full of over-enthusiastic reviews and ever-so-gentle interviews that we'd managed to blag by phoning record companies and pleading down the phone with them. Amazingly, considering we were nobodies, touting a fanzine that only reached the Manchester area, the response from the major labels was good. Records started arriving in the post for review and even a couple of things from The States landed on my doorstep. I felt like *Phoenix* could develop into something bigger, although I wasn't exactly sure what. I knew I loved writing about music and that when I thought about it, even the grind of producing and selling the magazine engrossed me. But the future was a nebulous area. The records, though, were very real. People wanted to give me albums so that

I could write about them, albums that I was already spending every bit of money I had on. That, I thought, I could get used to.

Soon I found that albums weren't the only things that record companies wanted to give me. Concert tickets, too, would get offered, so now I was able to go to gigs without paying either. I'd be able to blag tickets for most things without too much trouble. Later on I worked out that it must have been because I was based in Manchester rather than London, where press demands would have been infinitely more heavy. At the time, though, I wasn't thinking about the whys and the wherefores. I was just delighted to be getting in through the back door so to speak. So when it was announced that there was to be a second Castle Donington Monsters Of Rock Festival after the great success of the event

headlined by Rainbow the previous year, I was on the phone trying to blag my way in. I hadn't been able to go in 1980, I was on some sappy exchange scheme staying with a German kid in Freiburg, but this time my frankly thin social diary was unsurprisingly empty on the given day. Who were headlining? AC/DC, of course.

Since 'Back In Black' the previous year, AC/DC's popularity had skyrocketed. Admittedly, they'd had a decent-sized and solidly dedicated core of support since 1978. On my first live sighting at the Manchester Apollo on the 'Highway To Hell' tour the band were already doing two nights in a theatre that held just under 3,000, which wasn't exactly audience chickenfeed. But to move from being a solid first division outfit to European Champions in two years took some doing. I was

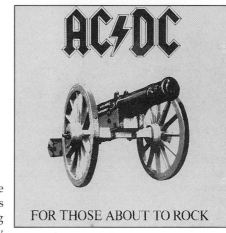

thrilled at having the chance to see AC/DC at Donington. The band had made their reputation as a killer live act and I certainly hadn't been disappointed by my one live experience. I was intrigued to check out Brian Johnson and although all my phone calls to get a free ticket to the biggest rock event of the year had proved unsuccessful, at least I'd been offered passes to the guest enclosure for the day. It had to be a good deal.

THE DAY ITSELF turned out to be a whole lot of fun. Wearing a *Phoenix* badge that I'd had made up in lurid, no sickly, yellow, I enjoyed hanging out backstage, where I met and interviewed Angry Anderson of Rose Tattoo, another Australian boogie band making a name for themselves at the time. I liked the group's music and I liked the group's singer – a tiny, bald yobbo who had the common decency to give me the time of day and pose for a photograph. I might not have been so

enthusiastic about the little guy if I'd known his propensity for walking around ships in Sydney harbour butt-naked, as I discovered reading *Sounds* later that year. And who would have thought he would have gone on to record that godawful wedding song for *Neighbours*? Never mind, eh? I think I got a bit pissed on the free beer that was being served in the various backstage hospitality bars – something I was going to get very used to in the future – and by the time nightfall came I was tanked up and ready to see AC/DC turn in the kind of performance befitting a band headlining in front of 70,000 odd rock fans.

Incredibly, the gig sucked. It was raining when the band took the stage, the sound drifted out of the natural bowl and up into the night air, swirling around while it made its mind up what to do, then drifting off in a hundred different directions so that you could hardly tell what the song was. Whereas in 79 I'd felt like I could have touched the band and in Angus' case literally did so, Castle Donington gave me nothing but a few distant pin-pricks on the horizon. This was a new festival and it showed, because it didn't feel as if anyone really knew how best to present the band to the public. It was just a shambles. Nothing about the performance sticks out in the memory at all. Johnson seemed to be an adequate performer, nothing more. The new songs didn't fare any better, sounding leaden and dull. There were no two ways about it. I couldn't help thinking that AC/DC had lost it. In retrospect there probably wasn't a band on earth who could have reached out to someone standing in the pissing rain half a mile back without any kind of decent sound system to speak of. Perhaps if I'd seen AC/DC indoors on that tour I'd have thought they were as brilliant as the first time I'd witnessed them. Perhaps I'd have thought that they were just as good a live band as ever. But as I started the trudge to whatever inadequate transport had been laid on

to get me back home to Manchester at the end of the night, I couldn't help thinking about what I'd just seen. The big cannons that had fired off at the end of the gig as a 21 gun salute to the power of rock or some other such cliché seemed to sum it up perfectly for me. AC/DC had misplaced their charm. And I just didn't know whether they'd lost it forever.

AFTER MY DONINGTON disappointment I was very, very wary of the forthcoming album. It turned out that I had good reason to be. Again produced by Mutt Lange, to my mind at least 'For Those About To Rock' marked the end of the band's golden era. For the most part as stodgy and leaden as its title, the record showed AC/DC moving away from the raw boogie that had typified their sound in the Seventies to a brasher, noisier, screechier approximation of heavy metal. The title had made me wary enough, but the music had pretty much turned me right off. By this time I was well enough in with Warner Bros, the band's UK record label, that I managed to blag a free copy of the record, but I still felt cheated by an album I hadn't even paid for; bad sign. Where there was once swing there was now bluster. Where there was once a sense of fun, there was now a nothing but a feeling of impending bombast. Everything sounded too over the top, which people who have spent their whole lives dismissing all rock as relentlessly ridiculous will utterly fail to understand. Hardcore AC/DC fans, however, will know that DC were never a heavy metal band, with all the huge stage shows, posturing and synchronised moves that the term so often seemed to insist on bringing along as hand luggage. They were never that calculating. Or at least I'd never believed they were. All of a sudden, though, that's exactly how it felt to me. The band had become just a wee bit, a teensy bit, cynical. ∎

Angus on the inspiration behind 'For Those About To Rock'...
"Bon had given me a book by Robert Graves called 'For Those About To Die We Salute You'. It was about the Romans and he knew I liked reading about history, so he gave it to me when he'd finished with it. The title just stuck in my head. Then we were in Paris recording when the Prince and Princess of Wales were getting married and the wedding was blaring on the TV in the other room. The cannons went off while we were recording and we thought it sounded great."

Rock Solid Cliff

The throbbing, low-end heart of AC/DC doesn't speak very often, so listen up to this 1994 interview...

You play such straight basslines in AC/DC; how can you get any satisfaction from that?
I get bored playing single notes just like anyone else. But in the band I play what's best for the song and get pleasure out of that. Do you understand what I'm saying?

It's been five years since the band last released an album. How come?
We haven't ever set out a specific plan. If the recording's bad, then we don't put it out. If we'd already committed ourselves, say, to touring next year, then that would mean we'd have to have

Isn't Rick Rubin producing the band at the moment?
Yeah, young blood. He's loved the band for years – at least that's what he says – and wanted to work with us some more. He knew that the band has its own sound and knew what we wanted to hear. He doesn't try to get us to do things that don't suit us.

So no big musical changes, then?
No. Angus and Malcolm write the songs and they've never tried to do something that didn't come naturally to them. 'Natural' is one of the

can get it down quickly or at least be flexible and be able to change things easily if someone says "We should do this or that".

What's the difference between recording and playing live?
Not a lot. I'm a bit more precise in the studio. So that means you're automatically more careful about what you do when you're in the studio.

How are you finding it playing with Phil Rudd again?
He was the first drummer I played with in the

"'Natural' is one of the key words for us. if something doesn't feel natural to us, then we leave it."

the record ready no matter what. We don't ever want to be in that position. When we're ready, then we're ready.

How does a typical recording session pan out, then?
We always play live, the four of us playing the instruments and Brian putting down a raw guide vocal. We try to record everything at once, but obviously we add overdubs when they're needed. "Keep it fresh and hot" is what we say. That's how we work best. The more you play a song, the flatter and more stale it becomes and in the end you just lose it. Over the years we've even stuck some of the first takes on the records, although I can't think of a specific example right now. Probably on 'Highway To Hell', because we were under a lot of time pressure on that one. That album had to be out so quickly that I wouldn't be surprised if one or two of them were first takes.

key words for us. If something doesn't feel natural to us, then we leave it. But yeah, the boys are writing the stuff and the rest of us try to interpret the songs as best we can.

How do you approach a song they've written?
They've already got a pretty good idea of how it should work, even before the whole band's had a run at it. The work is pretty advanced usually and they'll bring a complete demo to rehearsals. It would be frustrating for everyone if we had to start off trying to interpret something that Angus and Malcolm only had in their heads.

Has that helped to speed up the recording process?
Well, it takes as long as it takes. The teething troubles with the songs are ironed out because of Mal and Angus' preparation. Before we even get near a studio we know what each specific song needs. We know the tune inside out so we

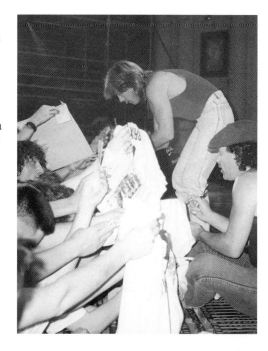

band, but he had to leave several years ago for various reasons. Now he's back and we're working well together. It's great that he's back. He was always the right man for the job.

What's the difference between him and the other drummers you've had?

Phil always had a natural feel for what the band was about. Chris Slade is a fantastic drummer and even Simon Wright's pretty good, but Phil fits us like a hand in a glove. So it's nothing specific, more of a feeling. He was in the band even before I joined and when I came in the group already ran like a well-oiled machine. I had to fit in with it and well, that's what I did.

So how exactly did you join?

I auditioned. The band wanted to improve their rhythm section so they came to London where there was a wider choice of players. They'd already made a few albums, they were very successful in Australia and had been touring Europe for a couple of months, though they hadn't yet been to the States. But they were in the process of promoting 'Let There Be Rock'. I got a call from a friend of a friend who thought I'd be the right man for the job so I ended up playing with them a few times.

AC/DC have got quite a specific rock/swing sound. What music influenced your playing?

For me it was always the old Stones, Beatles, The Kinks and a bit of blues. There wasn't as much blues music where I grew up in England as there was in the States. There wasn't really a market for it, so most people there didn't know much about it, except for a few things by Chuck Berry or Bo Diddley.

How did you learn to play?

I just sat down and did it. Listened to records and worked them out.

And why the bass?

When I was 13, everyone I knew had a band. It was the early '60s and rock music was just starting but there was a real buzz. A group of people hung around together and just ended up getting a band together somehow, saying "You do this and you do that". Then, when I was 16, a mate of mine who was already professional showed me a few riffs, but that's as far as my

"We've recorded so much stuff I can't remember half of it." – Cliff

formal training goes. I love playing the bass, but I especially love it with AC/DC, it's mega to play with them. They're solid and powerful... great in every sense.

What influence has Angus had on you?

He's taught me to keep out of his way on stage! I love watching him; he's such a bundle of energy. I don't know if there's anything specific I can put my finger on, but in certain ways I'm sure he's influenced me. He's turned me on to a lot of good music.

Have you ever had any accidents with him on stage? Collisions?

No, but there have been a fair few near misses. We opened for Blue Oyster Cult at Red Rocks in Denver one time a while back. They only let us have four white spots for our show, so the stage around us was really dark. At that gig I was really worried about Angus careering off the end of the stage.

Name some of your favourite AC/DC songs.

'Let There Be Rock', 'Live Wire', 'Gimme A Bullet' and 'Down Payment Blues'.

All old songs. Do you yearn for the old days?

Well you asked me the question and that's my answer. Everything was new to me at that time, 'Powerage' was my first album with the band. Truthfully, we've recorded so much stuff that I can't remember half of it unless there's a list in front of me. There are too many tracks! An old song called 'What's Next To The Moon?' suddenly came up again while we were all hanging around the studio. We hadn't played that one in years and I'd completely forgotten it.

Which bands and bassists do you like best these days?

I don't listen to any. Most of it just passes me by, I'm not really that interested. I saw a video by Green Day and that impressed me because it reminded me of The Who when they were first starting. As far as individual bass players are concerned, I have no idea.

Do you play solos?

No chance. Well, only if Mal and Angus' gear has blown up and the drummer's fallen over! Only in a ridiculous situation like that. I sound better with the rest of the band.

"It Affects People, Doesn't It?"

Back in 1981 Nikki Goff bought her first brand new AC/DC album. Now she runs the unofficial AC/DC fan club, Electric Outlaws, in Britain. Ever wondered why people perform such labours of love? Well now you can find out...

What are your first recollections of the band?

Well, I can remember hearing them on the radio a few times when I was really young, about 11 or so. They were playing some of the tracks from 'Highway To Hell' on Radio 1 and I just thought, "I've got to have that album." There was a lot of power pop going round at the time, stuff like Blondie, but AC/DC were just so exciting-sounding. I liked some of the other rock bands around at the time, but most of them were a bit too twiddly for me, not the same full-on sound that AC/DC had at all. So I heard 'Highway To Hell' on the radio quite a lot and 'Touch Too Much' as well. Then I heard a show with Pete Townshend from The Who playing his favourite records and 'Highway To Hell' was one of them. He said that the band were going to be very big and I couldn't help but agree with him. I really wanted to get the album, but I couldn't just go to the local record shop in St Helens, where I was living and pick it up. I couldn't afford it. I had to wait for my birthday. By the time I finally got 'Highway To Hell', Bon had already died.

Nikki. She quite likes AC/DC.

And did that have a big impact on you?

Well, I felt a bit sad. I was off school with the flu when I first heard the news on the radio and I remember thinking it would have been nice for him to have shared in the group's success, because they seemed to be really making it all of a sudden. But to be honest I just wanted to find out more about the group, really, which wasn't that easy. It was difficult to find out about anything new. There were a couple of record shops in St Helens, but they weren't much good. One was just a toy shop with a few records in and one was an electrical shop with the same kind of arrangement. Information on bands wasn't as freely available back then as it is now; there just weren't many magazines around. You had to rely on *Smash Hits* for little bits of info on rock bands, so when *Kerrang!* came out it was a godsend. I think at the time all I had was a picture of Angus cut out of a magazine that was stuck on the wall in my room.

"You had to rely on *Smash Hits* for little bits of info on rock bands, so when *Kerrang!* came out it was a godsend."

"They sounded like five desperate individuals who were trying

Nikki Goff

So when you finally got hold of a copy of 'Highway To Hell'...
I thought it was the most amazing thing I'd ever heard. I loved the raw-edged bluesiness of it. I got really into original blues much later on, and though I didn't know that music at the time, that bluesy feel was what appealed to me, what was different. I was brought up only listening to the occasional Beatles record – my parents weren't really into music or popular culture – but I was really excited about this particular band. I just started thinking about saving up to get the rest of the band's material. There were more second

hand record shops opening up, so I started getting all kinds of rock music, not just AC/DC, but Led Zeppelin, Whitesnake, all those kinds of bands. The first AC/DC album that came out when I was already into them was 'Back In Black', but I didn't manage to lay my hands on a copy of that for quite a while after it came out either. I couldn't afford it at the time and actually finally bought it second hand from a junk shop later on. The first album I went out to buy with my own money was 'For Those About To Rock'. I got that album the day it came out and that was a really nice feeling.

You first heard the band with Bon, then with Brian. What did you make of that?
I used to prefer Bon, but I like Brain too now – and he's been there a lot longer than Bon, of course. I thought Bon was a bit more bluesy and the way he came across, it seemed to me that he'd had more of a tough time and a more interesting life than Brian. His lyrics were a bit funnier. He was a real 'seize the day' kind of bloke. He was shipped out to Australia at the age of four or five and that must have had a big effect on him. Brian has never quite managed to capture the humour of the band the way Bon did.

hard to make something of themselves."

There's a really obscure song called 'Carry Me Home' which the band recorded around the time of 'Let There Be Rock', which is really hilarious. The lyrics are all about how Bon's drunk in a bar saying he's so smashed that he can't even find the door. That was the kind of stuff that he was great at.

Do you think there is a classic period of the band?
Difficult to say really. Perhaps '77-'79. Yeah, that was the classic period when they were at the peak of their powers. I think that around that time

they sounded like they were really hungry and that they meant everything they did. They sounded like five desperate individuals who were trying hard to make something of themselves. They've probably become a bit complacent because they don't have to worry about anything now.

So what made you decide that you wanted to take your interest in the band further than just being a fan?
It wasn't until much later, when I'd finished my degree really. I did a degree in fine art at Wolverhampton Poly and I'd been a member of

the official AC/DC fan club that was based in Bury St Edmonds since about 1981. It was run by Bob and Sandra Mundy, but they didn't even do a fanzine. They did a photocopied sheet of paper folded in the middle and for six quid you got four of these a year. You got cheap merchandise though, which was the only real incentive to be a member, but they didn't have any news on what the band were doing or what other fans were up to.

I wasn't very impressed by what they were doing, so in about 1988 I was down in London and I decided I'd drop in and see what was going on. They'd moved the operation to Morden by then. I was very shy, but I took my courage in both hands and knocked on the door. They invited me in and we spoke for a couple of hours, but I could tell that they were getting very jaded with it. The band had provided them with

"i've got a set of these Russian dolls that are painted like the band members. i paid for them with two pairs of Levi's jeans. Honestly."

merchandising and tour information and they had about 10,000 people in the club at that time, but they weren't doing much about it. I asked them why they weren't doing more for the fans. I thought that if they'd worked with the fans they could easily have put at least a magazine together, but they said they didn't have either the time or the staff. Bob and Sandra were employed and salaried as far as I know, and they were running it as a business, but to my mind it wasn't providing the right kind of service. You could sometimes get gig tickets through them, but you didn't even get news any quicker than anyone else. Anyway, I stayed in touch and I'd phone them occasionally to find out what was happening, but they closed the fan club two years later in 1990.

The band then toured in 1991 and I went to

see them at Castle Donington. I decided I'd start a petition there demanding a fan club and collected over 500 signatures. I sent a copy to the band's manager, Stewart Young, to see what he would have to say on the subject. No response. I sent a copy a few weeks later. No response. Anyway, I was going down to London that November on a Christmas shopping trip and decided to pay them a visit at their office down on the King's Road. I took another copy of the petition with me, went to the door and told the doorman I had a petition for Part Rock Management. He buzzed up and they got me up to the office to let me explain myself. They weren't very helpful and said "Well, you're just a fan, aren't you? What do the fans do?" I said "We pay for all this, so you should think about giving something back."

Well, they kept me stringing along for weeks and weeks and weeks without making any decisions about what to do. To be honest I didn't want to run the fan club or anything at first; I just wanted to pressure someone into doing something. But eventually a friend of mine suggested to me that I should just get on and do it myself. There were other unofficial fan clubs in Europe, so I thought that seemed like a good idea. I phoned Part Rock to tell them, and all they seemed to say was that they couldn't really stop me.

How did you feel about that lack of interest?
I thought "To hell with them. I'll do it myself." It was shortly before I moved to Bolton with my partner Clayton, but when I was back there I got stuck into it.

Did you know the band at all?

I'd only met them backstage at the NEC once, but I'd never had any deep conversation. Just "Hi, will you sign this?" I just started roughing out an idea for a fanzine and worked and worked on it, bought a typewriter and just got on with it. People I knew sent me a few bits and pieces and I put an ad in *Kerrang!* announcing that I was going to do a fanclub. About 10 people wrote back. I wrote to them explaining what I was doing and that it would cost £8 a year and, surprisingly, all 10 people wrote back and stumped up. I promised them four fanzines a year, a membership card and a certificate. Those people got the fanzine I sent them, they sent me stuff back for the next one and it just grew from there.

And how much did it cost to start with?

I got the first ones done cheap. It only cost about 20 quid at the local community centre. We advertised in *Kerrang!* about once a month and some friends put a bit about us on the Internet. We've got just over 50 members these days. We had about 100 when the band last toured.

AC/DC sell out 10,000 seaters, but you've only got 100 members. Why do you think that is?

I think a lot of AC/DC fans keep their love for the band very quiet. I wouldn't say they're embarrassed exactly, but a lot of people think it's almost socially unacceptable to like them. They think they're not very fashionable. That, and some people think joining fan clubs isn't cool.

When did your first issue appear?

The first issue came out in the Autumn of 1992 and it was just a mixture of personal stories and memories. People's experiences related to the group, especially if they've visited anywhere that's important in the band's history, are always really good. Things like Ashley Court in London where Bon was living, the Southampton Gaumont where he played his last gig, they're fascinating.

And how much involvement do you get from the band and their people these days?

Well, we've been to video shoots and stuff like that, but only because someone from the record company contacted us. I've never had a band member ring me or write to me personally and I

Only hardcore fans were unconcerned about being left alone with such a disturbed individual.

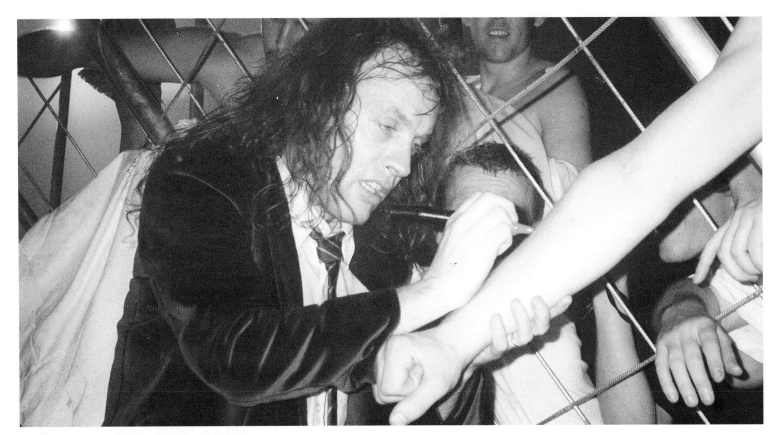

don't think anyone else who does a fanzine has either. I've heard that band members have asked fans to help them get a particular record or a particular guitar and have then written to say thanks, but that's about all. I did get an interview with Angus for the fanzine once. The PR company set it up for us.

So you don't think the band are particularly interested in what you do?
Well, I gave them all a copy of the fanzine at a gig in Aberdeen one time and it was after that that someone got back to me and said Angus wanted to do an interview with me, which I was over the moon about.

Do the band know who you are, then?
I think they do. We've mentioned the fanzine to them several times, but whether they actually take any notice or not is another thing.

Do you resent that lack of general interest?
I've got used to it. So long as I get enough material from everyone to do another fanzine

and keep it going, that's what's most important to me. We get people who are interested in all sorts of different sides of the band too, from collectors to tribute bands, and I enjoy that just as much as the contact with the group. You have people who are all into different things. Some people are more into meeting the band, some people are far more into collecting. We had some people from a French fanzine staying with us once and all they wanted to do was talk about serial numbers till three o'clock in the morning. I was just sitting there with a glazed look on my face.

So what have you learnt about AC/DC fans since you've been doing *Electric Outlaws*, apart from an obsession with serial numbers?
I think they're a good bunch. They don't have a bad reputation at all and there's no trouble or any of that sort of baggage with the them.

What's your most bizarre piece of AC/DC memorabilia?
I've got a set of these Russian dolls that are

painted like the band members. I paid for them with two pairs of Levi's jeans. Honestly.

What kinds of functions have you organised?
We organised an AC/DC day in Bolton back in 1994, which turned out to be an absolute disaster. We had two bands on, had people coming along with memorabilia displays, there was a raffle and disco and we were going to show videos all day. It was on the anniversary of Bon's death. We did some publicity, but the local paper ignored it, so we put notices in the pubs and what have you and sent out flyers to all the fan club members. We actually had people turn up from Australia and Ireland. The trouble was that the venue let a load of people in before we had even arrived, so we couldn't charge them. In the end only about 40 people actually paid to get in. We had to go to the bank to draw money out to pay the bands about £250 each, so we lost about £500 that day. The bands said they had to get paid and the venue said they had to get paid too, even though it was them who screwed up by letting people in. It was an absolute

nightmare. I was totally out of pocket and had to scratch the money back through the fanclub over a number of years, really.

Did that put you off that kind of event in future?
I guess it has up to a point, although we did have one in Scotland last year which was a roaring success; it sold out completely. Someone from the fan club who lived in the area organised it for us in Hawick and the place was absolutely jammed to the ceiling. It was brilliant. There were a few people there who had seen AC/DC in the early days and they said it was just like those Marquee gigs.

We tried to organise another similar event this year. Some people from London said they would

take care of everything for us, so the concert was booked for a place called The Standard in Walthamstow and the tickets went out on sale, but at the last minute the organisers changed the date and decided to have it in the first week of September. That's always a disastrous time for doing stuff, because people are all still on holiday. It really bombed. We only sold about 10 tickets from our end and they did even worse. They tried to bill us for £500, but it was really nothing to do with us and we'd already been burnt once.

What would you say is the most rewarding thing about doing the fan club?
The most rewarding thing is when you get your

stories together from people, you put it all together and then you actually get the magazine out. When people appreciate what you do it's very nice too. We helped get 200 fans to a video shoot in London one time and when the band came on there was this guy next to me and he just froze. He couldn't believe it. He said, "This is a dream come true, I've got to thank you guys for this." He'd been a fan for 20 years, and he said, "I never even dreamt about this moment." It's times like that that make all the hard work worthwhile. It affects people, doesn't it?

If you want to join The Electric Outlaws, then contact Nikki Goff at 10 Windsor Grove, Bolton, Greater Manchester BL1 3BR, England

We Salute You

Monsters Of Rock – The Alternative View By Wayne Etherington

Saturday 22nd August 1981, destination Donington Park for the second Monsters of Rock Festival. After three uncomfortable hours driving up the motorway, me and my mates clambered out of the van and walked up the path towards the entrance gate. There were all sorts of stalls selling T-shirts, posters, programmes, flags etc. I bought a large T-shirt (which sadly doesn't fit any more), a programme and two patches, which I'm proud to say I still have.

It was a long and very wet wait for AC/DC. By 10.05pm the atmosphere was electric. Excitement, anticipation and impatience were all at a peak when out of the dark night came the loud toll of the now-familiar one and a half tonne 'Hell's Bell'. Brian rushed onto the stage with a mallet in his hand and struck the bell four times. Angus then ran on accompanied by cheers from the crowd and chucked his schoolboy cap up into the lights. Into 'Hell's Bells' and as Brian sang "I'm rolling thunder, pouring rain", he threw a roll of toilet paper back into the crowd. Malcolm was playing his Gretsch White Falcon guitar (a rare sight these

days), while Angus was playing an English-built Gibson SG.

"Nice to see ya. Nice to be back in England. Here's one for everybody. I'm sure you know this one," Brian shouted. Then Angus blasted out the opening chords to 'Shot Down In Flames'. Then it was the classic 'Sin City' and 'Back In Black', then the strip tease to 'Bad Boy Boogie'. By now Angus was in the mood for a moon under the stars. Everybody sang along to 'The Jack', then it was a big surprise to hear 'What Do You Do For Money Honey?'. Brian said over the PA "Right lads, I've got one can of Heineken left," then launched into another Bon-era song.

During 'High Voltage' Brian shouted 'This is the first gig we've done in six months and it's lovely to be back in England. We've been busy in Paris recording a new album. It's a great album and it'll be out soon. 'Whole Lotta Rosie' started with everybody chanting Bon's lyrics. It was so good to hear the classic 'Rocker' over a loud PA system with Brian singing the original lyrics. Unfortunately the rain during the day had knocked out some of the PA, but there was

just no stopping the band. "Put some tatties on the bonfire lads," said Brian as he spotted a fire being lit in the crowd.

Angus started the encore with a solo leading into 'T.N.T.', then came 'Rock'n'Roll Ain't Noise Pollution' and 'You Shook Me All Night Long' from the 'Back In Black' album. The last song was 'Let There Be Rock'. "God bless you," shouted Brian and one side of the huge PA lit up with the AC/DC logo while on the other showed a burning Angus in fireworks. In a word: magic.

Chapter Six

FOR THOSE ABOUT TO WRITE

As a fella with bluer eyes than mine once sang, 'When I was 17 I had a very good year.' Well, good for Frank and good for me too. I too had a very good year. And a lucky escape. It was in 1981. The year of 'new romantic' if you peruse the rock history books. Of flouncing about in your mum's frock, applying your make-up with all the dexterity of a bricklayer and thinking that effete was the way to go. The papers were full of Steve Strange, the Blitz club and Spandau Ballet, people experimenting with gender-bending images in the way that each pop-literate generation seems to want to do. It was nothing new, of course. Just a twist on the old glam theme of a decade or so earlier. But new romantic was big news and everyone seemed to want to be seen as part of the movement. Well, not everyone, exactly. There was me, for starters...

In 1981 musical fashions were passing me by with fearsome speed. Not that I gave a toss. I'd

place), then you'd have a crack at it. So I had a crack at it.

Looking back I don't think I ever truly believed that I belonged there. I accepted the challenge because it was expected of me. I was told that I should apply for Downing College, Cambridge and so I did. I'd already passed my A Levels and got two As and a B. Pretty good. I was invited down for interview and, I think, some other entrance exam. So I went. It was as simple as that. I did it without thinking it through, and I really didn't have any burning urge to go to Cambridge. I thought that it would be full of toffs and packed with hard academic graft, two things which I had next to no time for. No doubt in my guileless 17-year-old manner I found it hard to hide my lack of interest when I sat in some tutor's beautiful study for my interview and the old boy was probably right when he stuck me on what they call 'The Reserve List', the semi-obscure place where they call you up if someone who's been offered a bona

been utterly ignored by most of the music press – except when it was being ridiculed, of course. Lewis and Barton recognised that metal was loud, brash, colourful and exciting and managed to persuade their bosses to invest in a new, monthly magazine with one major difference to all the other music papers that were around at the time. They would make it in colour.

Now putting together a colour magazine hardly sounds like the kind of inspirational notion that can make a career, but that's only because we now take colour music titles – the perfect medium for garish rock'n'roll of course – for granted. *Q, MoJo, Select, Mixmag* and all the rest of them didn't exist in '81. Only *Kerrang!*. And you can't imagine how excited I was when its imminent arrival was first announced through the pages of *Sounds*. At last. A magazine that loved metal, that didn't sneer at it like it was some Neanderthal nonsense played by juveniles obsessed with the size of their dicks and loved by acne-infested no-marks. When I finally

"The image of a sweat-drenched Angus rocking like a bastard perfectly summed up what *Kerrang!* was about."

already decided that rock was my drug of choice – despite my abject disappointment at the fall of DC at Donington that summer. And besides, make-up was absolutely, definitely out of the question. That, as the saying goes, was for the birds. How soon my viewpoint, my prejudice, would come back to haunt me, though that's another story. Two things did happen in 1981, however, that would bend my future into shape.

The first thing was that I failed to make my dad's life complete by not getting a place at Cambridge University. My school, Manchester Grammar, prided itself on the number of its pupils who succeeded in the Oxbridge exams. The two highest seats of learning in the land had a long-standing and 'firm handshake' relationship with the school and the assumption was always there that unless you showed the academic inclination of a monkey or a football hooligan (unlikely, since you'd had to pass a tough exam to get into MGS in the first

fide place at the college actually decides not to take it up. Chances of that, barring some terrible family catastrophe? Nil. I went to Birmingham instead, jewel in the crown of the Midlands.

WHILE I WAS SITTING on Cambridge Station feeling strangely ambivalent about my big chance of going to one of the world's greatest universities, Geoff Barton was sitting in an office directly above London's Covent Garden tube station plotting the rise of *Kerrang!*. *Kerrang!* – that's the sound made by an electric guitar when struck in anger, for the uninitiated – had been launched by Barton and publisher Alan Lewis earlier that year to capitalise on people like me who had been buying *Sounds*, the paper where they were both working, for the two, maybe three articles on metal that they put in each week. Back in 1981 *Kerrang!* was a unique concept, identifying that there was a massive groundswell of support for a style of music that had

got a copy of *Kerrang!*'s first issue in my hands, I was delirious to find that it didn't disappoint. And it had AC/DC on the cover.

The spurious idea for that first cover story hinged around the fans voting for the greatest metal track of all time through the pages of *Sounds*. And when the fans – probably all 150 of them – 'spoke', they voted for AC/DC's 'Whole Lotta Rosie'. Now the publishing game being what it is, you have to wonder how much the vote was influenced by the fact that not only were DC headlining that year's Donington Monsters Of Rock Festival, but that Barton and Lewis had found an incredible colour picture of Angus Young that absolutely captured everything they thought *Kerrang!* should be about. There was Angus, shirt off, sweat pouring from his body, hair drenched and flying all over the place. And he was rocking, well, like a bastard. The image was the very epitome of excitement and perfectly summed up what *Kerrang!* was supposed say to ➤

say to its readers. Whether the fans really rated 'Whole Lotta Rosie' above 'Stairway To Heaven' or 'Victim Of Changes' or whatever else was in the chart was almost irrelevant.

So when *Kerrang!* first emerged early in '81, I was in hog heaven. I'd been scouring the shelves at Smiths in Altrincham for a couple of weeks, hoping each time that this would prove to be the day when the magazine would finally hit the shelves. When I finally saw it, I bought it and scoured every single page on the bus home as if it was, I don't know, some sort of manifesto. I knew that this was simply the only magazine that truly spoke to me about the thing I loved most in the world. If someone had walked up to me on that bus and told me that within a year I'd be working for *Kerrang!*, travelling around the world at somebody else's expense watching the greatest rock bands on the planet and getting paid for it to boot, then I doubt I'd have been able to summon the strength to get off at my stop.

The truth was, I'd already had a piece published in *Sounds* when *Kerrang!* first appeared. I'd phoned Alan Lewis, who was swivelling in the editor's chair at *Sounds* in 1980, explained that I was running my own metal fanzine and that I wanted to do an article on the European rock scene. Incredibly, he agreed to the notion without seeing either references or a copy of my *Phoenix* fanzine. It took a while for the piece to run – a real filler if ever there was one in Alan's eyes, no doubt – but my joy when it finally did was unbounded. The joy I felt when a cheque for £129 plopped through the letter box for my work a few weeks later was even greater. Hold on. So you get paid for doing something you love, do you? And no catch? Frankly, I couldn't believe it.

I couldn't believe it either when the phone rang at home in Altrincham one day and the fella on the end of the line introduced himself as Alf Martin,

HEAVY METAL SPECIAL

KERRANG

No. 1 June 1981 50p

featuring the official All-Time HM Top 100!

In colour...
MOTORHEAD!
GIRLSCHOOL!
UFO! SAXON!
KISS! TRUST!
SCHENKER!
WILD HORSES!
PAT BENATAR! Z Z TOP!
STYX! VARDIS! TED NUGENT!
BLACKFOOT! GRAHAM BONNET!
RONNIE MONTROSE! ROSE TATTOO!
Deep Purple Family Tree! Black Axe! Handsome Beasts! Venom!
Silverwing! HM Quiz! Elitist LPs! Gross pix! Mayhem! Etc!

editor of *Kerrang!*. I didn't know what had happened to Geoff Barton, that familiar name from *Sounds* who, as far as I was aware, was the man in charge of all things metal. Mind you, I didn't care. Not when this Alf Martin was saying he liked what I'd done in *Sounds* and was asking if I had anything else knocking about that hadn't been published; interviews, features, whatever. Now of course any experienced journalist would have smelled a rat. No magazine editor rings you up, no matter how good a journo you are, just on the offchance that you might have a couple of things that you tossed off kicking around. If only things did work that

way! But I wasn't an experienced journalist. I was a hick from the sticks thinking that "Hey, maybe this guy, like, really likes my work, y'know?". I racked my brains for anything that I'd done that might interest him. I'd done a couple of interviews for the fanzine, one with an American band called Riot who'd been up in Manchester supporting somebody or other and another with a local group, A II Z, who'd just been picked up by Polydor. The bands would have merited a page at most, maybe even just a news story, but not in Alf-world. "Can you manage to do me a couple of pages on each?" he asked. Oh, I thought I could possibly manage it.

AND SO, WITH no more song and dance than that, I became a *Kerrang!* freelancer. I submitted the pieces, which were duly published, got asked to do an 'on the road' with Sammy Hagar and finally ended up taking up smoking on my first visit to the *Kerrang!* offices to meet Alf. I was so nervous, eager to please and keen to appear worldy-wise, that when he asked if I smoked I immediately claimed that I did, took one of his fags and proceeded to put in a piss-poor performance of someone who actually knew what he was doing with a Marlboro. Incredibly, it didn't stunt my chances at *Kerrang!* – although it may have stunted my growth, of course – even when Geoff Barton mysteriously returned to the helm. It was some time later that I discovered that the reason why my 'work' had been held in such high esteem was because there had been an NUJ strike. Alf Martin had been a strike-buster and, deprived of his regular writers, he'd been desperate to get his hands on absolutely anything with which to fill his pages. I could have been writing fourth form poetry and it would still have made the cut. Quite possibly I was. Amazingly, though, the rest of the staff who returned after the politics had been worked out never held it against me. ∎

Dirty Deeds

Thomas Schade has been running *Daily Dirt*, a brilliantly-detailed German AC/DC fanzine since 1987. What gives him the strength to do it, especially when he gets precious little help from the band?

When did you first hear AC/DC and what are your memories of that moment?

I've been a fan since 1980 and have since seen the band live 33 times! My first concert was in Frankfurt on 12th December 1980. I remember it really well, because it was really hard to get my parents to let me go. It was a month before my thirteenth birthday and because my parents had heard that AC/DC was an ugly and noisy band with a guy who showed his ass off on stage, they really didn't want me to go.

Fortunately my cousin (who was the same age) and some other schoolmates were all keen to go too, so eventually sheer weight of numbers forced a climbdown. I still remember being really envious of my cousin who'd been allowed to wear a denim jacket with a big AC/DC logo on the back ,while I had to wear a polo neck sweater and a thick corduroy jacket. What a disgrace!!!

What was it about the band that obsessed you so much?

I think it was just the simple yet powerful music, the fantastic, catchy guitar riffs and those unbelievable live performances. Everything is based on genuine rock'n'roll. AC/DC have never gone for gimmicks.

What gave you the idea of starting the fanzine? When did it come out and how did you go about producing the first *Daily Dirt*?

The first issue of *Daily Dirt* was published on 26th May 1987 and I only did 50 copies. Three years

As you can tell, this man runs a serious, detailed and brilliant AC/DC fanzine!

ago I decided to stop re-printing that first issue, because I don't think it's very interesting for the fans any more. I'd sold 670 copies of it by then (originally at 4 DM, but later I had to raise the price to 4,50 DM when the cost of postage went up).

The idea for *Daily Dirt* came from Jens Birkenfeld, a guy from Bremen. In 1987 he asked me if I was interested in putting together an AC/DC fanzine. At first, I told him that I wasn't very keen, because I had no idea what I could write about the band, except for some boring stories about bootlegs or gigs. In the end we decided that I'd help him lay out the magazine,

print the copies and find people who might be interested in it, but that he would be the editor. When I got the first issue from Jens I was a bit shocked. The layout was terrible and the articles were mostly copied from other magazines. Of course, it wasn't Jens' fault, because he had no experiences of making a magazine. I'd been reading fan-magazines about other groups for many years, so I had at least some idea about how to do it. I made another first issue from scratch, so we decided that I would act as deputy editor. After two weeks all 50 copies were sold out and I had to print some more. After that first issue, *Daily Dirt* became more and more my baby, because Jens didn't have enough time to do it properly. His last contributions were in *Daily Dirt No.3* and after *DD 5*, he decided that he couldn't carry on with the magazine. though he is still a loyal reader with good ideas on how the mag can be improved.

After Jens left the editorial team I went on the lookout for new help, because it was too much work for one person to do (the mag had 400 readers at this point). Fortunately, I found Markus Eltschinger and Phillip Flury, who had real talent for making great magazines. We had some problems, of course, mainly that they both live in Switzerland whereas I'm based in Germany. Ultimately, this was the reason why we stopped our joint venture after *Daily Dirt No.11*.

While we were publishing the magazine a lot of hardcore fans found their way to us and contributed a lot of stuff; guys like Marco Weber,

Jens Liesenberg or Detlef Kamin. Jens, who lives in the same village as me, was an ideal partner because he was such a big fan and was really motivated too. For example he played a key role in organising the latest two international fan meetings we've had in Trebur. Marco Weber, head of the AC/DC fan club Problem Child, impressed me with the good work he did with his fanclub and finally, Detlef Kamin was great for PR because he loves having long phone conversations to get into contact with fans and AC/DC related companies and organisations.

that you know already. *Daily Dirt* is also a good way for fans to talk about what they're interested in. I think these two points, combined with the fact that we've been doing this consistently for 12 years, are why we've been successful.

How often did you decide you would put the magazine out and did it grow quickly?
I was going to put it out three or four times a year at first, but because of limited time and especially due to the fact that AC/DC no longer release a record every year, I decided to do just one issue a

that probably wouldn't have happened if I hadn't been editor of *Daily Dirt*. It's been interesting to meet them and to get to know what they're like when they're not on-stage. The music's the most important thing, of course, but the fans like to know what the people who make the music are like too.

Is it very frustrating that the band don't seem to have a great deal of interest in getting really involved with projects like yours?
Yes, a bit. Angus is a very nice guy with a brilliant

These guys seemed like good reasons for me to build a new *Daily Dirt* team and it seems to have worked, because we've now been together for more than seven years! At the moment, the *Daily Dirt* mailing list has about 1500 readers from all over the world (in 30 countries) and I hope that we'll be able to add to that number!

What's the reaction of people who've bought *Daily Dirt*?
I get the impression that people are happy to have something which is 100% based on AC/DC, because there seems to be nothing else on the market which gives background information that's of interest to the fans. Most of what you find out via the regular media is stuff

year. This guarantees that each issue is of high quality. I don't want the pressure simply of having to fill the pages.

What's the single most interesting thing that's happened to you in connection with the fanzine?
There are a few things. I've met many nice people all over the world which is one of the most important by-products of doing this. And *Daily Dirt* has opened the door to several interesting organisations, like radio stations that have invited me to put together AC/DC specials and AC/DC's German record company who invited me to the 'Ballbreaker' release party in Hamburg with Angus and Brian. Over the last 12 years I've also met Angus and the other boys several times, and

memory. He knows me and *Daily Dirt* very well, but unfortunately, there's no permanent feedback, particularly from the rest of the band. It seems to me that many groups underestimate the potential of a well-organised fan-scene. I think one of the reasons that there's a really big AC/DC fan family in Germany is because of *Daily Dirt*. In France, you had a similar situation when a magazine called *Let There Be Light* was still going and in England you find the same thing with *Electric Outlaws*. In Italy, the US or any other country without an AC/DC fanzine, you won't find such a strong fan-scene. This makes it much more difficult for record companies in these countries to get into contact with their potential customers to find out what the 'market' wants.

On the other hand, I'm surprised that the band and the record companies don't make more use of this connection when it does exist. The band have almost never taken the fans' ideas on board for projects (aside from the compilation of the 'Bonfire' box set or the choice of Brian Johnson as Bon Scott's replacement, which was apparently made after a fan's recommendation).

My most disappointing moment was in 1996 in Dortmund where I gave all band members the latest *Daily Dirt* (issue 15). All of them seemed to be interested in the mag, except for Phil Rudd (who was on the cover!). He didn't say anything about it, then forgot to take his copy away with him. Phil isn't typical though; the other guys are much more open towards the fans than him.

Do you ever worry that you are too obsessed with AC/DC?
In the past I did, but things have changed over the last few years. I'm still known as 'that AC/DC-obsessed guy from Astheim, Germany' but there are other things in the world which are more important to me now, maybe because I'm not 17 any more. AC/DC still plays an important role in my life, but not the most important role.

It seems that there is no-one out there who prefers the Brian period to the Bon period. Why do you think that is?
I don't think that's true. In *Daily Dirt No.15* we had a poll where we asked which singer the fans preferred. The result showed that most of the fans like both singers and that there are also a few fans who actually prefer Brian.

What's the weirdest letter you've had from a fan?
I don't know how many letters I've received over the years, maybe 15,000 or more, and of course there were several weird letters. But I remember one in particular that came to me via a very bizarre route. It was sent by a fan from Chile whose grandma worked for the German embassy there. This fan gave his letter to his grandma, who forwarded it together with the embassy's post to Germany. I was very surprised to get a letter from the German embassy in Chile, I can tell you!

You don't make money out of *Daily Dirt*. Are there times when you just think it's all too much effort?
From time to time I get that feeling, especially when I'm under pressure to get an issue out in

Thomas Schade. The man behind *Daily Dirt*.

time to sell when the band are on tour. Fortunately, this doesn't happen very often. I get angry when I get phone calls from fans late at night or from fans who don't want to pay 6 DM for an issue (which isn't very much for a magazine with 80 pages, colour cover and postage and packing included). These people don't seem to understand that I'm not employed by AC/DC or the record company. I'm a fan just like they are and it's my free time and my own money which I have to invest to serve as an 'AC/DC information centre'. To this kind of fan I only can say: If you don't like what I do, then go somewhere else for your info.

Are you still as interested in the band today as you were when you first got into them?
I think that my interest has changed over the last 10 years. In the '80s I was much more intolerant towards other music and more fanatical about AC/DC. Now there are things like family and job which play an important role in my life as well.

Do your friends, especially your girlfriend, think you're crazy spending so much time on the mag?
Maybe they do think I'm crazy, but on the other

hand they notice that there are loads of interesting by-products from doing this. I know lots of people from many different countries as well as from all over Germany, so I get to know different cultures (for example in Japan, Italy or England, where I've visited readers of *Daily Dirt*). It's also helped my computer skills, writing English and German articles, organising big events like international fan meetings, which comes in handy in my regular job too. I admit I had a few problems with my girlfriend early on in our relationship because I couldn't find a balance between her needs and my AC/DC activities, but as I said before, my focal points have changed over the last few years. I think I had a lot of luck that I found a woman in Steffi who

"i think one of the reasons that there's a really big AC/DC fan family in Germany is because of *Daily Dirt.*"

has enough tolerance for an AC/DC obsessive like me.

What do you see as the future for *Daily Dirt*? And the future for AC/DC?
The future of *Daily Dirt* is completely linked with the future of AC/DC. If it takes AC/DC three to five years to produce a new record and go out on tour, then it'll be difficult for me to put out *Daily Dirt* every year. After 18 regular issues with more than 1000 pages (and 8 extra issues with another 300-400 pages), AC/DC has already been discussed in such depth that it's getting harder and harder to uncover new info. Let's hope Angus and Co. get over their mid-life crises and release many plenty more records in the future.

If you're interested in DAILY DIRT, you can get the issues for the following prices:
- *DD 2-11 for 4,50 DM (each)*
- *DD 12-16 for 5 DM (each)*
- *DD 17-19 for 6 DM (each)*
- *DD Extra issue "The Tour Diary 1996" for 5 DM Postage is included.*
Money can be sent in a registered letter or via postal order to Thomas Schade, Bernhard-Lichtenberg-Weg 3, 65468 Astheim Germany.

IT'S A LONG WAY TO THE TOP...

Mike Jones decided he'd take time out on an Australian trip to check out some of the venues that AC/DC played in the band's early days...

While on a trip around Australia in February and March of 1995, I had a chance to explore a few places from AC/DC's past. I had a plan as I'd gathered some information on venues from the Clinton Walker book, *The Life And Times Of Bon Scott*, which I'd bought one day at the end of January in Brisbane. I read it from cover to cover that same day in the youth hostel where I was staying. The main idea was to travel down to Sydney, Melbourne and Perth. It all started well as on the first leg of the trip, from Brisbane to Sydney, I'd stopped off at a place called Byron Bay and while browsing in a Red Cross shop there I found a very good copy of 'Flaming Galah' by a band called Fraternity, with a lead singer who later became famous with another group! A bargain at $1!

Once in Sydney I visited the Hard Rock Café, the first of the many that I've been in where AC/DC are actually honoured. There was a plaque on the floor with the band's logo in a star, even though the slash was the wrong way round. The band recorded several albums in Sydney but some of the

The Melbourne Tennis Centre.

venues where they used to play have now been demolished as I found out later that same year when I spoke to Angus at the 'Hard As A Rock' video shoot. I did get one interesting story, though, from a guy who had a belt buckle stall in the Haymarket area of the city near the Entertainment Centre. He'd seen the band doing a gig on the back of a truck near the market sometime in 1975!

MY NEXT STOP WAS Melbourne which again had a few band connections. It was a special time to be there as it was 19th February, the 15th anniversary of Bon's death. He's still a hero in Australia and many hardcore fans there really appreciate what he gave AC/DC in his all-too-short time with the

The Sidney Myer Bowl, Melbourne.

band. Bon Scott T-shirts were still a 'seller' in shops in Melbourne and other cities. On the night of the 19th a pub called The Fox And Hounds in Flinders Street had a Bon Scott tribute night where well-known local band Dirty Deeds played a great set including a couple of covers I hadn't heard anyone else do, namely 'Long Way To The Top' and 'Can I Sit Next To You Girl?'

The following day I took a tram downtown to find a venue the band had played quite regularly in '75 and '76 – The Festival Hall. After a New Year's Day show supporting the Skyhooks in April 1975 it was here in June that AC/DC played their first headlining show in the city. Apparently the gig was videotaped so the band had something to impress

The Fox And Hounds pub in Melbourne.

his grave again. I'd bought a nice framed print of Bon in the local market and took it with me for some photos near the cask and seat. I was given a little information by a woman behind the desk at the cemetery about the service and all of Bon's details, like his last address, which were still on file on the computer. It was quite eerie seeing it all. I was also told that his parents still visited the grave every weekend and had done so for the last 15 years, which to my mind is real devotion. Unfortunately I was there on a Friday because I would have liked to have met them.

I wandered up to the chapel and had a look inside. Imaginary memories of a sad day flashed through my mind. Apparently only a few fans were outside the gates on that day back in 1980. Talking of 'fans', I was also told that the reason why the plaque on the memorial seat looked different to the last time I was there was because some US

Mike Jones at the Hard Rock Cafe.

"There was a plaque on the floor with the band's logo in a star, even though the slash was the wrong way round!"

'the right people' with and this led to the band trying their luck in the UK in 1976. I wasn't allowed to take photos inside for some reason, so I looked at the small stage and wooden floor and wondered what it would have been like 20 years previously. After taking a picture outside I wandered down to Flinders Park and had a look at the Melbourne Tennis Centre, a massive venue the band now play when they're in town. How things have changed!

Nearby was another old venue, the Sidney Myer Music Bowl, a massive outdoor canopy opened on 12th February 1959 by the then Prime Minister of Australia, R.G. Menzies. AC/DC played there in April 1975 in the 'Freedom From Hunger' show which I think was a mini-festival featuring quite a few bands and which attracted a large crowd.

Later on in the day I took a tram to St. Kilda, a part of Melbourne where the band hung out in the early days. I tried to find the house in Landsdowne

Road where they all used to live, but with only the memory of a photo once shown to me I found it hard work and gave up as it was getting dark.

NEARLY A MONTH later I arrived in Perth, Western Australia. I'd been in the Perth Entertainment Centre back in May of 1992 without realising that it was one of the band's old stomping grounds. The place holds around 7,000 people and I couldn't believe AC/DC played two nights there on an Australian Tour back in 1976. That's how big they were just before they came over to England where they only played in pubs, clubs and universities!

On 17th March, after a trip around the town of Fremantle where Bon's parents apparently still live, I visited

marines had helped themselves to the old one as a 'souvenir'. That was the end of my little tour of homage, and after taking some photos I made my way back to Perth, followed a week or so later by the long journey back to rainy Manchester!

Mike's souvenirs at Bon's grave.

"THEY'RE THE BEST!"

DC fan Paul 'Gooner' Elliott has met the band loads of times while working for Kerrang! Here's what he thinks of them...

You're a long-standing AC/DC fan, aren't you?
Sure. I was in the fan club years ago and the best thing about it was that you got this T-shirt. It was a lovely black one with a little AC-DC logo, sort of within a globe, with 'International Fan Club' up here on the chest. That was my favourite T-shirt for ages. I can't recall getting that much from the AC/DC fan club, though. The highlight might only have been getting that famous picture outside some studio when Brian first joined the band.

So when did you first actually get to meet them?
I think I first met a band member around 1988, the time of the 'Blow Up Your Video' album. I remember that time because the only song I really liked on the album was 'Some Sin For Nothing', which was sort of mid-pocket rifferama. 'Blow Up Your Video' didn't look like an album that was going to be timeless to me. It was very '80s and it felt very dated, what with 'Heatseeker' and all that stuff. But I remember doing the interview, I think it was for *Sounds*, and then I did another interview for a Japanese magazine within a short space of time. Both times it was with Angus and he was brilliant. I've done Angus several times for *Kerrang!* since, but I've never interviewed anybody else in the band. I have spoken to Brian, though.

What was Angus like first time you met him?
I don't recall with any great clarity the first time I met him, but I remember one time I interviewed him in Holland around the time the 'AC/DC Live' album was coming out and I was really ill. I would have cried off, but because it was AC/DC I thought, "No, I've got to go". I went somewhere like Amsterdam and I remember that his lovely Dutch wife was there, who was charming. She wasn't really beautiful or rock star wifey, which I thought was quite sweet. I remember Angus was sitting there and he was so small! He had his denim jacket on with his passport sticking out of the top pocket and he just seemed so nerdy... but when he was chatting he was great.

I took a real fan's perspective of that interview and I think he was really receptive to my approach. He's a really funny man, very aware, and I think he's in on the joke of how AC/DC are both brilliant and funny at one and the same time. He was very eager to send himself up and he didn't mind talking about Bon, which I

The Gooner meets The Beano. Yadaday!

"Angus is a very funny man, and i think he's in on the joke of how AC/DC are both brilliant and funny at the same time."

thought might be a sensitive thing. You know how some bands are really uptight...

It was a great thrill for me to have interviewed my favourite band and I got Angus to sign an album for me. He signed 'Highway To Hell', but I couldn't get him to sign 'Back In Black' because I didn't have a silver or gold pen to go on the black surface. That was an enormous shame, because I think it's the greatest rock album ever released. For my own personal satisfaction, not

just as a music journalist, I wouldn't want to sit here and think I'd never interviewed AC/DC. It would be a glaring omission.

What do you make of the other three band members?
Phil Rudd's a tremendous drummer and Cliff Williams does his job well, but in truth Malcolm is the essence of the band. I see Malcolm on the cover of 'Highway To Hell' with that little white

T-shirt on and when I think of AC/DC, that's the image that always springs to mind.

So why exactly are AC/DC so special?
Simply because the music's so strong. It was proved to me the other night because I was at a mate's wedding when they played 'Touch Too Much' at the reception disco and my brother, who isn't any kind of rock fanatic, was playing air guitar. He'd forgotten how great that song is. The

best thing about DC? Just the sheer balls. They just had something. I say 'had', though, and that probably says something about the way a lot of people feel about them. They haven't really made a great album for what, 20 years?

Like the Rolling Stones.
Well, my two favourite drummers in the world are Charlie Watts and Phil Rudd because they play it simple. Keith Richards, who I did interview amazingly enough, said that his favourite metal album was 'Powerage', and you can completely understand why that would be an album that he would love. He said AC/DC sounded like they meant it, and I sat there and I thought, 'fucking right they do'. He also said that Metallica sound like a plane rumbling along the runway unable to

The Way I Wanna Rock'n'Roll' is probably up there as a turkey. But if I had to nominate one tune, I'd go for something from 'Fly On The Wall'. That was a pretty poor album, wasn't it? I mean 'Shake Your Foundations' was really rubbish.

What's your feeling about Brian versus Bon?
Well, I don't have as strong an emotional attachment to Bon as a lot of people appear to have, because I didn't see the band live with Bon. I got into them with Bon because I heard 'Touch Too Much' and things like that, so when Bon died I was sort of puzzled, more than mortified. And I have such a feeling for Brian that when I picked up the 'Bonfire' box set the one picture that gave me the most pleasure was that one of 'The Beano', the one in classic pose, even

a masterpiece. It's just beautiful, the perfect rock album. And the sound. Everything's right. You couldn't imagine them doing 'Let Me Put My Love Into You' without Mutt, although I'd be concerned that if he came back now he'd put some of that Shania Twain cheese in there the way he does these days. No, not really. I'm sure it would be fantastic.

Have you met other bands who are AC/DC daft?
I went on the road with 3 Colours Red and they have 20 tapes that they'd stick on their little ghetto blaster at the end of a gig and ten of them were AC/DC, so I was impressed with that. The singer Pete's also got his Bonfire keyring, which I definitely appreciate. Then you've got the Stereophonics and they were at the *Kerrang!*

"i think AC/DC's still very valid without Bon. i had far more of a problem when Simon Wright joined than anyone else."

take off, whereas AC/DC sounded like a band that had true bollocks on them.

What's your favourite DC track, then?
I suppose it would have to be 'Hells Bells'; it's such a tremendously exciting start to an album, isn't it? It's got loads of brilliant lyrics like, "If good's on the left, then I'm sticking to the right" and "If you're into evil, you're a friend of mind", which is clearly not true. But it's obviously all part of that nostalgia too. I remember the first time I heard it so well.

Where was that?
Around my mate Jeff Dixon's house when I was about 13 or something. That was a fantastically exciting time when I was just discovering rock music and so for that reason alone I'd probably put 'Hells Bells' up there with 'Back in Black' as an all-time favourite.

And what's the worst ever track they've recorded?
There have been a few, haven't there? 'Mistress For Christmas' wasn't particularly good, was it? Although it was quite a good title. It was such a ridiculous idea that it was actually better than being just a really poor song, I suppose. 'That's

moreso than Bon as a small boy in a kilt. Much as I respect him and love hearing him, it's not a major thing for me. I think AC/DC's still very valid without Bon. I had far more of a problem when Simon Wright joined than anyone else.

Why him?
He was just a useless fat old bastard, wasn't he? He was just too spotty to be in AC/DC. It seemed that AC/DC was becoming like any old band. Some bloke who used to be in some hopeless British bands was suddenly in AC/DC. That didn't feel right.

You say they haven't made a great album in 20 years...
Well, maybe that's harsh, but there's no doubt that the album that I'd say was their last great effort was 'Flick Of The Switch' 'Ballbreaker' is the best AC/DC album in years, but classic? No.

So what should the band do to recapture the glory days?
I think that they should do anything to get Mutt Lange back to do an album with them, because he made them sound like the greatest rock band in the world. 'Back In Black' was so powerful. It's

awards going on about how they used to go to fancy dress parties as kids dressed as AC/DC. Kelly, the singer, did Angus and unfortunately his brother had to do Malcolm, which isn't quite so good really. Then of course there's The Cult...

I actually took a tape of 'Wild Flower' from their 'Electric' album, the one that sounds just like AC/DC, to an interview that I did with Angus. I played it to him to see what he thought and he just went "That's fucking ridiculous, isn't it? It's 'Rock'n'Roll Singer', isn't it?" Billy Duffy from The Cult once commented that 'some wanker' had done that and I just thought "Oh, that was me"; I was quite pleased with that! But it is exactly the same riff, isn't it? That was just Rick Rubin wanting to produce AC/DC and having to settle for The Cult. Oh, I remember when I first interviewed Metallica, Lars Ulrich was walking around in a 'Back In Black' tour jacket that he got from Peter Mensch, who'd managed DC before he looked after Metallica. I was pretty envious of that. Blaze Bailey, who was in Iron Maiden, said the two albums you always have to have on tour are 'Master Of Puppets' and 'Back In Black'. But let's face it, everyone in rock loves AC/DC. And we love them too, even though we have a laugh about them as well! They're the best.

BLACK SABBATH AND THE FLICK KNIFE INCIDENT

Not everyone likes AC/DC. Sabbath's Geezer Butler remembers one very unsavoury incident...

The knife wasn't drawn, it was a flick knife. I always liked flick knives when I was a kid and I always had them because my brothers were teddy boys. I used to love them. It was part of my growing up, all my gang had flick knives. They were banned in England which gave them a bit of mystique and for some reason when we were on tour in Switzerland one time I went into a shop where they had flick knives for sale. I thought "Great" and bought one.

I was sitting there in the hotel bar flicking this bloody knife and AC/DC came in. They were getting absolutely legless and Malcolm got totally smashed out of his brains. He started saying things like "I suppose you think you're hard with that, don't you?" and I was going "Eh?" Just out of the blue, it was. One of those drunken things. Stupid.

When you remember things like that you're glad you gave it all up, the drinking. That's how it started, him getting pissed and starting an argument with me, but there's no way I'm gonna bloody stab somebody! Their tour manager waded in then, threatening to beat ours up, so they dragged Malcolm off to bed and that was it.

Sabbath's Geezer Butler (big hair on the left) nearly had the off with Malcolm!

SURE BEATS WORKING IN TACO BELL...

'Back In Black' changed Al Narvaez' life. It often has that effect on people...

Let me tell you about the first time I ever heard AC/DC. I remember seeing the video for 'Thunderstruck' and laughing at the silly guy duck-walking, even though I thought that the song itself was great. Then years later, when I was working in my first job (at Taco Bell), I decided to join one of those CD clubs that offer 20 CDs for your soul or some such. I kind of remembered the band's name and knew I liked that first song, so I ordered both 'Back In Black' and 'Live' and hoped that they were good. When I got them I still didn't have a CD player, so I bought one on a Friday between school and work, but didn't get a chance to play with my new toy before I had to go out. I busted my butt for six hours and came back stinky, broke and tired to be greeted by my brother shouting, "You've got to listen to this!" He put 'Back In Black' on and hit track 6 (the title track). I heard the cymbals crash and the band kick in and I thought "THIS IS ROCK'N'ROLL!!" I heard that album backwards and forwards that night and went on to get all the albums and build a website in honor of the band. They've got me through many bad nights and I can't think of music without them. Years later and I still stick to my statement – AC/DC *is* Rock'n'Roll. Everything else plays off them.

THE ODD COUPLE...

...of tracks you might not be familiar with, that is. AC/DC are renowned for the scarcity of rarities and obscure tracks. If a song's good enough, then it seems to be band policy to put it on an album. But collectors can still track down a few oddball items. Here they are...

■ 'Can I Sit Next To You Girl'/'Rockin' In The Parlour' – the first ever AC/DC single, with original vocalist Dave Evans singing. Originally released by Albert productions in Australia (1974).

■ 'Stick Around'/'Love Song' – issued on the Australia-only version of the 'High Voltage' album, the band's first (1975).

■ 'R.I.P. (Rock In Peace)' – issued on the Australia-only version of the 'Dirty Deeds Done Dirt Cheap' album (1976).

■ 'Fling Thing' – issued on the UK only as a B-side to the 'Jailbreak' single (1976).

■ 'Carry Me Home' – issued as the B-side of the 'Dog Eat Dog' single in Australia only (1977).

■ 'Crabsody In Blue' – issued on the Australian version of 'Let There Be Rock' and vinyl versions only of the album in Europe

■ 'Cold Hearted Man' – included on some vinyl versions of the 'Powerage' album, the track was replaced by 'Rock'n'Roll Damnation' on later vinyl versions and on CD (1978).

■ 'Snake Eye' – bonus track on the 'Heatseeker' single (1988).

■ 'Borrowed Time' – bonus track on the 'Moneytalks' single (1991).

■ 'Down On The Borderline' – appeared on an Australia-only promo CD for 'Moneytalks'

■ 'Alright Tonight' – recorded for the 'Blow Up Your Video' sessions and widely-available on a bootleg single alongside an early version of 'That's The Way I Wanna Rock'n'Roll' with different lyrics and guitar solo.

■ 'Boom Boom Boom' – cover of the John Lee Hooker song recorded by Brian and Angus for a French radio broadcast in 1995 and widely available on bootleg.

Chapter Seven

ViDEO NASTiES

Bon: "Let there be rock..."

Hojo: "Let there be..."

In 1982 I walked onto the campus at Birmingham University as a fully-fledged student for the first time. Four years later I left with a 2:2 degree tucked under my arm, hair down to my arse, very little clue about how I'd managed to fool all of the people all of the time on my Combined Honours French and German course, some knowledge of sex and drugs and a feeling that I'd just had what people would call 'the time of my life'.

University these days sounds like a dull affair, full of people who are on courses simply to study and learn, spending money that they haven't got which they'll then spend the first few years of their working lives struggling to pay back, all in aid of getting some top brass job where the vast amounts of money they'll eventually make will compensate for the miserable time they had while they were 'making it'. Back in 1982 there seemed to be an entirely different reason for being at university; at least amongst the people I became friendly with. There's no other way to put this. University was seen as one great big doss, a fantastic opportunity to get away from your parents for the first time, to go to the pub every night, stay up till four in the morning watching videos, shag girls and smoke dope. The work was a minor irritant, something that got in the way of all that other stuff, but it never worried me much. I liked the languages, enjoyed speaking them, could get by quite easily without having to try too hard, but couldn't be arsed reading all those books they had on the course list. I was always convinced that with a bit of ingenuity, I'd be able to bluff my way through whatever exams came my way. And so it proved. Of course the thought of a load of long-haired layabouts boozing their way through life for four years without a care in the world while someone else foots the bill is absolutely horrific to me now, especially when I get my tax bill at the end of each year. But am I glad that I was allowed to do it! University was incredible.

I had money, too. Not real money, of course, but certainly more than most skint students. I had my six hundred quid a term grant or whatever it was, which covered my rent, food and transport onto campus. But by the time I started in the autumn of 1982 I'd already established myself as one of Kerrang!'s prime freelancers. The rate the magazine paid of £80 per thousand words is ridiculously low for a working man with responsibilities (and rumour has it that the rate has hardly improved to

this day, though I couldn't say for certain as it's not far off a decade now since I last wrote anything for Kerrang!.) Whatever, for a student with virtually nil outgoings, once the grant had taken care of basics, then I could live, if not like a king, then certainly like a lord. This meant that I got pissed three times a week at a conservative estimate, could travel to London every seven days to keep my contacts with Kerrang! solid and could spend money on clothes that in retrospect only serve as a sobering reminder of how ridiculous – not to mention colour-blind – young men of 19 can be.

The record collection was coming along nicely too. I was getting a whole load of albums for free in my new role as a writer, and was really enjoying one of the greatest perks in the world. Some of the stuff I was listening to, that horrendous '80s metal which was full of hair-raising guitar solos and equally histrionic haircuts, beggars belief now, but at least AC/DC was still on the Johnson playlist. And on tape, as it happened.

VIDEO WAS THE HOT new medium of the day and shops like Rumbelows and Radio Rentals had suddenly started offering great rental deals on video players. As soon as I'd moved out of the digs in hall that I'd been allocated for my first year and

moved in with three equally rock-oriented pals in Kings Heath, a once-swanky-but-by-then-had-seen-better-days suburb of Birmingham, we clubbed together and got the video in. I'd run into a guy in Birmingham called Video Paul. I never knew his surname and clearly wasn't feeling inspired the day I christened him with his nickname, but I was glad I'd made his acquaintance because he was the king of the illicit music video tape. I can't even recall where Paul used to get his material from, but I knew he had a hell of a lot of it. Some of them were grainy, third or fourth generation copies of copies, but I didn't care. I was insatiable for the stuff. Kiss, Black Sabbath, The Stones, Mötley Crüe, Van Halen. Promo videos, American TV shows, interviews, all kinds of weird shit was on those tapes. Oh, and AC/DC, who soon emerged as our collective faves.

In the three or so years that had followed 'Back In Black' and in the wake of Bon Scott's death, my interest in the band's music had dwindled to almost zero. Neither 'For Those About To Rock', nor the '83 album 'Flick Of The Switch' moved me. The band's music had pitched from hi-powered R&B and boogie towards a lumpen heavy metal mush and I pretty much hated it. I certainly all but ignored it. This now seems rather churlish when you consider the rest of the tripe I was listening to at the time, but that was the way of it back then. Where video was concerned, however, AC/DC still ruled the roost at 112 Station Road.

AC/DC's video career is littered with disasters. They are neither great fans of the medium, nor are they actors, and so their efforts to capture their essence on tape usually land somewhere between outright farce and cloying embarrassment. ➤

Unless, of course, you're stoned off your nut. Then AC/DC videos suddenly grow wings and become some of the funniest pieces of work ever laid down in the name of rock music.

I discovered this quite by accident. Before I went to university I'd never touched drugs. I'd fallen into the trap of smoking fags after the Alf Martin incident at *Kerrang!*, of course, but that was the extent of my debauchery. Birmingham University changed all that, though. My first experience wasn't good. A girl by the name of Tetsy had told my friend Barry and me that she could score for us. Curious and stupid in equal measures, we coughed up, then nearly spewed up when we rolled and smoked the bizarre array of seeds and weeds that we'd been assured was grass. Bollocks was it. All it gave you was nausea, exacerbated by the fact that I was sick with myself for getting ripped off so easily.

Still, I got by with a little help from my friends, as they say. After that first debacle I soon found out what it meant to be stoned. Some of the guys I

The paraphernalia that goes with dope-smoking has always amazed me. Maybe back in those golden days when everyone was smoking full strength tobacco out of a tin, sparking up a joint wouldn't have been a problem. After all, novices could roll a fag with one hand back then, while true smoking pros could do it behind their backs n'all. Not us 1980s bozos though. We tried the rolling malarkey and failed miserably, ending up with strangely-shaped efforts that looked like origami decorations, but which bore precious little resemblance to cigarettes. So we improvised, making our own bongs, which gave us two advantages. Firstly, we saved ourselves many man hours. All we needed was a beer can and a pin, or if were feeling really adventurous a couple of large-sized plastic cola bottles and a bit of rubber tubing. Then, with the most rudimentary knowledge of construction techniques we were soon bong-handed. And with the dope being fired up neat you could get stoned quicker – a whole lot quicker. The living room of

haloes attached to the back of the neck like kids wear in primary school nativity plays. Bon Scott stands in the pulpit, playing the part of a rock 'n' roll vicar, mugging furiously as he exhorts the congregation to get worked up about the powers of rock 'n' roll, before eventually discarding his ecclesiastical robes to reveal the customary naked torso and tight jeans ensemble, ready to do battle with the band's ever more frenetic power boogie. Led by an impossibly young-looking Angus, wearing his hair short and, incredibly, his trousers long for the one and only time as far as I'm aware, the band's blustering boogie is sharp, hard, tough and, quite obviously, incredibly loud. Angus bangs his head as he moves around, looking even more ridiculous than when he's wearing the schoolboy uniform as the choirboy gown gets in the way of his fingers and the wooden halo bobs about above his head like a sailboat being tossed in a storm. The music is absolutely irresistible, the video utterly preposterous and for a bunch of young men in

"AC/DC's video career is littered with disasters. They are neither great fans of the medium, nor are they actors"

knocked around with found someone to provide us with the dark, tarry resin that was the real deal. And Station Road became the meeting place for a bunch of stoners-in-training. Maybe three days out of five there wouldn't be lectures in the latter part of the day, which turned out to be our cue to head back to the house for an afternoon of video-viewing and pot-smoking.

> 'Highway To Hell' was once turned into muzak for shopping malls by some folk with no sense of decency. "If you can whistle the first few bars of AC/DC's 'Highway To Hell' then you'll remember the track and the era," explained Phil McCauley, MD of the company committing the crimes against music. "It helps you to bond with your shopping environment."

our house soon seemed to have a permanent mushroom cloud of smoke hanging over it, and you could pretty much get stoned just being in the room, never mind taking a hit from the bong. Within moments of starting this afternoon caper, a regular group of experimentalists were sitting in our living room flitting between two states, zombified or utterly unable to stop laughing. It was Maggie Thatcher's worst nightmare, the supposed cream of Britain's intelligentsia sitting there chonged off their chuffs.

Once the mood had been set, then inevitably videos would be demanded. And in our mashed-up state it seemed that only one video would truly hit the spot. In amongst the AC/DC material, the majority of which was filmed with Brian Johnson on vocals and held little interest for me, there was one little promo clip for the song 'Let There Be Rock'. The concept behind it was as cheap as the video itself. The band are filmed in a church, dressed in green choirboy smocks and with their uniforms topped off by those round, wooden

Birmingham stoned to the gills, it was absolutely the funniest thing we'd ever seen.

'Let There Be Rock' must have been played every single afternoon for, ooh, six months at least. It became part of the ritual. Have a smoke, get stoned, laugh at 'Let There Be Rock'. Things couldn't have been more perfect. God knows who'd persuaded the band that such a cheesy load of nonsense was a good idea, but whoever you are, sir, I doff my cap to you. Without your doubtless well-intentioned efforts, many university days would have passed much, much slower. Looking at the video again now, it's hard to believe such a ham-fisted effort could have been one small step on AC/DC's march to becoming a worldwide phenomenon. You could have bet your house that any group stupid enough to have let themselves be filmed doing *that* would have been back at their day jobs within weeks, let alone months. That the band's music could overcome such ridiculous drawbacks is possibly the most fitting tribute to its sheer spirit that I can think of... ∎

The Fans' Forum

The *Daily Dirt* fanzine conducted a survey of its readers in 1995 to find out more about the average DC fanatic. Here are the findings...

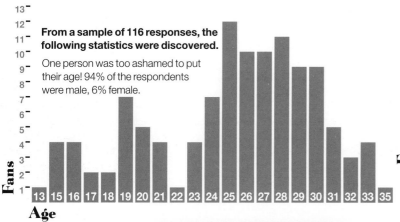

From a sample of 116 responses, the following statistics were discovered.

One person was too ashamed to put their age! 94% of the respondents were male, 6% female.

Age / Fans bar chart: ages 13, 15, 16, 17, 18, 19, 20, 21, 22, 23, 24, 25, 26, 27, 28, 29, 30, 31, 32, 33, 35

Number of Gigs...

Fans / Number of Gigs bar chart: 0, 1, 2, 3, 4, 5, 6, 7, 8, 9, 10, 11, 12, 13, 14, 15, 16, 17, 18, 19, 20, 20+

FAVOURITE TRACKS FROM BALLBREAKER

1) Hard As A Rock
2) Ballbreaker
3) Boogie Man
4) Hail Caesar
5) Burnin' Alive
6) The Furor
7) Cover You In Oil
8) Whiskey On The Rocks
9) The Honey Roll
10) Caught With Your Pants Down
11) Love Bomb

FAVOURITE AC/DC VIDEO

1) Let There Be Rock
2) Donington 91
3) Australian Songs
4) Fly On The Wall Collection
5) Clipped
6) Who Made Who

FAVOURITE SONG

1) Down Payment Blues
2) Highway To Hell
3) Let There Be Rock
4) Hells Bells
5) Touch Too Much
6) Whole Lotta Rosie
7) Back In Black
8) High Voltage
9) Thunderstruck
10) T.N.T.

Apparently it's too cheeky to ask if Beano is better or worse than Bon.

OCCUPATIONS

Working	60
Student	14
At School	13
Unemployed	10
Soldier	2

INSTRUMENTS PLAYED BY BAND MEMBERS

Guitar	12
Drums	6
Bass	4
Vocals	2
Keyboards	1
Management	1

FAVOURITE AC/DC ALBUM (INC. NUMBER OF VOTES)

1) Powerage	31
2) Back in Black	29
3) Highway To Hell	23
4) Let There Be Rock	13
5) T.N.T.	6
6) For Those About To Rock	5
7) Dirty Deeds Done Dirt Cheap	4
7) High Voltage	4
9) Ballbreaker	3
9) Live	3
11) If You Want Blood	2
11) The Razor's Edge	2
13) 74 Jailbreak	1

HAVE YOU MET A BAND MEMBER?

| 1) No | 73% |
| 2) Yes | 27% |

PERSONAL HABITS

	YES	NO
Smoker	73	42
Long-haired	67	48
Hard of hearing	100	15
Band member	95	20

SHOULD MALCOLM AND CLIFF MOVE MORE ON STAGE?

| 1) No | 67% |
| 2) Yes | 33% |

FAVOURITE BAND MEMBER...

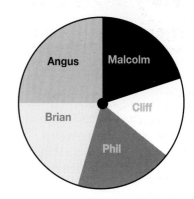

Pie chart: Malcolm, Angus, Brian, Phil, Cliff

FAVOURITE SINGER...

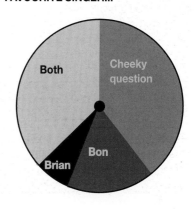

Pie chart: Both, Cheeky question, Bon, Brian

AC/DC LINE-UPS 1973-1999...

AC/DC - 1

ANGUS YOUNG – guitar (from Tantrum)
MALCOLM YOUNG – guitar (from
Velvet Underground)
DAVE EVANS – vocals
LARRY VAN KNEDT – bass
COLIN BURGESS – drums

AC/DC - 2

ANGUS YOUNG – guitar MALCOLM
YOUNG – guitar DAVE EVANS – vocals
ROB BAILEY – bass RON CARPENTER
– drums

AC/DC - 3

ANGUS YOUNG – guitar MALCOLM
YOUNG – guitar DAVE EVANS – vocals
ROB BAILEY – bass RUSSELL
COLEMAN – drums

AC/DC - 4

ANGUS YOUNG – guitar MALCOLM
YOUNG – guitar DAVE EVANS – vocals
ROB BAILEY – bass PETER CLACK –
drums (this is the line-up which played
the Chequer's club, 31st Dec 1973)

AC/DC - 8

ANGUS YOUNG – guitar MALCOLM
YOUNG – guitar/bass BON SCOTT –
vocals PHIL RUDD – drums (from
Buster Brown)

AC/DC - 7

ANGUS YOUNG – guitar MALCOLM
YOUNG – guitar BON SCOTT – vocals
GEORGE YOUNG – bass TONY
KERRANTE – drums (from The 69ers)

AC/DC - 6

ANGUS YOUNG – guitar MALCOLM
YOUNG – guitar BON SCOTT – vocals
drums GEORGE YOUNG – bass
(brother of Malcolm and Angus, from
The Easybeats)

AC/DC - 5

ANGUS YOUNG – guitar MALCOLM
YOUNG – guitar BON SCOTT – vocals/
drums (from Fraternity) BRUCE
HOUWE – bass (from Fraternity)

AC/DC - 9

ANGUS YOUNG – guitar MALCOLM
YOUNG – guitar BON SCOTT – vocals
MARK EVANS – bass PHIL RUDD –
drums

AC/DC - 10

ANGUS YOUNG – guitar MALCOLM
YOUNG – guitar BON SCOTT – vocals
CLIFF WILLIAMS (from Home) – bass
PHIL RUDD – drums

AC/DC - 11

ANGUS YOUNG – guitar MALCOLM
YOUNG – guitar BRIAN JOHNSON –
vocals (from Geordie) CLIFF WILLIAMS
– bass PHIL RUDD – drums

AC/DC - 12

ANGUS YOUNG – guitar MALCOLM
YOUNG – guitar BRIAN JOHNSON –
vocals CLIFF WILLIAMS – bass SIMON
WRIGHT – drums (from A II Z)

AC/DC - 16

ANGUS YOUNG – guitar MALCOLM
YOUNG – guitar BRIAN JOHNSON –
vocals CLIFF WILLIAMS – bass PHIL
RUDD – drums

AC/DC - 15

ANGUS YOUNG – guitar MALCOLM
YOUNG – guitar BRIAN JOHNSON –
vocals CLIFF WILLIAMS – bass (Paul
Greg acted as stand-in for some shows
on the U.S. leg of the 91 tour) CHRIS
SLADE – drums (from Gary Moore)

AC/DC - 14

ANGUS YOUNG – guitar MALCOLM
YOUNG – guitar BRIAN JOHNSON –
vocals CLIFF WILLIAMS – bass SIMON
WRIGHT – drums

AC/DC - 13

ANGUS YOUNG – guitar STEVIE
YOUNG – guitar (cousin of Angus and
Malcolm, brought in for U.S.A tour 1988
to replace Malcolm) BRIAN JOHNSON
– vocals CLIFF WILLIAMS – bass
SIMON WRIGHT – drums

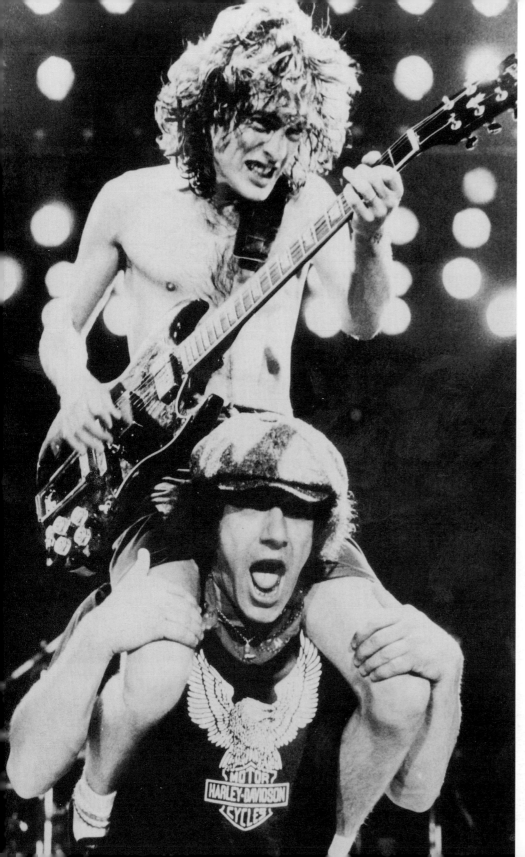

"I'VE SPENT OVER A THOUSAND BUCKS ON AC/DC"

Andrew J. Shal of Penn State University explains the attraction of buying everything he can find to do with the band...

My interest in AC/DC started roughly eight years ago, when I saw the video for 'You Shook Me All Night Long' on MTV. The mere sight of that lovely lady pulling on the sweater made me a fan for life! Soon afterwards I purchased 'Back In Black' and the rest, as they say, is history. I soon became quite the obsessive fan and made it my mission in life to own anything bearing the band's likeness that I could find. I've spent well over a thousand dollars on AC/DC items alone, and since I'm a student with no steady means of employment, that is quite a large figure! I began simply by collecting all the albums and accomplished that in a week, buying three albums a day. As my knowledge of the band increased, I learned of all the B-sides and non-American tracks, so I began my search for those songs as well, successfully tracking down all but the rarest of the rare (which to this date I still don't own). I do have all rare tracks on a dubbed tape and a CD-ROM, however.

At this point I thought that'd be enough, but before I knew it I was buying any promo items that had the logo on. I now have an almost complete collection of interview discs, picture discs, and books. I also own all of the commercially-released videos and hours worth of concert and promo footage. I also own a lot of bootleg material on CD and audio tape. I'm currently trying to finish off my album collection on vinyl, as to my ear they are superior to CD. My most cherished items are my original pressing of the Australian 'High Voltage' album, which is still sealed, and my 'Baktabak' interview picture disc that was mis-pressed with a Guns N' Roses interview instead. Even the "big" collectors have not seen or heard of that one, so to me it is extra special.

The song that has the most meaning for me would be 'Kicked In The Teeth', as it describes basically all my relationships with the opposite sex. However, if being an AC/DC fanatic has taught be anything, it is that 'Hell Ain't A Bad Place To Be.'

COLLECTOR'S CORNER

If you really want to get into AC/DC collectibles, then Jack Bonny will at least give you some idea of where to start...

You don't judge an AC/DC fan by the number of records and CDs he or she has got. To be an AC/DC fan means that you simply have to enjoy their music. But if, like me, you start to get the bug to be a completist, it can turn out to be a very expensive business.

It all started simply enough with a cassette of 'Highway To Hell', but now I have to collect pretty much everything the band puts out. And it's cost me a small fortune in the process.

I know of some AC/DC fans who have decided to specialise and are for example only interested in bootlegs, but it can be a very dear do. They seem to be worth more the older they are, but most bootlegs appeared between '89 and '93 and in greater quantities than before, so you would only expect to pay somewhere around the £20 mark for them. There are, of course, some exceptions, for example 'Monster Of Rock' from Modena '91, a very limited pressing that will set you back a whole lot more. The older recordings are more rare and so are by definition much more valuable. You won't get the 'Muscles And Missiles' bootleg, for example, for anything less than a hundred quid!

Bootleg CDs, rather than the more traditional vinyl, are becoming more of a player in the bootleg marketplace and I can particularly recommend '110/120' which came out in a steel box and is probably limited to just 100 copies. CD bootlegs cost anywhere between £15 and £70.

Even official releases can be expensive if they're rare enough. There's a multicoloured vinyl version of 'If You Want Blood...' and an orange vinyl 'Highway To Hell' that are both going to set you back plenty. Most fans will also know of the differences between the early Australian albums and worldwide releases in terms of covers, songs and running orders, but all those records are worth collecting if you don't already have them.

One of my favourite areas for collecting is the singles market, because there's such a variety of stuff you can hunt down from so many different territories. There are five different covers that you can collect for 'Rock'n'Roll Damnation', for example. The most important territories for singles are Japan, England, France, Spain, Holland, Belgium and Portugal. Singles will cost you somewhere between £10 and £20, although Japanese editions will be a bit more expensive. As far as I've been able to work out, 12" singles don't tend to have such a variety of covers, but of special interest is the 'Danger' EP from Australia, that's got some really original artwork featuring the fly from 'Fly On The Wall'. I really like the poster packages that they seem to specialise in in England, but the rarest EP is 'Dirty Deeds', which is 7"-sized. On the minimal side, America

You don't honestly fancy collecting these, do you?

seems to issue a lot of 12" promos without any sleeves at all.

There are plenty of picture discs and interview discs available and some enterprising companies have even tried to do picture disc bootlegs. Best of the batch? 'Live In Stockholm '91'

If you like buying your records as a set, however, there's still something for you. There's a Swedish steel box set that has a chain on it so you can hang it up. And each box has a different selection in, so it's a bit like a lucky dip.

There are plenty of fans who collect videos and tapes too. Most interesting are obviously recordings that you can't get on record, CD or video. People like to track down stuff that features, say, songs that were only performed once or twice on a particular tour. There are quite a few examples of these songs that have hardly been played live, like 'C.O.D.'. 'Sink The Pink', 'Inject The Venom' or 'Rock'n'Roll Singer'.

As far as video is concerned, it's quality that matters most. There are plenty of tapes out there that you can barely see, so they're not really worth more than a tenner. What many people like is to get hold of videos of gigs that they've actually been at, of course!

Other stuff that people collect? Flexi discs, live pictures, posters, reviews, T-shirts etc etc The choice is endless. Just don't forget though, that it's the music that matters most, not the one-upmanship of collecting.

SMOKING!

AC/DC's last major video project, a 'Live In The Studio' performance at music channel VH1, has already been hailed as a classic. Producer and DC fanatic Jim Parsons explains how it all came together...

Tell me how you ended up producing this amazing VH1 session with the band then, Jim.

Well, back in 1996 we didn't really do very many big, full band performances at VH1; it was all little acoustic things. I can't remember if this was the very first big electric one, but whatever, it was an interesting idea to do a full band, because the studio we had in London's Camden area is really tiny. The drum riser's only about 8'x8', so the distance across the back of the stage must only be about 20 foot. It's about 12 foot deep and most of the studio's taken up by cameras anyway. I thought that to get a band like AC/DC to perform there would make for an incredibly intimate show. I was involved in helping to get the bands to perform and it was after the 'Ballbreaker' tour that I tried to get AC/DC to come in and play. I spoke to the department that actually books bands and they said they'd see what they could do. Not very much, it turned out. So I rang the band's label, East West, and spoke to Dante who was their main guy there. He said "We can hardly get them to *talk* to us, never mind do any promo, so forget it." Everyone said you've got no chance of getting them.

So how did you pull it off?

The key to it all was a guy called Mike Kaufmann who was Head of Production at VH1, because he knew Malcolm and Angus' guitar roadie. He spoke to him at the Wembley gig on the 'Ballbreaker' tour, asking if they'd consider a live performance thing. He said "I doubt it. They don't do much and we're off to Europe anyway. But drop us a fax and we'll see if they're interested." So I sent them a fax originally, asking if they'd just come in to do an interview. I added a bit more, though and said "If you'll do a

performance in our little studio, then that would be great. If you'll do an interview, then that would be great too. If you send us a letter telling us to fuck off, then even that would be great." We didn't expect anything, but we sent them the fax anyway. I wrote it for Mike and Mike signed it and I faxed it off. Two or three days later we got a call from someone whose name I can't remember and he simply said, "They'll do it."

Just like that? No conditions?

None. Apparently they just remembered working

The VH1 crew together with the band. Jim Parsons is middle row, second from the left.

with me and Mike and thought we were OK, so they said they'd come in and do it. They had a day off on tour between Madrid and Lisbon, I think it was, so they could fly in. And that was it. It was on.

And they didn't go, "We need to know a load more. What gear have you got in there? What size is the studio?" and all the rest of it?

I'd given them the basic outline of what we wanted, but they didn't really seem too worried about firm details. The roadie then phoned a couple of days later and said, "You'll need to sort out some gear. I'll bring guitars, but you need to call Marshall and they'll sort out the amps they

need." He then said "Malcolm needs one head, Angus needs one head. Talk to Ampeg about Cliff's bass gear, talk to this guy at Sonor about a drum kit." It was all pretty easy. The only thing that was difficult was that we needed to get this particular microphone from Bayer because it's the only one that Brian uses, it's the only mic he likes and there are hardly any of them about. Of course I rang all these companies and said "Can I get this gear?" and they all went, "Yeah, for AC/DC, no problem." Everything was brand new and they all delivered everything. It was incredibly simple. The only real expense for me was that I had to send a bike to somewhere like Woking to pick up that mic and that was it. I think Phil Rudd asked for some special monitoring, which I couldn't organise, but he didn't kick up a fuss or anything when he was told it couldn't be done.

So when the day arrived, how did the band handle it?

It really wasn't a problem. They arrived in a couple of cabs about three or four o'clock in the afternoon and sat in the hospitality room, smoking a lot of cigarettes while we got things ready. They didn't even bring their own sound guy with them. They were very relaxed and professional about the whole thing. I asked them if they could play something a little different for us and they came back and said they'd play four songs which I believe they'd never ever played with Brian before. I think I'm right in saying they'd never played a couple of them live in their history. The songs were 'Go Down', 'Down Payment Blues', 'Gone Shootin'' and 'Riff Raff'. Brian didn't even know the words to 'Go Down' and they had actually phoned us up beforehand and asked someone to write the words to some songs down on a load of cue cards. They'd written some of them down on the plane, but couldn't remember all of them. We had one of the girls in the office transcribing the words, which was funny. She was saying "I think he says 'Licking on my licking stick' here." I was going "That sounds about right." I don't think we knew what songs they were going to do until the day of the filming. I went out and bought a cassette of 'Powerage' and a CD of 'Let There Be Rock' from Record And Tape Exchange in Camden, so we could get the lyrics!

How long did they have to sit around and wait for until they could actually start playing?
They were sitting around for about two hours before we were ready to go, but I don't remember being antsy about keeping them waiting because I was too excited about the whole thing. I wanted to hang out and chat with them, but there was work to be done unfortunately. I explained to them they they'd have to do each song a couple of times, which they were pleased about because they didn't really know them that well. Originally they were only going to do those four numbers that I mentioned earlier, but in the end, they did 12. I think once they got going they were enjoying themselves, so just decided to play more songs. It even got to the point where they were saying "What songs do you want us to do now?", which was amazing, especially because I couldn't think of any at the time! I went a bit blank, to be honest.

What did you feel the relationship between the band members was like?
They all seemed very comfortable together; very, very relaxed with everything. There were no big egos at all. I don't think there was a cross word at any point. Phil and Cliff were quite quiet and Angus and Malcolm are obviously in charge. They were the ones who would say, "We'll do this, we'll do that." They obviously run the group. I got the impression that Malcolm was the one who ran it on a business level and on a musical level I think it was Malcolm and Angus together.

> *'Ballbreaker' was originally going to be called 'Crossed Wires', then 'On The Brain'. There were even T-shirts produced with the phrase written on.*

Brian just wears the hat really. It didn't seem like a hierarchy, though. It just seemed like five blokes arsing about, having a bit of fun.

And how were the band with you?
Really nice. Not over-friendly. There was no "Thanks ever so much for having us," but why would they have said that? They're AC/DC. I think we got on quite well because I'm such a fan of the band and I also play guitar. I spoke to Malcolm and Angus for ages about guitars. Way before the tape even started rolling I was looking at Malcolm's guitar and talking to his roadie who was saying, "This is the guitar that every single AC/DC song except for one was recorded with." I can't remember what song it hadn't been used on, but I was in awe of that guitar. It's a wood-coloured Gretsch that looks really knackered and is probably the most horrible guitar I've ever played.

The most horrible?
Well, the strings are 11 to 56 gauge – really madly thick – and the action's ridiculous. There's no possibility of any solo widdling on it at all, which I like to do. Malcolm came out and I asked him about the guitar, where you could buy them. He told me that he didn't think you could, they were made especially for him. I said, "Do you mind if I have a little go?" and he said "Go ahead." I started playing 'Back In Black', but I couldn't play it because my fingers weren't strong enough. It was *so* hard to play.

Was he there when you were trying to play?
Yeah. He was just laughing. I said it was impossible with that guitar, but he just said, "You get used to it." He said "My guitar's not designed for playing anything other than big fat chords." Talking to Malcolm and Angus was like talking to people in a guitar shop rather than rock stars. Angus was using an SG that his roadie had found in a junk shop and he said it was the nicest one he'd ever had. He said "To you it probably wouldn't be that noticeable, but I play an SG all the time and this one is just brilliant." He offered me a little go on it. I felt a bit embarrassed playing Angus' guitar in front of him, but it was still a real thrill. I was tempted to ask if I could play a song with them, to be honest. It would have been so cool and I could have got the whole thing filmed. I really wish I'd asked now, but there was just that element of professionalism that held me back.

Live in the VH1 studios, Camden, England. "The whole vibe was just great."

Apart from guitars, what did you talk about?
Not that much, really. They kind of wandered in and out. If I'd tried to talk to them about their tours and albums then I would have sounded like a tosser. One thing I did regret, though, was not inviting anybody else down to share the moment. So many of my friends would have absolutely loved it.

Did you have a chat with Brian?
Yeah, but I can't understand a word he says. He laughs after every other word, chuckles all the time and he's still got a really strong Geordie accent. The whole thing was very mellow, though. One of them had a couple of beers – I think it was Phil – but that was it. The one problem I had with my Studio Manager was that when they first arrived I asked them if they had any foibles about what they do and they all said, "Well, when we play, we smoke all the time. Is that a problem?" And I went, "Yeah, there's no smoking in the studio." And they all went, "Oh,

jaded because they do TV stuff all the time. This was different. They were very focused to start with, because the first four songs they were doing were the ones they hadn't played before, so they were thinking about the words and getting it right and that sort of thing. Brian was reading the lyrics to 'Go Down' off the monitor. But once they got going, they really got into it. I think we had the studio booked until 10 o'clock that night, but they didn't stop playing until about a quarter to one. I got screamed at the next day, but I wasn't bothered.

fucking hell," and I said, "Don't worry, I'll sort it out." I went to the Studio Manager and said "Look Jason, it's either smoking and AC/DC or no smoking and no AC/DC." Jason looked at me and said, "What happens if I say 'no smoking?'," and I said, "I'll have to kill you. I don't care, they're going to smoke in there." Jason could tell... he's known me for a long time and he kind of went, "If I say they can't smoke, then you'll kill me? Then they have to smoke." He went on to say, "No bottles on amps, no cigarettes on the floor or ashtrays on the drum riser." So I just told them to try not to drop fag ends on the floor as it was against the rules and they went, "Fine."

Did they think it was quite good fun for them, despite the 'fag trouble'?

The whole vibe was great. They knew they were going to be there until late, but they weren't flying out until the next morning, so they just got on with it. There was no, "Oh god, do we have to do that *again*?" I think that other bands get a bit

What about the quality of the performances?

I spent most of the night watching Malcolm. I couldn't believe how brilliant he was, especially watching from just four foot away. I don't think he played a bum note all night. Angus screws up because he's running around so much, but not Malcolm. I think his rhythm playing is almost perfect. He must've got through 40 picks. They're really heavy and he was ripping them in half.

Angus is one of the few guitar players who has such a distinct sound that you know who it is the minute he starts playing. Even on those over-produced, horrible records they made in the '80s, you still knew it was him. Who else do you know immediately? Brian May? Eddie Van Halen? Considering the fact that they hadn't ever

played those four songs with Brian – and he's been with them almost 20 years now – they were pretty damn good. They had no audience in a tiny studio, but they were still really into it. I really loved 'The Jack', where Brian went walkabout into the gallery. He didn't know where he was going or what he was doing. There was only Mike Kaufmann there, clapping out of time and not knowing the words!

So everything went incredibly smoothly?

Well, Angus made a big fuss about wearing the school cap. He came on with a cap on and I said, "Do you really want to start with a cap?" and he was very insistent. When you see them actually start playing, within three seconds of the first track, 'Riff Raff', the cap's gone anyway, I think it lasted about two bars... as soon as the song picked up it was gone! I really wanted him not to wear the schoolboy stuff, because I thought it'd make the event unique. It's a bit silly, isn't it? But there is a pressure on them to do it – in the same way that, you know, if they didn't play 'Whole Lotta Rosie'...

And after the session? Were they bothered about having approval of the recordings?

Not at all. All they said was "Can we have a DAT?" and I got a fax from Malcolm a week later saying "Please don't use 'Let There Be Rock' because Phil thinks he drummed really badly on it." I thought it was great, but Phil said it was too fast. So they let us use 11 out of 12 songs. Good deal. They weren't bothered about seeing the footage or anything.

So how did you rate the whole event?

I've produced things that were more glitzy and more complicated and more challenging for me, but as far as I'm concerned it's still the best thing I've ever done. Out of all the bands that I've worked with they're the one group I've loved most. They couldn't remember the last time they'd done a TV appearance either, so knowing how rare an event it was made me very happy. I really wanted the night to end on a high note rather than try dragging more and more out of them, but in the end it simply reached a natural conclusion. I knew that if they finished on a high they'd remember the whole thing as being a good experience. And I think that's what happened.

"CLASS. ALWAYS HAVE BEEN. ALWAYS WILL BE!"

Kerrang! editor Phil Alexander on the phenomenon of AC/DC and their effect on him...

What are your recollections of your very first AC/DC gig?

It was on the 'Back in Black Tour'. How old was I? Fourteen, I think, and the one thing I'll never forget is the fact that I realised I'd missed seeing Bon Scott. I was gutted. Here's an interesting bit of trivia which you may appreciate more than anybody else, though. You know the French rock band Trust were big mates with Bon. On their second album, 'Repression', which they were recording in London at the time of his death, there's a dedication to him on the inner sleeve, but there are two versions of the album, an English and a French one, and the date given for Bon's death is different on both of them. I haven't got a clue which is the right one.

Anyway, so back to the 'Back In Black' thing. I read something that Sylvie Simmons had written in *Sounds* about Bon's death at the time and it said "Imagine losing a brother or a sister, then multiply that feeling by ten and you'll be somewhere close to what AC/DC are going through having lost Bon." That really struck a chord with me, so I think I developed this really sentimental view of the band from day one, even though I'd never seen them. That first gig I went to was at Hammersmith Odeon and all the way through I was asking myself "How would Bon have done this?"

The big problem with the Odeon was that anytime you tried to get down the front you'd get the security guys stepping in your way. As I learnt in later life though, if you went to every heavy metal gig you'd suddenly find that this decent security guy let you through and you'd get to Row B. But at that gig I tried to go down the front, got repelled immediately, of course, and spent the rest of the time in my seat with my knees wedged against the seat in front. You were allowed to stand up, though, and a bit of the old loosening of the dandruff occurred.

I can't even remember who supported them that night, although I was meticulous about that kind of thing at the time. I had an exercise book noting all the bands I'd seen, including support bands. But the thing that shocked me about AC/DC when I was a kid at school was that I went through this phase where I was in DC denial.

How come?

There was this geezer called Tim King, who was in the same year as me in school and he was totally into metal. But me and him really hated each other and I remember having this argument with him about DC one time and he said, "They're the greatest band on this planet." Because I hated him so much I said, "No they're not, they're fucking rubbish," and he went,

"What bands do you listen to then?" At the time I was listening to a lot of Hawkwind, so I just turned around and said, "Nick Turner's Inner City Unit are better than AC/DC and I'd rather go and see them any day of the week!" The boast that Inner City Unit were better than AC/DC was something I wholeheartedly disagreed with, but I had to front it out with Tim King! He never knew, of course, that I was going home and putting on the classic DC albums and giving it the big'un... playing the guitar with the headphones on and the lights out when your parents have gone to bed and all that kind of stuff. So when I went to see them on the 'Back In Black' Tour, I couldn't admit to this guy that I'd gone to see AC/DC at all. He'd gone a different night from me and he said, "I went to see AC/DC," and I went, "Oh, right, must have been *rubbish*." But I'd been there the night before myself! What a joke!

I was a weird kid, though. When Tim King used to say to me AC/DC are great and I'd say, "No, you're a tosser," I would then have virtually the same conversation with somebody who liked the Stray Cats. I'd go, "The Stray Cats aren't rock'n'roll. Fucking AC/DC are rock'n'roll. Motörhead are fucking rock'n'roll. Grow up, get with the programme." I also remember that I used to comb my hair to make it as big as possible and I can only describe it as a pyramid

"The thing about AC/DC is that they have never done anything that's uncool because they have a brilliant sense of humour"

with the top lopped off. I looked an absolutely ridiculous sight.

Less of your hair now. How had you got into the band in the first place?
I remember stumbling across the live album and thinking, "Bloody hell, look at this, this is fantastic. There's a guy with a guitar plunged through him!" I think I was interested from there. I went and got my copy from 'LPs' in Bexley Heath, a now-deceased second-hand shop and I paid £1.50. When I actually heard it, though, I could never really understand why people were chanting, "Angus, Angus." I was bemused. I thought, "What's made them do that? It's not a natural place to chant, 'Angus, Angus'" I thought it was a bit silly. It was really that imagery that got me hooked.

Did you think it was funny?
You know, the thing about AC/DC is that they have never done anything that's completely uncool because they have a brilliant sense of humour. At a time when everybody was in mid-'70s excess mode, seeing someone dressed as a schoolboy seemed to make sense to me and it was funny. After the image, of course, it was the sheer attitude of the music that truly shook me up. If Angus had come on dressed as a fucking fire-breathing dragon and played *those* riffs with *that* attitude, it wouldn't have mattered.

At home, when there was the odd programme that would show an AC/DC video or some footage of them on television, my mum always said, :Ooh, he's gonna make himself sick if he carries on like that." It was funny because at the time she was worried for Angus Young and I'd say, "Don't be silly. Headbanging is all part of natural evolution mum."

So, when you went to see their first gig, did you think AC/DC were a special band?
Definitely. That gig was a confirmation that rock music could be streetwise, sussed and make you feel like you were in a gang. It was a

Brian, Phil and Angus having a reasonably good time at the *Kerrang!* awards.

confirmation that streetwise rock'n'roll was what I actually loved. All the bands I liked after that were not poncy bands. They didn't nonce around on stage, they were just delivering the full, 200% aggression kind of thing; Motörhead and Rose Tattoo, Trust and Girlschool. I liked DC's sense of humour too, like I said.

Did they lose that sense of humour when Bon died?
I only ever realised that in retrospect, but I never realised it at the time. When 'Back In Black' came out I didn't think it was as good as 'Highway To Hell' and I still don't. But it didn't seem to me as if they'd lost their bonhomie or their sense of humour. But I agree now that all the fun seemed to have been taken out of it. I don't think Brian could have sung 'Big Balls'. Songs

like that were what had made them very weird, very eclectic. My dad got quite worried around that point, because I'd also be listening to '2112' by Rush as well as AC/DC. On the back on that sleeve Rush all looked like women. So my dad discovered that not only did I listen to an album by a bunch of blokes who looked rather camp – you know, all the white, flowing clothes and what have you – but I was also listening to a band called AC/DC. He said, "AC/DC? You do realise what that means, don't you?" Well, of course, at that time I didn't really have a clue. It turned into a massive issue in our house. I'd only just started reading porn mags really, so it was quite a shock to suddenly understand the idea. I just thought 'AC/DC, power supply!' My dad was quite concerned, though. Then I played him a couple of tracks and it was all OK. My mum and dad liked rock music and so my dad went, "Excellent, 'The Jack' I'll have some of that."

What else did you love about the band at first?
The logo was classic. I had it on the inside of my desk at school, right next to a Jam logo. I liked punk too, so it made complete sense to me. Of course, I used to get beaten up by everybody just because I liked music.

So when was your first meeting with them?
I've never actually done a sit-down interview with them, though I did a phoner with Brian Johnson around the summer of 1988. It was for a thing in *RAW* magazine called *Rogues Gallery* and I was absolutely gobsmacked. Someone had said to me, "Will you do this interview with Brian

albums and we thought, "OK, they're not the kind of band that likes to come to an awards ceremony, but we are the kind of magazine that has put them on the cover several times, maybe they'll take notice of this and they'll come." They'd changed labels in this country from Atlantic to EMI, so we called up EMI and we said, "Will you invite AC/DC and will you let us know what they say?" We then got this phone call back saying, "AC/DC will come, they'll send Malcolm Young," and we said, "Well, much as we love him, we feel that Malcolm on his own will not represent the band entirely, so how about sending Malcolm, Brian and Angus?" Then we heard absolutely nothing back, radio silence. So we called up this woman called Jacqueline who's worked with them since 1976 over at Elektra and she had always said, "If you need anything with

Sam Lock from EMI called up the number she had for them – a recording studio somewhere. She called up and she goes, "Hello, this is Sam from EMI. Could I speak to someone who is looking after AC/DC?" and it was Brian Johnson on the other end of the phone. He goes, "Oh, hello, it's Brian here, the singer from the band." She told him she was just checking whether he was still planning to attend the *Kerrang!* awards on August 25th, and he goes silent for a bit while he checks, then says, "Aye, we've got in penned in on the wall planner!" And that was it, that was how they turned up, Angus and Brian.

And how did they enjoy the day?
I think they had a good time, but they were kinda like observers. They don't go to any kind of award ceremonies usually, so it was a bit alien to

"People go on about how important Bon was, but no-one should underestimate Brian's contribution to the band."

Johnson at 6pm on the phone?"; and I was like, shaking. I called up this number and said, "Hello, is that Brian?" and it was like, "Yes, speaking." I said, "Oh, hello, this is Phil Alexander. I'm not sure if you're expecting me to call or not", "Oh, yeah, yeah, I've been waiting for your call," he said. I think one of the questions was "What's your favourite drink?" and he goes, "Oh, I do love Newcastle Brown," and I was like, "Oh, where are you at the moment then?" They were out in the States, and he goes, "I really do miss a bottle of dog, you know," and we then had this long conversation about Newcastle Brown. It went on for about 10 minutes, you know, how some people have said it's been chemically-enhanced and all the rest of it. I just couldn't believe that I was talking to the singer of AC/DC about Newcastle Brown. I was blown away by his decency. But the first time I actually met them in the flesh was last year at the *Kerrang!* Awards

So how did you get them to show?
Well, we thought it was about time the DC got some kind of recognition. We knew they were doing the remastering and reissuing of the

DC, just call us." She put a load of calls in and ended up calling me back saying, "I'm getting nothing back, they must be on holiday, they must be doing something else, I don't know where they are." I was like, "Oh, that's it, it's over."

Anyway, we called up EMI and said, "What's going on?" Six weeks go by and we're starting to get a bit worried. Eventually we get this phone call back saying, "No problem, Brian and Angus will be delighted to come and will be really honoured to accept the *Kerrang!* Award." I was like, "This can't be right," because even the smallest bands take longer than that to get back really. Anyway, I checked again and this woman,

> **Angus' first band was Kantuckee, a four piece featuring vocalist Bob McGlynn, bassist John Stevens and drummer Trevor James. The band lasted from late '73 to early '74, before it mutated into Tantrum, with one additional member Mark Sneddon joining on guitar and vocals.**

them, but I think they appreciated the warmth that everyone had for them. There were bands who were there, like The Stereophonics, who were such massive fans that they couldn't believe they were in the same room as them. Brian found that funny, but he was flattered all the same. Angus was just there, this little guy in his denim jacket, not saying too much.

So how influential do you think the band have been?
Massively influential. I put them up there with the truly great rock bands of all time. They've been absolutely true to their vision and they've never played the record company game. Their songs and their incredible energy has always made them stand out and I think they've been criminally underrated over the years, especially the Brian Johnson era. A load of people go on about how important Bon was and of course, he *was* important, but no-one should underestimate Brian's contribution to the band. No-one, but no-one, could ever dare to say that Brian had short-changed the fans or had ever given less than 100 per cent. AC/DC? They're class. Always have been and always will be.

Chapter Eight

DAWN TO DUSK

The name Dawn After Dark came to us lying in bed one night. I was in the final year of university and was back living in Station Road after spending my third year abroad. Not at the same house. No, we'd gone upmarket and moved to number 37, which was a bigger and therefore, we assumed, a better student gaff. Well one thing you could say for 37. It was certainly colder.

Between shivering and studying and writing for *Kerrang!*, now I decided that I wanted to have a crack at being in a band myself. Most people do it at some stage if they really love music, dreaming of making the grade and living the life of luxury. I'd seen so much of it at first hand by then that I couldn't see much of a downside there, so why not try and grab it for myself? I answered a small ad in the *Melody Maker* music paper. 'Birmingham band wants singer: Influences, Cult, New Model Army' or something like that. I phoned the number given

a big thing of it. I was sure I couldn't sing either. Dave was a good bass player, Rich a competent guitarist, but we had a bit of fun that night, me warbling along to the racket they were making. I was 21 and was convinced that it wasn't enough for me to be interviewing rock stars for *Kerrang!* any more. Oh no, now I wanted to *be* one, didn't I?

I got the gig. They phoned me a day or so later and told me I was in. Of course, what they didn't tell me till much later was that only one other person had replied to their ad and he'd turned out to be someone who not only looked like Catweazel, but sang like him as well. The competition for the vocalist's berth had not been intense. What did I care? I was a singer in a band now, wasn't I?

THE NEXT COUPLE OF months were spent writing and rehearsing, while I was supposed to be concentrating on university finals. It turned out we had the same taste in music, a penchant for the gothicy rock that in my new-found musical

the toss and blagged the room when we'd first moved in.

That room was *cold*. In the winter icicles would form on the *inside* of the windows, which I worked out somehow meant that it was colder sleeping inside than it would have been kipping out on the street. Ridiculous. The three of us would lie under the covers of the bed fully dressed, me curled up in an enormous green army great coat that I'd picked up in Leamington Spa of all places and Rich still wearing the calf-length biker boots that seemingly never left his feet. It was like those old Eric and Ernie sketches with added poverty, but it did have its advantages. It was often too cold even to think about sleep, so we'd spend most of the night talking shit and dreaming about what we'd do with our as-yet half-formed group. It was during one of these bizarre late-night debates that we stumbled on Dawn After Dark. We liked the name, its symmetrical feel, its allusion towards positivity. We were paranoid about being seen as goths. The

"Rich wore a sheepskin coat that even fourth division football bosses would have dismissed as being too low rent."

and spoke to some strange, disconnected and decidedly Brummie voice about the band. It turned out there wasn't really one as such, just three lads rehearsing in a factory unit over the other side of town. I arranged to meet Dave and Rich outside the Birmingham Odeon on the city's main drag and will always remember their first words to me when I first met with them. Maybe it was a look of disappointment that I couldn't hide when I saw their short barnets. 'Don't worry mate, we're growing our hair.' Both lads seemed unremarkable. Rich wore a sheepskin coat that even a fourth division football boss would have dismissed as being too low rent. Dave was a bit overweight, but seemed friendly enough.

Back at the rehearsal room I met Lee, the band's drummer, and we had a bash at The Cult's 'A Flower In The Desert' and 'Spiritwalker' as well as something or other by New Model Army, though I can't remember what exactly. First impressions? Lee couldn't drum, though I wasn't about to make

maturity I'd decided was a better bet than the hairspray and widdle stuff that was passing itself off as metal at the time. None of the lads had any interest in more traditional rock, but they seemed reasonably impressed by AC/DC when I played some for them one night in Station Road.

Since Rich lived over the other side of town and Dave still lived with his parents, they would both often end up staying at my place. I was sharing with four other guys – my mates Barry, Keith and Paul and another lad, Duncan, an unlikeable weirdo with a flat top who claimed his granddad had built the Taj Mahal and who was attempting to learn the saxophone. I'm not making this up! There were no spare beds, so there was nothing for it but for Dave and Rich to share mine. Except that it wasn't so much a bed as a double mattress slung on the floor. To be honest I was glad of the company. My bedroom, the biggest in the house, also happened to be the coldest. Which probably served me right for the obvious glee I'd displayed when I'd won

press hated goth music, goth imagery and goth fans and it seemed that anything that featured rock guitars, but which couldn't be categorised as heavy metal, was lumped into the goth category. And besides, we just didn't feel like goths were supposed to feel; gloomy, mysterious and nocturnal. We liked beer and fags, parties and women, traditional pursuits for the twenty-something male. And we pursued those goals relentlessly.

DAWN AFTER DARK flourished. We got rid of Lee and replaced him with a psychiatric nurse called Tony, a lad whose musical background was pure rock. He'd been drumming in a metal band, hilariously called Shere Khan, and was playing all that typically flash stuff, drum rolls all over the place. It matched his personality, I suppose, loud and obnoxious. We added a second guitarist, George, a far better player than Rich and the most musically talented of all of us, and we developed our own sound the way all rock bands do, by gigging. We would play anywhere, anytime, to any number of people, adding one or two new fans everywhere we went, eventually getting a record deal with one of the more celebrated independent labels at the time, Chapter 22, home of such acts as Pop Will Eat Itself and The Mission. We felt like a real band and we were nothing if not dedicated. Gigs two or three nights a week and rehearsals just as often too. We'd begun to need somewhere permanent where we could play, a place where we could set the gear up and leave it. We had such a lot of stuff that it was getting really difficult to store it at Station Road and cart it to whichever rehearsal studio we were booked into in the back of the white Datsun van I'd managed to cobble together enough cash to buy. Which was where The Pits came in.

The Pits was situated up at the top end of Birmingham, on a backstreet of a tiny industrial enclave on the way up to Five Ways. We'd seen an ad for the place in some local paper or other as a rehearsal complex and so decided to have a look at it. To call it a complex, though, was stretching things a bit. The Pits looked like one of those old grain depositories built around the time of the industrial revolution and, to be honest, it didn't seem like all that much had been done to it since. It was run, I found out when I went to scope the place out, by a guy called Fraser Young. Fraser was probably in his early 30s at the time, small, thin and wiry with a broad Scottish brogue. He looked like a crumpled version of Angus Young, which turned out not to be all that surprising when I found out that he was indeed part of the Young musical clan. Cousins, I think he said. Whatever, I was impressed by this fame by proxy, the straightforward manner he had with us and the fact that he was prepared to let us have a basement room at The Pits for what I seem to remember was fifty quid a week. At the time it was a heavy commitment for the five of us.

The band was always a bottomless pit for our meagre funds. Rich and Dave had never been off the dole since I'd met them, while both Tony and George had been forced to give up their jobs as nurse and contract hire driver respectively due to the sheer volume of gigs we were doing. I was still doing my *Kerrang!* writing, but the money coming in each month varied from somewhere between three and six hundred quid. It was a great added bonus if you were a student, but after graduation in the summer of 86 I was forced to leave Station Road when the rest of my mates packed up and

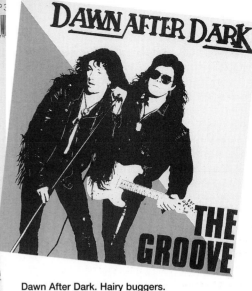

Dawn After Dark. Hairy buggers.

headed off into the big, wide world of work. I moved into a shit-hole of a bedsit in Moseley, home of UB40, which cost an arm and a leg compared to the house I'd been in with four other guys. Money was, as the song, says, too tight to mention.

I WAS INSPIRED BY the attitude of the guys at The Pits, though. Besides Fraser there was a guy called Steve Burton living there. 'Burtie', as everyone knew him, had a ramshackle bed set up at the top of the building, a mattress tucked up in the rafters. He had a little Jack Russell-type mutt that lived there with him and that seemed to be pretty much his only responsibility. He seemed to wear the same clothes – black leather jacket, dirty old jeans – every day, topped off with a red neckerchief that looked like he wasn't averse to wiping his nose on it should the need arise. Burtie had been in Starfighters, a Birmingham band who'd sounded like AC/DC and had made a couple of albums at the start of the '80s. I'd liked their gritty, more urban take on AC/DC's style and had actually seen them live at

Birmingham University once, so I had respect for what Burtie had achieved musically. I also admired the fact that he was a true outlaw, the living embodiment of what in the end I realised I was just pretending to be. Burtie genuinely didn't give a fuck. He loved rock music and loved the lifestyle. He didn't want to live the workaday, nine-to-five, happy-go-lucky thing and if it meant that he'd never have more than the price of a pint in his pants, then that was OK by him. I can only imagine Burtie's still knocking around somewhere in Birmingham today, probably still wearing the same jeans, jacket and neckerchief, still singing for his supper, still refusing to settle down. Good luck to him, I say.

The third member of The Pits crew was Stevie Young, who'd also been in Starfighters. Stevie was Angus to a T, moreso even than Fraser. He was short with wild, unkempt hair tumbling down onto his shoulders. You never saw him without his jeans and denim jacket, he talked in that strange Scottish/Aussie hybrid drawl that Angus and Malcolm have and, like Burtie, he just seemed happy getting by without a pot to piss in so long as he could play his music. He'd put together a little 8-track recording studio upstairs and was always tinkering away on something or other. He was very guarded about what it was he was doing. He never told me, but I suspected that he'd been burnt by his experiences in the Starfighters and was cagey to ➤

the point of paranoia about his bands ever after. We never really talked about AC/DC; he was cagey about that too and didn't really seem to appreciate my fan's eye interest in the band whenever I brought up the subject. 'Aw, they're just my cousins,' he would say, before quickly changing the subject. Still, I wasn't going to let this opportunity go to waste and somehow eventually persuaded him to produce what was to be our third single, 'Maximum Overdrive'. The sessions, in some Birmingham studio that was totally inadequate, were disastrous and poor Stevie didn't seem able to pull either a great sound out of the building or a great performance out of us. We scrapped the whole lot of recordings and started again at a studio called Rich Bitch in Selly Oak, where we'd rehearsed in the days before The Pits. Stevie gave us a hand, but it was obvious that after his bad experiences, his interest was waning. Although his name was on the single sleeve (or at least his pseudonym, Casper Wyoming), his interest in Dawn After Dark had dwindled to nothing. Maybe his mind had been on other things.

One day we turned up for rehearsals and got talking to Fraser. We hadn't seen Stevie for a few days and wondered aloud what he was up to. 'Ach, he's just gone off to America for a while to play with AC/DC,' said Fraser, as if that was as normal as rehearsing in The Pits. We were gobsmacked. What? *The* AC/DC. 'Oh aye,' Fraser informed us. 'Malcolm's had to pull out of the American tour and go home. He's not well. Stevie's filling in.' I suspected it was booze with Malcolm, but I was more in awe of Stevie and his new gig. Fraser seemed disinterested and toddled off to do whatever he did to run The Pits. We went off to rehearse in the basement, inspired by what we'd heard.

'I reckon we should do this,' I said, slipping the cassette into the ghetto blaster we kept in the basement to record our ridiculously loud

rehearsals. The chords fired up. Dah-na-na-na-na-na-noh. I was trying to sell 'Sin City' from the 'Powerage' album to the boys. Tony and George knew the tune instantly, while Dave and Rich listened intently, trying to make the chords out. It wasn't difficult. Most of AC/DC's music is simple to play, but that's not what's special about the group. Capturing a feel is their genius and this song was a perfect example of it. It's still a favourite of mine, the epitome of leery rock that's high on life and taking no prisoners. And as I soon found, when we'd cobbled the chords into shape, it's a fantastic song to perform. The way that DC's best songs are constructed give the rhythms such power that you get into another zone entirely, lost in music... sweaty, dirty, rock'n'roll music. We all looked around the room at each other after a couple of run-throughs of 'Sin City', delighted with the vibe we'd captured. I'd barked myself hoarse screaming the lyrics, but that was nothing unusual. I always had to do that just to get myself heard above the monumental racket that we made. But I'd enjoyed the experience immensely. We'd never been that big on covers. They never seemed to sound exciting or appropriate. At one stage we'd done The Who's 'Substitute' in our live set a couple of times, but it stank and was quickly dropped. I think 'Sin City' was the only cover that stayed with us for a while, maybe as long as a year. It was awesome playing it live. A lot of the people who followed our group had never heard the tune, but once they did they were always turned on to it. I reckon AC/DC must have sold, ooh, at least an extra hundred albums because of our

You'll be surprised to hear we didn't think of ourselves as goths!

efforts. I wonder if they'd consider cutting us in on the royalties?

PERFORMING 'SIN CITY' in most of Britain's rock dives remains one of my best memories of Dawn After Dark, because as is the way with so many of these things, the group ended in acrimony. I was getting sick of doing all the leg work, using the contacts I'd made through writing to further our career, and had demanded that a publishing deal which looked like it might soon be on the table should reflect the extra work I'd put into the group in the way the money was split. The answer I got wasn't even a discussion. I was unceremoniously fired from the band in that self-same rehearsal room where we'd, well, rocked. I was devastated. I'd put four years of solid graft into the group and it had come to absolutely nothing, except a drained bank account and no prospects. Well, it had come to something, actually; bitterness and recriminations and not having anything to do with any of the band members for many years. Some of them I still haven't spoken to to this day. Dawn After Dark got another singer, made a demo that sounded great to me, even more AC/DC-like than before, but went nowhere and disintegrated without doing another tour. I admit I felt a certain amount of schaden-freude when they found out the hard way that things weren't as easy as they'd suspected. Me? I thought about putting another band together for about a nanosecond, then decided I didn't have the strength for another four years like that. I hung up my mike and carted myself off to London with my girlfriend at the time to start another life entirely. That particular chapter, with all its delusions of rock star grandeur, would remain closed forever. ■

COVER CHARGE

Bill Vocchia of New York AC/DC tribute band Ballbreaker on why DC matter...

I've been a huge fan ever since I first heard AC/DC back in 1980 and even at the age of nine they became my number one all-time favourite band. They've stayed as my favourite band ever since and I'm now 29. I began collecting AC/DC 'stuff' early on. I started buying pretty much whatever I could afford – buttons, pins, patches, posters, etc. – and records, of course. I owned all the albums and then discovered that there were other 'collectibles'. I found the band had European import versions of albums, and Australian versions – with different covers! It was like they'd released a whole new slew of music all over again! It was fantastic. Not to mention all of the 7" singles you can collect with different picture sleeves.

I moved on to collecting any of the band members' pre-AC/DC music; Bon Scott with Fraternity, the Valentines, and the Spektors, Brian Johnson with Geordie, Cliff Williams with Home

NY's hottest tribute band... and portrait of the artist as a young Ballbreaker.

A quiet word with the Ballbreaker...

How long have Ballbreaker been together?
I've been in Ballbreaker now for almost two years. They were an existing band before, but had broken up. I knew Mike (Angus) from a long time ago (we were trying to get an AC/DC band together back in 1990-91, but we never found a singer) and I was in an AC/DC tribute band for two years rehearsing, but without a singer. We auditioned so many singers, but no-one could do it right.

Meanwhile, Mike, Tommy (Cliff), and Joey (Phil) were playing in an AC/DC tribute band called Heatseeker with a different rhythm player and singer. They had a falling out with the singer and broke up, then re-formed as Ballbreaker with a new singer, who didn't really fit the part too well, so it didn't last too long. I contacted Mike soon after and the band was reborn, with new singer Chris Antos who does Bon and Brian brilliantly!

What inspired you to join the band?
I've played guitar since I was a kid, so I've always been in bands playing covers, originals, whatever. I always enjoyed playing AC/DC songs and have fun doing it. So what could be better than doing an AC/DC tribute, playing all AC/DC songs, and emulating the band in every way; how they play, perform live, etc? It's the next best thing to actually being in the real AC/DC.

How much do you think you sound like the real thing?
Very very close. It's scary sometimes. Our fans who attend the shows regularly say we sound just like AC/DC. Being such a huge fan, I say we could use some work if we want to sound *exactly* like them, but sometimes during a gig I listen to us as we play and have to say 'COOL!'

Bon or Brian era? Which is best and why?
I enjoy the Bon era much more, though I love both. Bon's voice is unmatchable by any other singer to this day. His range and uniqueness is amazing. His lyrics are also better than any other

and Bandit, Phil Rudd with Buster Brown, etc. etc. It's a great hobby and fun to try to find and collect all of the bands' releases, though I have to say I'm far from being finished! At this point I also try to find anything and everything to do with AC/DC; books, magazines, fanzines, tour programmes, 7" records, 12" records, CDs, promotional items, pretty much anything.

AC/DC's music means a great deal to me. No other band, albums, songs or musical 'entity' has given me such a great inner feeling the way AC/DC does. They are truly the world's greatest rock n roll band of all time. Not The Who, Zeppelin, The Stones... not Metallica, Guns N'Roses or Van Halen. AC/DC are the ultimate – and what's more they've sold more albums than all of the above worldwide to prove it! I think this should be mentioned in the book that AC/DC are the all-time best-selling rock band worldwide. They were even given an award in recognition of over 100 million album sales in 1997.

When the band sells a lot of records I'm proud of them and I hope that they continue to do so. They were also the first hard rock band ever to have a number one Billboard album ('For Those About To Rock') and they have the best selling hard rock album of all time, 'Back In Black', which made the *Guinness Book Of Records* in 1999.

This year marks AC/DC's 25th anniversary and I'd like nothing more than to see the band make the Rock And Roll Hall Of Fame. If any band deserves it it's them. And why not a Grammy? The awards shows and ceremonies are so bogus at the moment. AC/DC have done more in their career for music than most of the bands that get the credit for it. And I reckon it's about time they started getting the recognition they deserve!

"Sometimes during a gig i listen to us as we play and i have to say 'COOL!'"

songwriter's out there. Who can write such catchy songs other than Bon? My favourite album is 'Highway To Hell', followed By 'Let There Be Rock'. I love Brian's stuff too and love AC/DC's music as a whole. It was great to see the band release the 'Bonfire' box set. I thought it was about time for a Bon tribute. The only disappointment was that there were only a handful of truly 'unreleased' songs. We all know AC/DC must have tons more unreleased and rare tracks with Bon Scott left in their archives. Hopefully these will be released someday! The fans want to hear all his music. AC/DC say that they don't want to rip people off making money from Bon's name, etc. Well, how about this for an idea? Release a package in Bon's memory with all the rare archives, recording sessions, out-takes and everything and donate the profits to Bon's estate or to a memorial for Bon!?

Have the band heard you? What do they think?
No – at least not that I know of. However, it'd be great if they could. I'd love to meet AC/DC and

Angus on his two singers...
"Bon had seen Brian in Geordie and told us about this wild guy rolling around the floor, screaming his lungs out, so we thought we'd try and find him... The funny thing is that when I asked Brian about it he said 'After that show I had to go off to hospital. I had appendicitis, that's why I was on the floor screaming.'"

have never had the fortune to do so. I hope to meet the band someday before I die.

What's so special about AC/DC?
Their music is the ultimate. Their lyrics, songs, vocals and guitar riffs say it all. No band or performer has come close to AC/DC to this day.

Do you make good money out of your band?
We do OK. Nothing we can quit our day jobs for,

but it's more for the fun of playing and actually 'being' AC/DC for that time than to make money.

What's the biggest crowd you've played in front of?
About 650 people, during this past summer at an outdoor show in Manorville, NY. It was great!

What's the toughest song to play and why?
Probably either 'Beating Around The Bush' or 'Night Prowler'. Tough backing vocals in 'Night Prowler', keeping it tight and correct. Also, the opening riff on 'Beating Around The Bush' has to be kept tight and together.

Who's the best muso in DC?
Bon Scott was the best, and Malcolm's great. Angus as well, if you include live performance. No-one can compare to Angus Young at a live concert. Eddie Van who? Not to mention his burning lead playing. Check out 'Whole Lotta Rosie'. He should be on guitar magazine covers more often! But all the band members are great at what they do.

DC ALL OVER THE WORLD

AC/DC superfan Gary Campbell has seen every single DC show in the UK since 1986, but he's done a whole lot more besides...

There have been several occasions when I've been fortunate enough to have met AC/DC – the first time at the 'Heatseeker' video shoot back in 1988. I hadn't been so lucky a couple of years earlier when I spent a very cold January night sleeping under tarpaulin with several other fans at the back of Wembley Arena after one of the 'Fly On The Wall' shows. We'd missed the last tube home after hanging around trying to meet the band, then, and it was one of the longest nights of my life; it was so freezing and I was desperate for a cafe to open to get some hot food inside me! Mind you, it was good practice because it wouldn't be the last time I'd freeze my balls off following AC/DC around. I've seen every gig the band has played in the UK since 1986, many of them during my student days when I could barely afford a ticket, and I had to sleep rough on plenty of occasions. I used to pray that when new tour dates were being announced that the band would decide to play the UK in the summer, but it was always spring or winter! Still, the guys I shivered with on that freezing night at Wembley have become good friends. We still keep in touch and meet up 13 years later.

AC/DC get a rough deal from the press in the UK because people think they're inaccessible, but they're the exact opposite when it comes to the fans. I've lost count of the number of times one of the band members, mostly Angus, has stopped on the way in or out of a venue to sign autographs. I remember hanging around with about 10 fans after one of the Wembley 'Blow Up Your Video' shows. It was around midnight and a limo came out of the arena gates and stopped. Then Angus got out and spent 15 minutes chatting and signing autographs, and at least this time he got some recognition from the press for what he was doing. Dante Bonutto, who was the editor of *Metal Hammer* at the time, walked past Angus as he was signing and wrote an editorial in the mag the next month saying that the band clearly did care about their fans and that while they might not have time for the press, they always had it for the people who mattered.

IN JANUARY 1996 I fulfilled my ambition of seeing AC/DC in the US. We flew into Greensboro, North Carolina, to see the opening night of the 'Ballbreaker' world tour. There were about 20 fans who had travelled from all over Europe for the show. AC/DC's tour manager arranged after show passes for everyone. We waited in a room after the

> **Angus On Influences...**
> "I was never into modern day sorta music. I get off on all the old stuff; Elvis, Chuck Berry, Little Richard, Jerry Lee. Swing records, Louis Armstrong and stuff like that. All the other stuff seems poor in comparison. You get Little Richard's 'Tutti Frutti' and put some music from today next to it and it sounds timid in comparison."

Gary with the boys.

gig with about 60 others – competition winners, guys from local radio stations and some people who looked like they'd never owned an AC/DC album in their lives! The tour manager came and told us that the band were having a meeting to discuss the first night's technical problems so we wouldn't be able to meet them. Then he quietly ushered all the Europeans into another room where the band came in to meet us! They were tired and wanted to get back to their hotel, but they made sure they met the travelling fans first. America was having some really bad storms at the time, so the band checked that everyone had places to stay and that no-one was sleeping rough; one fan had arrived late and didn't have a hotel booked, so Angus arranged for one of the road crew to phone around and find a room for him. Incredible!

I went on to see the next four shows of the tour before I had to fly back to reality... and work. Following AC/DC in America was totally different to following them in the UK. It involved a lot of travel as the shows were so far apart and the Greyhound stations were always in a rough part of the city; in some towns the taxis wouldn't either pick up or set down at the Greyhound station. Some of the motels we stayed in were dubious, to say the least. One in particular was over-run with drug pushers and we went to sleep to the sound of gunfire in the distance! We didn't care, though, there was another show tomorrow!

IN 1997 I WAS backpacking in Australia with my girlfriend. We were staying in Perth for a few days so I decided to take the opportunity to get the train down to Fremantle and pay my respects to Bon. I can remember that it was a scorching hot day and it was about a two mile walk from the train station to the cemetery. Once I got there I started to look for Bon's grave. I knew there was a bench nearby donated by Bon's family, so I walked around looking at all the benches I could see. After about an hour I was about to give up but finally stumbled on it right by the entrance where I'd come in! Luckily there's only one cemetery in Fremantle otherwise I'd have been in real trouble! On the walk back to the centre of town I had time to look up Bon's high school. That was strange – walking about the place knowing it was where Bon had grown up.

When I was in Perth, there was a travelling rock exhibition on at a museum for a few days. It had displays relating to Australian music from the '50s through to the present day. The item of most

The travelling exhibition featuring Angus' SG and Bon's leather jacket.

"America was having some really bad storms at the time, so the band checked that no-one was sleeping rough."

interest was a display cabinet devoted to AC/DC. Besides one of Angus' SGs and Bon's leather jacket there was a hand-written setlist that someone had picked up from a dressing room floor after an early gig. The setlist contained 'Soul Stripper', 'Jumpin' Jack Flash', 'Stick Around', 'Little Lover', 'School Days', 'Honkey Tonk Women', 'Shake Rattle & Roll' and 'The Jack'. There was also a booth that had an electronic drum kit with a choice of four songs to play along to. One of them was 'Thunderstruck', so I had a go, even though I had a little too much hair to do a convincing Chris Slade!

"PEOPLE WHO SING ABOUT POLITICS ARE DUMB"

Back in 1988, Jens Birkenfeld met with Brian Johnson for this exclusive interview...

What do you think about the relationship between rock'n'roll and technology?
Forget about it! If you get involved in trying to marry the two of them, then it'll end in tears. I've got a mate who owns a studio in England and I go down there just to take the mickey. I ask him what synthesisers he's going to be buying next. He's mad about technology! But if you start with that stuff you can lose your perspective. Well, there are some bands who use that kind of stuff really well, but there's nothing in it for us.

Do you think that rock'n'roll's coming back?
Sure. Rock'n'roll is around in the way that Strauss and Wagner are. Their music's still alive today and so is rock. It just has to re-invent itself and it's already done that in the '30s and '40s. There's rock out there that I don't understand, but it's about the fans. They understand it. Your parents understood Bill Hayley and Elvis.

Things are going well for you at the moment. You've sold out eight of the 11 gigs here in Germany. Why do you think you're so successful right now?
No idea. The last time we were here hardly anyone showed up. I've got no idea. I think my mum was here selling tickets. She must have been going around saying "Help my son, help him. Please help him!" I don't think anyone knows why we're doing well. Maybe everyone just said "Come on, let's go and see AC/DC again." Maybe it's because there's a new album out, a really good album, because last time the songs weren't really all that good. This is a really good album with great songs on it. People are telling us to just carry on doing what we've done this time.

How do you stay in shape for the gigs? Beer?
I've given up drinking so much actually. I go to the gym, lift a few weights and I do a lot of

breathing exercises. I've cut down on the ciggies too. I used to smoke three packs a day; now it's a lot less, a packet at most. They were knackering me. I hope I'll give them up completely one day. I feel a whole lot better because this is the first time in ages that we're doing a really major world tour. I wanted to play in Europe again and here we are. We were in Australia, now we're in Europe and then we're straight into America, followed by Japan.

In the latest video, for 'Heatseeker', Angus is perched on a Pershing missile. Is there some kind of political statement going on here for Reagan and Gorbachev?
No, no, no, no. It was just co-incidence that we were making the video when all the peace talks were going on. Good timing, maybe? It was just an idea that was done for fun, that's all. Angus just wanted to have a go at it. Maybe he should be a politician.

It's Angus' birthday on 31st March when you play in Essen. Any special plans?
Yeah, we were talking about it on the plane but I can't tell you anything about it – it's a surprise. It's

weird, but it's the first time ever in the history of the band that Angus will have been onstage on his birthday.

What have the highpoints of the tour been?
Well, we've only just started, but I think that being in Australia was already a highpoint. We hadn't played there since 1981 and of course it's where the band's from, so we had a few good parties there. We played our arses off over there. The gigs were great, but all the gigs have been great, especially Wembley and Birmingham in England. I've just thought of one special moment, though. We played in Arnhem a few days ago. It was amazing, the kids were fantastic, but the place was dripping with sweat. After the gig Angus showed me his finger and all the skin on it had peeled off. All we could say was "Oh shit." I won't forget that in a hurry.

What's your favourite AC/DC song?
Up to now it was always 'Down Payment Blues', it's amazing, but since recording 'Meanstreak' that's taken over as my favourite.

Mine's 'Two's Up'
That's my second favourite. Do you know what that one's about? It's about the fact that every man should have two women. You should always have two women with you.

Does that mean you've got two wives, then?
Everybody should have two wives! Then you can have double the fun.

Why are there so many different pressings of AC/DC material?
I've never got to the bottom of that. I don't really know anything about it. I saw an AC/DC single in America that was on sale as a special import for 50 bucks. The record company puts them out and we have nothing to do with it. I asked the kid who was in the shop why he was buying the record and he told me it was 'cos he loved me! I said "Right!"

'For Those About To Rock' was recorded with a mobile studio. What happened to it?
I dunno.

I heard it cost two and a half million dollars to build.
Well it still wasn't that good. I don't know what happened to it, though. Maybe it was put up for sale. It wasn't that special, though.

Why does Angus drop his trousers during the gigs?
He's wild. I don't know why he does it, but if he doesn't people start screaming for his arse!

I heard that Angus once played guitar with his dentures. Why?
He doesn't have dentures. Where did you hear that one from?

> **Brian is crazy about cars and bikes. At one point he owned a Jaguar V12 with the terrible numberplate 'HOT TO ROCK'.**
>
> **Brian's all-time singing hero is, you won't be surprised to hear, Joe Cocker. Favourite tracks? 'Delta Lady' and 'Bird On The Wire'.**
>
> **After the demise of Geordie, Brian ended up singing on a vacuum cleaner commercial to make a few quid.**

There must be a lot of things that piss you off, but why haven't you ever written a song about it?
'Cos that's got nothing to do with music. You shouldn't mix music and politics. People who sing about politics are dumb. I hate it. I hate 'Rock Against Drugs', 'Rock Against Life', 'Rock Against Puffs', 'Rock Against Unemployment'. Music's got nothing to do with all that. Music is entertainment. There are enough idiots out there singing 'Jesus loves you'. I wouldn't do it even if I was a born again Christian. I can't be doing with all that shit. It doesn't matter whether Communism is good or not. I've seen musicians who want to stand up for their point of view and I've asked people who went to their gigs how they found it and they said "That wasn't a gig. They just talked about the farmers in America." They didn't want to hear that shit. There are plenty of other people who are on about that stuff, so why musicians as well? There are plenty of people who are only using their position to

make money. John Cougar Mellencamp? What an arsehole. I've had enough of his nonsense. He's full of shit.

Let me ask you this then. Why do so many AC/DC fans have to get absolutely tanked up before they go to one of your gigs?
That's not true. Were you in Sydney? Or Melbourne? Or Birmingham?

No, but there are loads of people like that in Germany.
Nobody does it in London. OK, they have a few drinks, but no more than that. I don't get it when people are completely out of it, but if Cliff Richard was playing it would probably be a bit different. Still, I don't get it if people are only there for the booze. I thought it was for the music.

How do you think rock's going to develop?
No idea. There are loads of new things happening. Speed metal, thrash metal and other shit like that.

Metallica are the kings of that kind of music.
I don't get it, though. People are always asking me if I know about thrash metal and I say 'No, I don't know this shit'. People in England seem to be getting into Metallica though.

They write about politics, war and what have you. People like it.
Have you heard our song 'This Means War'. That's just another way of telling the same story.

OK Brian, last question. AC/DC's been going for 14 years. Are there moments when you think about the end?
I reckon that as long as there are people who like what we do then we'll carry on, but when I start writing tunes like 'Save The Whale' then I'll give up 'cos that will be me finished. When you know that you aren't into it any more, then the fans will feel it too. Then you've got to give it a rest. Plenty of people say it's easy to make music, so why isn't everybody doing it? It's really hard to make it to the top. Think how many singles and albums come out every week.

One last question, then. Tell me, what's under your cap?
Plenty of hair, mate, plenty of hair.

UNDERCOVER

'What's your favourite favourite?' ran the slogan for those TV ads for some chocolate or other. Strawberry Cream, maybe? Noisette? Whatever, it seems that when it comes to AC/DC fans have just as much trouble plumping for their absolute favourite tune. Excellent. That simply means there are plenty of bands covering plenty of different numbers. Here's a selection of tribute albums, covers and bands.

TRIBUTE ALBUMS

WELCOME TO ROCK'N'ROLL HELL
A weird album featuring one side of bands covering Motörhead songs and the other side of bands attempting AC/DC. The running order on what's called the 'Hell Side' is:

Jingo de Lunch – Overdose
Slowheads – Sin City
What... For – Love At First Feel
The Angels – Problem Child
Billy Button & The Knockwells – It's A Long Way To The Top

FUSE BOX – THE ALTERNATIVE TRIBUTE (BMG Ariola)
17 unknown Australian artists paying homage to their hairier roots.

Anti Anti – Riff Raff
Front End Loader – Let Me Put My Love Into You
Yothu Yindi – Jailbreak
Fur – Ride On
Ed Kuepper – Highway To Hell
The Meanies – It's A Long Way To The Top
Regulator – Back In Black
Suciety – Night Prowler
Nitocris – Dirty Deeds Done Dirt Cheap
Downtime – Walk All Over You
Spiderbait – Rocker
Don Walker – There's Gonna Be Some Rockin'
Electric Hippies – Whole Lotta Rosie
Rig – Baby Please Don't Go
Blitz Blitz – Livewire
Frenzal Rhomb – T.N.T.
Automatic – You Shook Me All Night Long

THUNDERBOLT (De Rock Records)
Album which features top '80s rock stars including Sebastian Bach (Skid Row), Phil Collen (Def Leppard), Scott Ian (Anthrax), Lemmy (Mötorhead), Whitfield Crane (Ugly Kid Joe), Bob Kulick (Meatloaf), Warren DeMartini (Ratt), Dee Snider (Twisted Sister), Joe Lynn Turner (Rainbow) and Simon Wright (Dio and… er AC/DC).

TRACK-LISTING:
Highway To Hell
Little Lover
Back In Black
Live Wire Sin City
Ride On
Shake A Leg
Whole Lotta Rosie
Night Prowler
It's A Long Way To The Top
Walk All Over You
T.N.T.

COVERED IN BLACK – An Industrial Tribute To The Kings Of High Voltage AC/DC'
(Cleopatra Records CLP 9811-2)
An acquired taste of industrial takes on the standards that makes up in originality what it lacks in listenability.

The Electric Hellfire Club – Highway To Hell
Genitorturers – Squealer
Die Krupps – It's A Long Way To The Top
Spahn Ranch – Shot Down In Flames
Godflesh – For Those About To Rock… We Salute You
Joined At The Head – Whole Lotta Rosie
Pigface v Sheep On Drugs – Back In Black
Birmingham 6 – Thunderstruck
Razed In Black – Hells Bells

Psychopomps – Badlands
Sister Machine Gun – T.N.T.
16 Volt – Dirty Deeds Done Dirt Cheap

HIGH VOLTAGE (Tribute records)
A bizarre 'Stars On 45' style medley of the band's songs, including 'Highway To Hell', 'High Voltage', 'Who Made Who and 'Jailbreak'. Crap, obviously.

A SALUTE TO AC/DC (Tribute Records)
Various Swedish bands paying their 'respects' to the band with varying degrees of success.

AB/CD – Riff Raff
Belt – The Razor's Edge
Violent Work Of Art – Hell's Bells
Straitjackets – Hell Ain't A Bad Place To Be
Diamond Dogs – You Shook Me All Night Long
Masquerade – Whole Lotta Rosie
Tornado Babies – Jailbreak
Trilogy – Sin City
Fistfunk – Back In Black
Downstroke – Overdose
Transport League – Let There Be Rock
Feed – Send For The Man

COVER VERSIONS
By no means a definitive list, but as much as we've been able to uncover

ALIVALTIOSIHTEERI – Highway To Hell (from 'Yeah Baby Yeah' Hill 009)
BEASTS OF BOURBON – Ride On (from 'The Low Road' Red Eye)
CPR – Back In Black (from 'CPR' CDGRUB 26)
BRUCE DICKINSON – Sin City (from 'All The Young

Dudes' single EMI 12 ENG142)

EXODUS – Overdose (from 'Fabulous Disaster' CDMFN 90)

EXODUS – Dirty Deeds Done Dirt Cheap (from 'Good Friendly Violent Fun' Roadracer RO 92351)

JOHN FARNHAM – It's A Long Way To The Top (from 'Age Of Reason' RCA PL71839)

FEMME FATALE – It's A Long Way To The Top (from 'Falling In And Out Of Love' single Geffen)

GUNS N'ROSES – Whole Lotta Rosie (from Japanese EP Geffen 25XD-977)

HARD CORPS – Back In Black (from 'Def Before Dishonour' Interscope 791756-2)

HULLABALOO – Back In Black (from 'United Colors Of Hullabaloo' EFA 11377-06

IRON FISH – Big Gun (from Various Artists album 'Rock Ballads' MARK 149)

JOAN JETT – Dirty Deeds Done Dirt Cheap (from 'Dirty Deeds' single CHSCD 3518)

KANUUNA – Touch Too Much (from 'Kanuuna' AMTCD 2042)

SAM KINISON – Highway To Hell (from 'Leader of The Banned' WB 9 26073 -2)

ED KUEPPER – Highway To Hell (from 'A King In The Darkness Room')

ALAN LANCASTER – High Voltage (from 'Life After Quo')

HERWIG MITTEREGGER – Crabsody In Blue (from 'Deutsch Läuse')

OMEN – Whole Lotta Rosie (from 'Nightmares')

ONSLAUGHT – Let There Be Rock (from 'In Search Of Sanity' FFRR828142-2)

PARTY BOYS – High Voltage (from 'Party Boys' EPC 460485-2

HENRY ROLLINS AND THE HARD-ONS – Let There Be Rock (from 'Let There Be Rock' single)

SCREAMING JETS – Ain't No Fun (from 'Living In England' single RooArt 4509-91158-2)

SIN CITY – Down Payment Blues (from 'And There Was Rock')

ANDREW STRONG – Girl's Got Rhythm (from 'Strong')

THE SURF RATS – Baby Please Don't Go and Rocker (from 'Straight Between The Eyes')

ANDY TAYLOR – Live Wire (from 'Dangerous' A&M POL900)

THE MOTORCITY TUFF GIRLS – Girl's Got Rhythm (from 'The Motorcity Tuff Girls')

TRUST – Love At First Feel (From 'Paris By Night Live' Melodie 63001-2)

TRUST – Ride On (from 'Trust' CBS83732)

TRUST – Live Wire and Problem Child (from 'Trust Live' Epic 472671-2)

UGLY KID JOE – Sin City (from 'I Hate Everything About You' single MERCD 367)

VULCAIN – Hell Ain't A Bad Place To Be (from 'Live Force' New Musidisc 2382)

W.A.S.P. – Whole Lotta Rosie and It's A Long Way To The Top (from 'Black Forever' EP Raw Power)

TRIBUTE BANDS

SIN CITY
German covers outfit who have added originality to the standard formula by performing AC/DC songs acoustically. Their set list includes 'It's A Long Way To The Top', 'Ride On', The Jack' and 'Highway To Hell'. The band have also recorded an album which comprises nine originals and a cover of 'Down Payment Blues'.
LINE-UP:
Eddie Eisenbarth – Guitar, vocals
Nelli Brill – Guitar, vocals
Dschurgen J. Young – Guitar
Patrick Puddah Apel – Bass
Lars M. Lunova – Drums
Eule Seiler – 'Joker' guitar

EL SIIS/ON SIIS – Letut Ja Rocka (Fazer Records 0630-11897-2)
TRACK-LISTING
Riff Raff 5:34
High Voltage 4:15
Heatseeker 3:24
Highway To Hell 3:16
Hell's Bells 4:52
Shoot To Thrill 5:08
Problem Child 3:58
Dirty Deeds 4:04
Whole Lotta Rosie 3:53
T.N.T. 3:56
For Those About To Rock 5:11
A fan's eye view of the band's gig at The Tavastia Club, 27th August, 1994
"As the first chords of 'Riff Raff' blast the Tavastia club, the audience is wild and noisy, just how the 'Letut Ja Rocka' album begins. 'Shades Of Donington' is a festival that's taken place four times to date. There have been lots of covers bands, performing Kiss, Judas Priest, Van Halen etc. But AC/DC is the only band whose songs have been performed at all four festivals. The band responsible? Ei Siis/On Siis, who performed as headliners each time. If you can't get to see them, listen to 'Letut Ja Rocka' – an energetic live recording that really shows the band's enthusiasm. I

would recommend Ei Siis/On Siis to all Finnish AC/DC fans and to all other rockers. The band only play one or two gigs a year, but they're really 'professional' – you never hear them play a bum note.

"As Mirka Lindstrom (bassist) says, 'We're doing it out of respect for our idols and we try to play as near to the original as we can.' Ei Siis/On Siis aren't here to do some crap interpretations of perfect songs."

ACTION IN DC
Dutch-based Bon-era covers band with a singer who does a good impression of Scott. Songs attempted include Dirty Deeds, Hell Ain't A Bad Place To Be and a Brian Johnson-era Thunderstruck.
LINE-UP:
Bon – Mario Vermulst
Angus – Stefan Verstappen
Phil – Jan Laugs
Cliff – Nick McGrath
Malcolm – Sebi Floris

POWERAGE
Newcastle-based band
LINE-UP:
Bon – Shaun O'Brien
Angus – Terry Simm
Malcolm – Mick Conroy
Phil – Vic Gazza
Cliff – Mick

THE JAILBREAKERS
Another German act, this time out of Halle, who concentrate on Bon-era material. Formed in 1994, the band perform a 90 minute set including songs such as 'Highway To Hell', 'T.N.T.' and 'Dirty Deeds'.
LINE-UP:
Angus – Harry Greiner
Malcolm – Michael Horntrich
Bon – Jens Thorun
Cliff – Geier Büttner
Phil – Jies Hündorf
Contact: Michael Horntrich, Georgstrasse 9, 06108 Halle, Germany

If you can track down an album of country rock by Aussie band The Stetsons titled 'The Stetsons 97', it features a cover of a Bon song, 'Up In The Hills Too Long', which he wrote while he was in the Mount Lofty Rangers

HIGH VOLTAGE

Band from Belgium who released an album titled 'If You Wanna Rock'n'Roll – Tribute To Bon Scott, Live At The Spirit Of 66'.

SAMPLE SET LIST
Riff Raff
Hell Ain't A Bad Place To Be
Sin City
Bad Boy Boogie
Down Payment Blues
The Jack
Gimme A Bullet
Whole Lotta Rosie
Dirty Deeds
High Voltage
TNT
Highway To Hell
Let There Be Rock
Live Wire

HELLS BELLS

CD available featuring 'Whole Lotta Rosie', 'Touch Too Much' and 'Riff Raff'. Singer's voice sounds more like Brian.

BALLBREAKER

French act

DIRTY/DEEDS

Danish band who cover plenty of more modern DC tracks. DC fan Tommy B Jensen wrote this review:
"When we arrived at the venue the stage was already set, with the band's own cannons, Hell's Bell and Jack Daniels Bottles and flags everywhere. I had been to one Dirty/Deeds show before, but I was still excited. I didn't know the set list, but when the hi-hats on 'Back In Black' sounded it brought back memories of AC/DC's gig in Copenhagen in '96 where they also started with 'Back In Black'. Then it just went rocking ahead with 'Highway To Hell', 'Dog Eat Dog' and 'Moneytalks', which included the band's own bank notes thrown into the crowd. The first half ended in 'Jailbreak'.

"After the break, the show went on with 'Hell's Bells' and 'Dirty Deeds Done Dirt Cheap', which is a must at every Dirty/Deeds show. I'll never forget 'The Jack', because halfway through the song a stripper came on stage! Everybody loved it (mostly the men). When the band had finished 'T.N.T.' they said goodnight and went backstage. But everybody knew there was more to follow and after five minutes they went back on to play 'Thunderstruck' and then line up the cannons for a 21 gun salute, going into 'For Those About To Rock

(We Salute You)'. Afterwards the band said their thanks-yous and good-nights and then disappeared into the smoke from the cannons."

DIRTY/DEEDS SETLIST 25/10/97
Back In Black
Shot Down In Flames
Sin City
That's The Way I Wanna Rock'n'Roll
Highway To Hell
Dog Eat Dog
Money Talks
Jailbreak
Hell's Bells
You Shook Me All Night Long
Dirty Deeds Done Dirt Cheap
High Voltage
The Jack
Whole Lotta Rosie
T.N.T.
Thunderstruck
For Those About To Rock (We Salute You)

LINE-UP
Angus – Tim Andre
Malcolm – Brian Dan
Bon – Jimmy Olsen
Cliff – Peter Spelling
Phil – Kenneth Nygaard

AC/SEEDY

LINE-UP
Angus – Kenny Couzins
Malcolm – Tony Savage
Brian – Grant Foster
Cliff – Steve Clews
Phil – Gary Hitchens

"Attention to detail is AC/Seedy's watchword. Angus wears a schoolboy uniform? So does Kenny. Malcolm plays a Gretsch? So does Tony. The bell at the opening of 'Hell's Bells'? It's there. These boys are so spot on that 'For Those About To Rock' wasn't performed live until they could replicate the cannon fire authentically! With a set list that spans '76-'96, AC/Seedy are AC/DC when they hit the stage." – Details from the band's biog

THE BON SCOTT BAND

Barcelona-based band

AB/CD

Cut The Crap
Rock'n'Roll Devil

Not a covers band per se, but a Swedish group who have built new songs out of old DC sounds and as

often as not old DC riffs. Numbers include 'Jackpot Bingo', 'Your Name On My Bullet', 'The Masterplan' and 'Have You Got The Guts'.

BAROCK

German act who have done mammoth two and a half hour sets including 'Live Wire', 'T.N.T.', 'Highway To Hell' and 'Hell's Bells'

LINE-UP:
Brian – Jabbsy
Angus – Walter Thomas
Malcolm – Eugen Turscher
Cliff – Markus
Phil – Martin

BIG BALLS

German band whose album features nine songs, five of which are DC covers. Track listing:
What's Next To The Moon
Walk All Over You
Down Payment Blues
Rock'n'Roll Singer
Carry Me Home
Lady Whisky
Gis A Smile
Thank God It's Friday
Loch Lomond

LINE-UP:
Lead Guitar – Dirk Reinking
Rhythm Guitar – Christian Sender
Vocals – Thomas 'Chicken' Klaus
Bass – Matthia Haverkamp
Drums – Jorg Klute
Contact: Big Balls, Zur Wehme 10, 32289 Rödingshausen, Germany

CRAZY CROWD

This German band, from Weimar, are known for putting more obscure songs such as 'Deep In The Hole' in their set. They've also got their own website at http://home.t-online.de/home/crazycrowd
LINE-UP:
Bon – Michael Brust
Angus – Peter Weidemann
Malcolm – Robert Kaltofen
Cliff – Walter Waldmann
Phil – Fips

Note that this is the info that I've been able to put together to the best of my knowledge. There are bound to be omissions and errata, but you'll just have to live with that, alright?

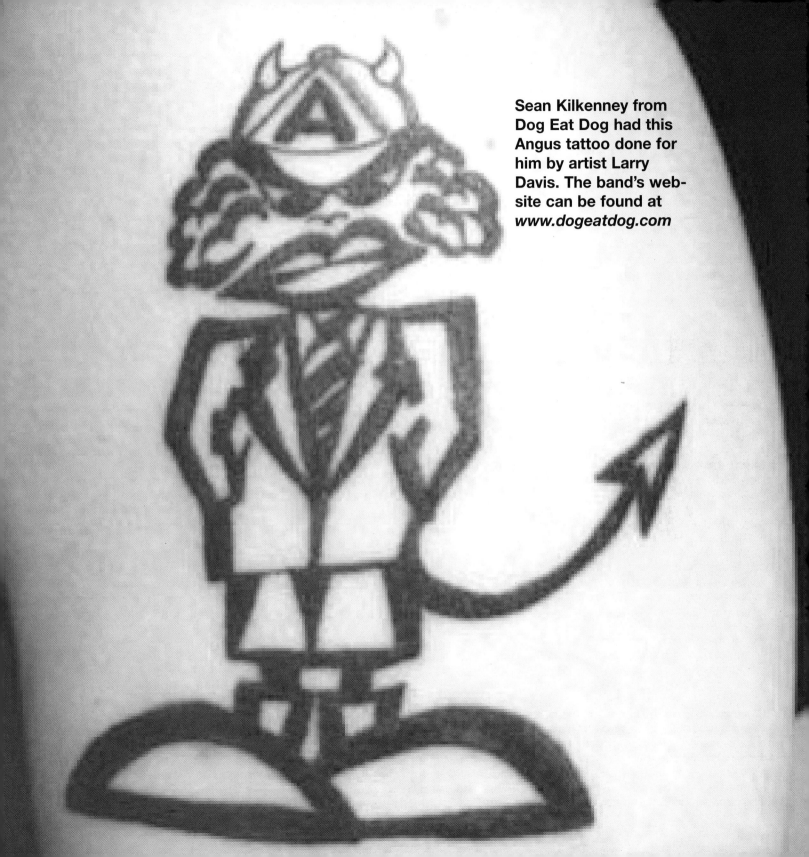

Sean Kilkenney from Dog Eat Dog had this Angus tattoo done for him by artist Larry Davis. The band's website can be found at *www.dogeatdog.com*

CAP IN HAND

Diamond Dave is a well-known figure on the British rock scene. Not because he's worked with Therapy?, The Wildhearts and 3 Colours Red amongst others, but because his impressions of Brian Johnson are the stuff of legend...

So how did your obsession with AC/DC start?
I grew up in Belfast and got into rock because of my uncle Michael, who was right into all that stuff, but when I moved to Ascot in England in 1982 I met a guy called Stuart Duckworth and he had a copy of 'Highway To Hell'. I would've been about 10 or 11 at the time and the big band for me was Status Quo, but I was impressed by the cover, that little staring face that Angus had and Phil Rudd looking like a girl. Then I really got into 'If You Want Blood...', which I thought was so much better than the band's studio albums that I'd heard. That really hooked me. I must admit that my interest in the band has tapered off after the last couple of albums, but I'll always go and see them on tour. I don't think I've missed one since 1983.

So why do you like them live so much?
I'm not exactly sure, but I think it's because somehow they manage not to be corny. They're the missing link between '50s rock'n'roll bands and the music of today. It's a purist thing, I suppose. I don't think any other band comes close live. The last time I saw AC/DC was at Wembley Arena on the 'Ballbreaker' tour back in 1996 and it was amazing. Brilliant to watch... and then those songs! I also like the fact that they realise that they're older guys and they're removed from what's going on in the music industry. But they're really truthful, because they don't give a toss about what's fashionable. I like that.

How did you become a roadie, then?
I was in a disco in Belfast one time when I'd gone back home and heard this song that I thought was amazing. Someone told me it was Therapy? and it just so happened that a couple of the band members were in the club that night. I was introduced to Michael, the bass player, that night

and started following the band. In 1990, after I'd been following them around for a while, Andy the singer said "This is ridiculous, you turning up everywhere we go. You might as well sell the T-shirts." That's how I ended up working with them. I took a couple of years off and went to college to learn to be a drama teacher, then came back and started to work with other bands

Diamond Dave:
He just can't stop.

too, including 3 Colours Red. Everyone I've ever worked with closely is mad about AC/DC.

In what ways?
Well I've never seen a band that has such a ritual where AC/DC are concerned, the way 3 Colours Red do. If they were on tour for a month you'd have AC/DC on the sound system on the bus

every single day. After you've been on the bus for a couple of hours, 'Back In Black' always comes out. Without fail. They're absolutely obsessed.

So how did you discover your undeniable talent for impersonating Brian?
I ended up working for the Wildhearts for a while, and when they supported AC/DC on the 'Ballbreaker' tour back in 1996 I went along to the show with 3 Colours Red. We were all there with our guest tickets, so we were right at the side of the stage at Wembley with a great view. We were all pissed, so when they started playing 'Back In Black', which is my favourite song, I was going mental at the side of the stage, of course. Now Brian came right up to where I was sitting, he was only about six foot away, and did that funny little dance that he always does on stage – just for me! I was knocked out by that and so I just started impersonating it in a very camp manner, probably due to the alcohol, and it sort of stuck. Everyone loved it, so it's almost became like a nervous twitch now. Nowadays any time I'm out of my mind, ripped to the tits on drugs and drink, I just start doing it all night long. I just can't stop. It's bizarre!

It's very good, though. You should do it on *Stars In Their Eyes*!
Well, I do like to get up and sing a song every now and again. I've done 'Back In Black' with Therapy? and I've even done it live with 3 Colours Red one time, with the cap and everything. I've got a high voice, so I can get away with it. It was so hot on that particular night with 3 Colours Red that I sang the first line and started seeing stars. I thought I was going to pass out. I love doing it, though, because it makes people laugh. I'll have to shave off the beard and if I can find a little guy with long hair, then I'm going to have to have a go for *Stars In Their Eyes*. I'm serious!

What about doing it in front of Brian?
Oh, I don't know about that. I mean, I've got big balls, but I don't know... I'd be nervous just about meeting AC/DC, never mind impersonating them. What I do know is that if anything happens to me, God forbid, then I'm putting a request to them right now via this book to play a benefit for me at the Haverstock Arms, Belsize Park, London! What a fitting tribute that would be.

Chapter Nine

A MEETiNG OF (TiNY) MiNDS

"So I'm a preacher, right?"

Considering I first started writing for *Kerrang!* back in '81, it was amazing that it took me until 1990 to get around to actually interviewing AC/DC. Well, 'get around to' sounds pejorative, like it was up to me as to where and when I would deign to meet the band. It wasn't like that, of course. I would've jumped at the chance to meet them anywhere, anytime. It didn't matter to me that I hadn't really liked anything much of their output since 1980, they were still heroes of a sort. Not in that awful hand-clasping, open-mouthed adulation kind of way. I'd met enough rock stars not to be fazed by anyone walking in the room. Unless they were Bob Dylan, maybe, but that's another story entirely. No, Angus and Malcolm were heroes because the records that they recorded in the early part of their career had such huge importance in shaping my life. I sit in my office in my lovely house nowadays, surrounded by the computer equipment that's now

the tool of my trade, with CDs and books stacked up high on the shelves behind me, with my son screaming downstairs and my wife running round looking after him, and the journey I've travelled seems so... so long. In many ways I'm a totally different person to the youngster standing outside the Manchester Apollo blinking up at the lights and wearing those shorts. And yet 'Powerage', 'Let There Be Rock', 'Highway To Hell', 'Dirty Deeds Done Dirt Cheap', 'High Voltage' and 'Back In Black' still mean a lot to me. They're such great records, full of cockiness, rage, humour and above all, honesty, that they still form an essential part of my listening habits. I don't play much other rock now. Much of it seems brash, stupid and crass. Yet those AC/DC records are amazingly enduring. They haven't paled at all, still the epitome of what's good about rock when it's played full-on, from the heart and with its feet on the ground. Anything that proves itself a constant thread through your life for over 20 years has proved its own worth, no matter

what anyone else may think of it. It's for that reason that Angus and Malcolm are heroes and for that reason that I was excited when I finally got the chance to interview Angus.

THE LITTLE MAN was in town to promote 'The Razors Edge' album. Since I was going to do the cover story interview for *Kerrang!* I'd been sent an advance tape of the band's latest work. It was produced by Bruce Fairbairn, a Canadian more famous for working with soft rockers like Loverboy, but I was still hoping for a return to the swinging days of old. Of course I was disappointed. As usual there were a couple of great tunes. The opener 'Thunderstruck' was a groovy rocker, despite the fact that Brian's vocals were puzzling. He sounded like he'd lost all the power from his once incredible lungs. 'Fire Your Guns' and 'Moneytalks' were also good medium-sizzle rockers, but the whole package was still a good few notches down from the glory days of 'Back In Black'. I'll be digging out

"But I'm supposed to be a bit rock'n'roll as well, yeah?"

"And if I wear this ludicrous outfit, then we'll give a bunch of wasters in Birmingham a good time, right? Er, OK!"

"i didn't tell Angus that i was a fan at all. That i'd pissed my sides laughing at his antics on the 'Let There Be Rock' video while stoned out of my mind."

the interview in a minute to see what I said about the album at the time. I imagine I would have lied and claimed it was a return to form, a big return for the original bad boys of rock or some such nonsense. I'm ashamed to say I would have lied, because being on the front cover of *Kerrang!* meant that it was in everybody's interests to make the band look good. Maybe I'm being too hard on myself, though. Maybe I was being more honest than that. Maybe in the euphoria of the moment I really believed that 'The Razors Edge' was a great album from start to finish. I now know better, of course. But what the heck, I was getting to interview Angus.

FOR REASONS BEST best known to themselves, it had been decided that I'd be doing my interview on a Saturday morning, so it was quieter than usual when I arrived at the offices of Stewart Young of Part Rock Management, a glass and chrome building standing ostentatiously at the side of London's super-fashionable Kings Road. I remember as I

headed towards the entrance feeling that this London town, big business bollocks seemed utterly inappropriate for a band that prided itself on being a rootsy operation. In retrospect, maybe they weren't any more. Maybe the reason their music had lost its way was because the band members were no longer hungry, living in the lap of luxury that God knows how many gold and platinum albums around the world inevitably brings.

I jumped into the lift, one of those all glass jobs that shoots up the side of the building like something that Schwarzeneggar always seems to be falling out of in his movies. I'd piled in just as the lift was about to zoom skywards and just slipped through as the doors slid shut. All of a sudden I found myself standing next to Brian Johnson, who had obviously got in the lift just before me. Beano looked exactly like you would have expected him to; small (all rocks stars are small, except for Darryl Hall), unassuming-looking, maybe a wee bit older than he looked on stage, but nothing special at all.

No aura around him. No charisma. He seemed to feel as uncomfortable as I did in this hi-tech, big-business empire, head down, shuffling his feet. I thought it would be a bit presumptuous somehow, to introduce myself. I let the doors slide open at the appropriate floor and out he hopped, scuttling along the corridor towards the office. I let him go. If Brian Johnson didn't want to let on, then Howard Johnson didn't either.

ANGUS YOUNG, YOU will not be at all surprised to hear, is very, very small. But not only is Angus small, Angus is quiet too. Some shortarses try to fill up every room they walk into with their personality, almost like they're compensating for their lack of physical stature by proving what a big character they are. The guitarist isn't like that at all. When I was escorted into one of the rooms of the management office and plonked onto one of those leather sofas which were the stock in trade of '80s rock management company offices, Angus was ➤

already sitting opposite., drinking a cup of tea and smoking a fag. Over the course of the next hour I was to discover that smoking fags and drinking tea were two very appealing and all-consuming pastimes for Angus, clearly far more enjoyable than talking to some poxy music journalist, no matter how much of a 'fan' he professed to be. Actually, I didn't tell Angus that I was a fan at all. That I had worshipped him from afar when I was a kid. That I'd run out of the house in shorts against my mum's wishes. That I'd pissed my sides laughing at his antics on the 'Let There Be Rock' video while stoned out of my mind, that I had covered one of his songs in a band that I'd only just been given the boot from. No. For the sake of professional decency I didn't let on about any of those things. I simply sat down and did my interview for the cover of *Kerrang!*

The wee man was polite at all times, but never once did he really give me any insight into either what makes him or the band really tick. I Iis utterly bizarre speaking voice was hard to decipher even when I was giving it my fullest attention, but even when I could get a grip on what he was on about Angus was so cagey, so non-committal, that I felt for the most part that I was doing nothing more than circling around him, jousting for position, never once penetrating his armour of suspicion. If I asked a serious question: 'What kind of state had Malcolm been in that he was forced to get off the road in '88?', 'How much have the band missed Phil Rudd's distinctive drumming?', more often than not I was dismissed with a quip, a smart remark, a joke. For a band that prides itself on being unaffected by rock stardom, of being a band of the people, the greatest contradiction in AC/DC is that they have a paranoid fear of giving anything away, of opening up. Maybe their reticence and refusal to let anyone into their own private worlds is an integral part of their appeal, of course. Maybe the uncertainty about their motivations has contributed to their endurance. After all, what do we really *know* about the group? That they don't like modern music, are only really moved by the blues, smoke a lot of fags and drink a lot of tea. That's about it, really – which for a band that has been in existence for over a quarter of a century is pretty incredible. Has there ever a been a band as big as AC/DC that has been as private as they are? I doubt it. And, of course, I failed where many before me and plenty since have failed too. I didn't really get anything revelatory out of Angus Young. I got the usual perfunctory comments about the usual

perfunctory things, which you can read about for yourself elsewhere in this book, but as for the reasons why a man in his forties still sees fit to run around in a schoolboy uniform, still doesn't want to kick back, chill out and head into his 'rural phase'... well, you're just going to have to whistle for that stuff.

TOWARDS THE END of our allotted time together someone from the management company stuck their head around the door as they are often prone to do and said 'Five minutes', indicating that Angus had all but spent his time in hell and was about to be released from purgatory. Truth is, I wasn't that upset. As far as pointless exercises were concerned this ranked right up there with looking for that needle in the haystack. We wound things up sharpish, both glad that the formality produced by a tape recorder whirring away in the background recording your every word was finally at an end. Angus stood up for the first time since I'd been in the room, which merely confirmed just how tiny he really is. We shook hands and he prepared to scarper. Just as he was about to leave the room I remembered something. Angus had a talent for drawing little caricatures of himself, all long curly hair, thick lips, schoolboy's uniform and devil's tail. The fan in me finally got the better of me. "Er, Angus, if you don't mind, my girlfriend's a big fan of the band. Would you be able to draw her one of your little Angus devils, please?" For the first time all morning his eyes lit up like beacons. "Sure," he grinned, grabbing a pen and a piece of paper and proceeding to knock out one of the cartoons he must have been able to draw with one hand tied behind his back by then. After just a few deft movements with the pen the little Angus devil was complete, he signed his handiwork with a flourish and was gone, with as little ceremony as possible. It was time to leave.

I looked around to see if I could clock Brian Johnson again as I left, but he was nowhere to be seen. I put the drawing into my bag carefully, thinking that was the best thing about the day and that at least I would always have some memento of my meeting. I was wrong about that. I split with the girlfriend and she got custody of the cartoon, of course. I'll never be able to pin down exactly what happened to that little drawing. Just like I'll never be able to pin down the little man who drew it so expertly. ∎

CHRIS SLADE

The drummer who was too perfect for AC/DC...

Born on 30th October 1946 in Pontypridd, Wales, Chris Slade left school at 17 to join his first professional band, Thommy Scott And The Senators, in London. The band's singer was Tom Jones and a year later the group changed their name to Tom Jones And The Squires. When Jones opted for a move to America and recording with session players in 1965, Chris had the opportunity to jam with the Count Basie Band and Ted Heath in various clubs. Then, when The Squires finally split in 1969, Chris hooked up with the band Tomorrow, which featured Olivia Newton John. He recorded an album, 'Loudwater House', with Tony Hazzard, which came out in 1971 and also recorded an album with Tom Paxton, 'How Come The Sun' that same year.

In 1972 Chris got his first big break, joining Manfred Mann's Earth Band. He recorded nine albums with them between '72 and '78. After recording the 'Watch' album in 1978, Chris left the band and joined the Frankie Miller Band in 1979, as well as recording an album, 'Crazy Love', with Kai Olsson. A year later he joined up with Uriah Heep for the band's 'Conquest' tour, but when the band split in 1981 Chris joined up with Gary Numan for the 'I Assassin' album.

By 1983, though, he was back playing rock with The Mick Ralphs Band and The Firm alongside Jimmy Page and Paul Rogers. The band's first album came out in February 1985 and a second, 'Mean Business', appeared a year later. It wasn't a success and the band splintered. It wasn't until 1989 that Chris then replaced Cozy Powell in Gary Moore's live band, learning their set in four days flat! He was never short of offers of work, and there were talks going on with former Aerosmith guitarist Rick Dufay and ex-Colosseum man Chris Farlow when Malcolm Young got in touch, giving Chris the chance to work with AC/DC:

"I'd seen him with Manfred Mann in Sydney years ago," said Mal. "I remember thinking that he worked really well with the bass player."

There were rumours that AC/DC were thinking of working with former Guns N'Roses drummer Steven Adler after Simon Wright left the band, but there was never any confirmation of that. Angus spoke of the auditions, saying:

"We tried out a load of guys and most of them were great – for the first number. But after three or four songs they were all tiring and we had to find someone who could give us the right kick all the time. That's what Chris could do."

"They told me play as loud as I could, so I did," Slade said of the audition. Chris played on the earliest demos for 'The Razor's Edge' and after the recording of the album proper was asked if he wanted to stay with the band. In January 1990 the group celebrated his arrival with a meal at the notorious London restaurant School Dinners, where the waitresses all dress as schoolgirls. Brian Johnson, at least, was delighted with the new member. "It feels like he's always been there," he said at the time. "The kids will be amazed by his playing and his energy, which is far better than Simon's." Angus was in agreement. "He's a bit frightening, like Phil."

Chris made his live debut with the band on 2nd November 1990 in Worcester (USA, not Britain) and stayed with the band right up to the return of Phil Rudd in 1995. Malcolm explained:

"The stuff he did with us was great. We had no musical problem with him and there wasn't anything personal either. He's a perfect drummer, probably a better musician than any of us. But it was about a specific groove that we wanted. We just wanted to get back to the feel we had in the early days."

Angus on Phil Rudd...
"Chris Slade was a great drummer and a great guy, actually. I think though, whenever we've had someone since Phil come in and play the drums, you've sort of got to direct them towards your style, whereas Phil is our style."

THE INSIDE STORY

Dante Bonutto worked very closely with AC/DC as Head Of Rock at East West Records, so has a unique insight into how the band works...

You ended up working with AC/DC eventually, but your first met them when you were a rock journalist, right?
It wasn't exactly a meeting. When I was working on *Kerrang!* many years ago Mark Putterford was the guy who did most of the stuff on the band at the time, but I did do one interview with Angus on the phone. He was in Australia, I was in London. This would have been around the time of *Maximum Overdrive*, the Stephen King film. He was telling me that he always thought *Kerrang!* was a piss-take of his name – Kerr-Ang. He always thought it was weird. I remember asking him the question that he must have been asked the most of all time. I asked him about 'Whole Lotta Rosie', which I'm sure he was delighted with! But he was a gentleman when he answered though. I also remember that it was a bloody bad line and his accent was weird, somewhere between Scotland and Australia. There was no great connection between us at the time.

Were you a fan of the band?
I was to a degree, but my taste was more for the flamboyant side of rock. I think the first time I really took notice of AC/DC was around the time of 'Let There Be Rock' or 'Powerage'. Angus was on the cover of *Sounds* a lot in those days. There was a shot of him with his teeth missing that I really liked. I actually had tickets to see them live at Hammersmith Odeon with Bon Scott one time, but something came up and I couldn't go. I've still got the ticket at home, I

think. I did see them with Bon, but only on the television. My first gig would have been the 'Back In Black' tour with the bell. That was fantastic. I still think it's one of the best moments ever in rock, when that bell comes down and the track starts up. You know it's going to happen, but you always get excited.

So when did you first work with them in a professional capacity?
I guess the first time I worked with them would have been on 'The Razors Edge' album and I went on to work with them on 'Ballbreaker' too.

So when did you start at East West?
Around 1990, I think. I remember not long after I started there getting invited to hear the new album at their manager's office. When I got there Stewart Young said "No, not in the office," and we went down to the car park. He'd just bought one of those flash Japanese cars, a Lexus, a huge thing. He was one of the first people to have a CD in his car and he blasted the whole of 'The Razors Edge' at me. I thought 'Thunderstruck' was absolutely fantastic and I have to say I did think it was a pretty good album overall.

Dante Bonutto. His faultless filing system impress[ed] AC/DC so much they decided to work with him.

Was the record company contact mainly with Stewart?

The contact was always with Stewart. The band had rules about what they would and wouldn't do and I sort of knew that from being a journalist and watching them over the years. Stewart was the enforcer. I knew they weren't a normal rock'n'roll band. They'd never courted publicity,

"Angus always wore the same clothes. it never came into your head that he was a millionaire. No-one in the band ever had the trappings of all that stuff." Dante Bonutto

were never snapped at fancy places, were never in gossip columns. I worked out that it was a different beast we were dealing with here. You had to deal with them differently to how you would deal with other groups. I knew a lot about them, so I wasn't surprised by that, but Stewart was a strong manager. When we had meetings at East West, *Top Of The Pops* was always suggested and the answer was always no. It was probably the right thing to do as well. AC/DC were never a band that felt comfortable doing anything that wasn't totally honest and true. I liked Stewart. He was very good and I think he represented them honestly and faithfully. It was a difficult job for him because there were a lot of things that weren't on the agenda with them, but he protected their interests well.

Was the band pushed onto you because you were the company's rock fella? Did anybody else

over at East West really care about the band?

Well, I ran the rock department, so it was my job to assess the record, work out what we should do with it, what formats the singles should have and to vibe people up. I don't think it was a question of other people not caring about them, but they kept a distance between themselves and the record company. The promotion was always really limited because there were so many things they just wouldn't have been comfortable doing – and they were never going to change. I suggested they should do some club shows, which almost happened, but even they fell through in the end. They always felt they should be presented in context, but I thought they should have broken the rules occasionally and do something like a Marquee show. They never felt comfortable doing that, they always wanted the whole nine yards when they played live. I think there was interest in them at East

West, though. They're one of those groups that are considered crossover.

They weren't very hip though, were they?

They just were what they were. You knew Angus was never going to get out of the schoolboy uniform...

What was your first meeting with them?

I can't remember to be honest. I know for a fact that they would never come to the record company for a meeting, so it would have had to have been at a video shoot, a gig. Possibly a gig. I remember for some reason or other that I was asked to take them out for a night once. That might even have been the first time I met them. The Hippodrome in London had a rock night so I took them there and we were put into some VIP box. They clearly hated it and felt very uncomfortable – as did I. Well, the bass player

"Angus is an incredible performer live, and they saw that as what they really were."

was sort of OK having a drink and chatting up all the women there, but the rest of the band couldn't wait to leave.

Women? They don't get mentioned much in the AC/DC story, do they?

They're mostly married as far as I know, but the way with AC/DC was still that if you introduced a woman into the equation, then they got a lot more interested. I used to have a tall blonde secretary and so I took her with me whenever I went to see them. That made a big difference. They seemed to like very tall women. But it didn't help on that night at the Hippodrome. It was

terrible... I do remember that they ordered loads of drinks and put them on my bill. They enjoyed that, they thought that was very good. But the night just wasn't them. I still don't know what is them though.

I only went out for dinner with Angus once. He was being honoured by being invited to Warner Music publishers at Baker Street and I persuaded him to go with me. There was a bit of a do in the boardroom with people walking round with things on sticks because he'd sold so many records for them and of course he turned up in jeans and T-shirt. The big wigs from the record company made a speech and then me and

Angus went for a meal around the corner. He was very quiet.

I wanted to talk to Angus about the Mutt Lange albums, but he clearly wasn't mad about them. He obviously liked to get in and out and record quickly and that wasn't Mutt Lange's forté. I remember we talked about 'You Shook Me All Night Long' and he tapped out the way Mutt wanted it on the table, a much more poppy rhythm, and he said they changed it back to how they had originally wanted it. Clearly there was a discrepancy in the way they saw the records, but when it worked, like on 'Highway To Hell', it was amazing.

Vatican officials identified AC/DC as one of the most extreme examples of bands sending out "diabolical and satanic messages." They claimed that the band's initials stood for the satanic phrase 'Anti-Christ, Death To Christ'. Sadly for the Pope, the band actually took their name from a sticker they found on a hoover!

What did you make of Angus as a bloke?

You never felt he was someone who had a lot of money, except for cigarettes which he smoked constantly. He always wore the same clothes. It never really came into your head that he was millionaire. No-one in the band ever had the trappings of all that stuff. You never even saw them in a car; they just seemed to go around with Stewart and that was it. They always turned up in jeans and T-shirts and seemed very normal to me. They seemed not to like the ceremonial side of the industry. Getting him to go to that dinner is probably my greatest achievement. Even when he got that award last year at the *Kerrang!* Awards he didn't seem that comfortable with the whole affair. I'm not sure how AC/DC measure their success. I never really thought it was about the sales. It was more about the music and how they felt about the records. You always felt they were much warmer towards the albums they'd made with their brother. 'Powerage' and 'Let There Be Rock' seemed to be their records of choice.

Did you ever feel you got close to them?

Considering I was working at their record company, the fact that I even got to talk to them was a major achievement! I suspect that to win their trust it would take many, many years. You had to change your approach with them, but I never felt I got beneath the surface with them. I don't think many people ever do. A lot of the suggestions I made they took on the chin, but at the end of the day they pretty much always went with their own instincts.

What kind of things did you suggest?

More interesting artwork, more zany artwork. More interesting B-sides...

Like?

I think I wanted them to make use of the 'Live At Atlantic Studios' stuff, which eventually came out on the box set. I think they always had the plan to hold a lot of stuff back for a box set, but I kept mentioning 'Live At Atlantic' because it was so great and at one point I even got a DAT of it, which was a major achievement. But I never got to use it. I presented lots of wacky artwork and they did actually go for a couple of them. There were certain things we did do; bank notes with 'Moneytalks'. The cover for 'Hail Caesar' was

quite different. I would have liked to have taken that a lot further, but they were very careful about breaking the formula. Not changing had worked for them and they didn't want to be seen as competing in anybody else's game. They wanted to be their own thing. They had a very simple view of who they were and what they wanted to do.

Once I had to buy them all a present and that was really hard. When bands come to town you put a little something in their hotel room for them. Usually it's fruit, but I decided that was too boring, so I tried for a more personalised gift. I bought Angus some kind of Chuck Berry boxed set, but it was really hard to find things they might like. They weren't interested in competing with the modern bands, which was why getting them to work with Rick Rubin on the 'Ballbreaker' album was so hard. I didn't think he did the best job in the end, but it took a lot to get them to work with him in the first place.

Did you feel slighted that you couldn't get close to them?

Not really.

Are they boring people, then?

I think there's the onstage and the offstage thing. Angus is an incredible performer live and they saw that as what they really were and offstage wasn't that much a part of it. I wouldn't say they were boring. In a way they were refreshingly different. With the other bands there was almost a formula you could tap into to get along with them. You couldn't do that with AC/DC. They had a different aura about them, so no, I never felt they were boring.

You never hear 'sex and drugs and rock'n'roll' stories about them...

I got the impression that a lot of that had gone on, but not any more. By the time I worked with them it had longed ceased to be a part of things. Angus' wife was around a lot and there was only really a lot of tea-drinking and a lot of cigarette smoking. But all that seemed to make some sort of weird sense with them.

What about the chemistry between them. What did you learn?

That whenever it was business it was always down to Angus and Malcolm. It was those two and then the rest of them coming up behind. I think everyone in the band accepted that position quite happily. I've no idea what the business arrangement was in terms of who got what financially. I think Brian was just quite grateful to be in the band at all. There was one thing that showed me that there wasn't that great a communication between them all. It was when I was at *Kerrang!* We decided to convince one of the photographers that David Coverdale had joined AC/DC, just as a wind-up. We even mocked a cover up and then I got a call from Peter Mensch, who was managing the band at the time, saying "I hear you've been spreading a rumour that Brian's out of the band and he's just phoned me up and even he believes it!" That probably proves that there wasn't any great communication between them. I think it was hard for Brian to follow in Bon's footsteps because Bon's lyrics were so brilliant. I don't think the band was ever quite what they were after he died.

AC/DC is, which is a spontaneous rock'n'roll band. I think it's because they were spontaneously recorded. Whenever I go into recording studios 'Powerage' is the album that rock bands mix against. Sometimes 'Back In Black' for the drum sound, but 'Powerage' for the sheer excitement on the record. I know Keith Richards always mixes against 'Powerage'. It's one of his favourite records as far as I know.

Tell me about 'Ballbreaker', then. You were involved in that project from the ground up.
Well, I was involved with the 'Big Gun' single before that, too. That was the single where they gave Rubin a chance and I did encourage that association. I'd talked to Stewart about him, how I kept reading that he would kill to produce AC/DC. I mean he'd already 'done an AC/DC' with The Cult's 'Electric' and with a band called The Four Horsemen and I thought they should give him a go. I don't think it turned out that well

asked everyone to turn around. At the back of the hall was the cannon and I put some shades on expecting there to be this almighty boom. All that happened was this horrible 'phutt'. It was very low key. It was quite funny, but the response, it must be said, was poor.

You've mentioned your disappointment with Rick Rubin a couple of times. Why was that?
I detected that it wasn't a smooth working relationship with Rubin. Everyone who's ever worked with him says that he's never there in the studio and I think the band felt that. Maybe he

"i think AC/DC are more relevant than ever now. Rock music has taken on a greater sense of irony and i think they've always had that."

Did you talk about Bon's death with them?
I think they were very upset by his death, but I never talked to them about it. Someone told me that when they flew back to Australia for Bon's funeral that they'd specifically asked not to be on the plane with the coffin, but due to some mix-up that's exactly what happened and they were very upset about that. To be honest Bon's are the albums that have stood the test of time. Those early records captured the essence of what

in retrospect, as I said, but at the time it seemed right. Rubin was very cred then.

I actually came up with the idea for the sleeve for that single too. We were going to do a lot of different versions; a big gun by Trafalgar Square, a gun by the Eiffel Tower, a gun by the Leaning Tower Of Pisa. That got whittled down to just one sleeve in the end, but I went to Diss in Norfolk where they store all their cannons to photograph one to get the right perspective for the sleeve. They had all the old sets there and because after that shoot I then knew where they kept the cannons, I got them to drive one down to our sales conference one time. This must be going back four or five years now. I think I was presenting 'Ballbreaker' to the company, so I made this speech, went offstage, pretended I'd forgotten something and came back on again. I said 'There's one thing I forgot to mention' and

wasn't musical enough for them either. They started on drum tracks in New York and then scrapped them all and moved on to LA. There was a lot of hassle about that as I remember.

'Ballbreaker' was of most interest to hardcore fans because it marked Phil Rudd's return. Phil was already back by the time we started working on the album. There wasn't any fanfare about it; he just came back. They'd had a few drummers in between, Simon Wright and Chris Slade, so we were kind of used to rotating drummers. I thought it was a bigger deal than they seemed to believe it was. I don't know if Rick Rubin had any part in it, but he could have done since the idea of the album was to go back to the roots and recapture that early sound and feel.

How does the band work when they're recording?
They're very autonomous. I don't think they even

played demos for their manager, never mind the record company, so I think Stewart heard it pretty much when it was mixed the same as we did. I think they always felt the music was their thing and the business was everybody else's. I think Malcolm sings on a lot of the demos as far as I know, but I certainly never got to hear them.

What did you make of 'Ballbreaker' when it was finally finished?

In retrospect I thought the production could have been better. If someone had asked me to produce them, then I think I would have broadly done what Rick Rubin did, come up with something that was more like the 'Powerage', 'Let There Be Rock' era. But 'Ballbreaker' didn't quite match those records overall. It was almost a pastiche and didn't quite capture the band's power. I'm sure Rubin put a lot of effort in because he was working with his favourite band. But maybe working with your favourite band isn't such a good idea. I think it had to be tried though; he was a hot producer at the time and they were his favourite band. They're a lot of producers' favourite band, actually. Loads of them have said to me "If you can get me one track with AC/DC I'll be your friend for life." Everyone wants to work with them.

Are there things you find embarrassing about the group? The schoolboy uniform. The crassness they sometimes show?

No, I never have done. I've never been besotted with them either, though, even though I think the last tour was the best of that year. But I think AC/DC are more relevant than ever now. Rock music has taken on a greater sense of irony and I think they've always had that. Plus they've never liked that inflated ego shit and all the bands who've worked with them love them. The Wildhearts supported them on the last British tour and they thought they were great blokes, they treated them brilliantly.

So what are your favourite memories of working with AC/DC?

Going to the videos, I think. 'Thunderstruck' was a good one. They asked us to find an audience and I think we put an ad in *Kerrang!* saying if you wanted to be in the video then you had to meet

outside the Hammersmith Odeon at a certain time on a certain date and we carted everyone off to Bray. When we got there we still didn't have enough, so we were dragging people in off the street. The videos were one of the few times when the band and the fans met. I thought they'd stand around for hours after gigs signing autographs, but that wasn't really them either.

And who did you like most in the band?

You just can't separate Malcolm and Angus like that. Brian is clearly a very funny guy. He was the

"I think the band were very upset by Bon's death, but I never talked to them about it."

guy you'd bump into backstage most, sort of wandering around holding court. He would sit with anybody – telling jokes. I could never understand his accent that much. I can't say I knew any of the rhythm section. I liked them all, really. I thought Malcolm was an excellent bloke and he had a good understanding of the business. He lives here, so I think he was very in touch with how difficult it was for them in this country. I think they wanted to work with people who liked what they did and understood it. They hated all the '80s metal thing and didn't want to be any part of it. Most bands I've worked with I'd

know more about, but you never really got the chance to hang out with them that much. People who are fans do tend to be very hardcore and I think the band were always taken aback by that kind of response. I don't think they were ever comfortable with that kind of adulation. Maybe they were just shy.

They do inspire that level of devotion, don't they?

God, yeah. A friend of mine went out in an old AC/DC T-shirt recently and he said he had the best night down the pub ever because everyone wanted to talk to him. The band was a real ice-breaker. I think they're very fashionable. In Duffer Of St George, which is one of London's trendiest clothes shops, they have designer jeans with AC/DC on the back pocket. That band A have the A the same as the AC/DC logo and 'For Those About To Rock' on their T-shirts. AC/DC are fashionable because they've been going so long without ever changing. So they have fewer embarrassing photos than most.

Is it very much a boy thing with AC/DC?

Yes. It *is* very much a boy thing with AC/DC, because their music makes far more sense if you're a bloke and you're drunk. Their gigs are certainly more male-oriented. Maybe it's got a certain puerile element which men find funny. They definitely make a lot of sense in the 'Laddish' era, though I have to say, they made absolutely no sense at all when grunge was at its height, though.

People like me still hanker after the early days and the early sound...

The early days are always the ones that people remember most fondly and those are the days that make the most sense to bands. That's when you're breaking down barriers, but there are different challenges when you're as successful as AC/DC are. It's about keeping that success buoyant. I think the best thing about them is that they haven't changed, and I don't think they ever will change. If they'd chosen to change style they wouldn't still be around. There's been a formula kept. They've never embraced technology or whatever. They know how to do what they do and they think it's their strength – and who am I to argue with that? ∎

THAT ANGUS INTERVIEW IN FULL

First published in Kerrang! dated September 29, 1990...

Did you choose Bruce Fairbairn to produce the new album because you saw what a shot in the arm he's been for Aerosmith's career?
Nah, not really. We were gonna use my brother George, but he had other commitments, so we were on the hunt looking for someone new. These days I think it's pretty hard to find someone to produce you who's really into rock music, so we asked around and the word came back that Bruce Fairbairn was the best around.

So my brother Mal went out to Vancouver to have a chat with the guy, shoot the breeze, 'cos there was one thing that we were worried about and that was the fact that people on the US side like to be very commercial, y'know, rock ballads and all that. But the first thing that he said was that he wasn't gonna change us. You're hardly gonna be able to change a band like AC/DC anyway, but that was a big plus in his favour.

When we got there he was very smooth to work with; he just wanted us to be happy. There's no point trying to play something you're not comfortable with, and he never tried to make us do that. I think it helped that we had everything written before we went in this time so we weren't working while still changing this and that.

Was he expensive?
On the business side it wasn't that tough to come to an arrangement. He was very keen to do it because he told us in the past that a lot of bands had come to him and asked him for the AC/DC sound. So he said that instead of having to copy it now he could have the real horses, see how it's really done. It's difficult for us to be anything else, anyway, to go into a studio and come out all tra-la-la.

Someone told me you and Mal went to a great deal of trouble writing songs this time round; that you wanted to record the best AC/DC album ever. In retrospect do you think you achieved that?
It's all relative, isn't it? You always make the best record you can for that period. We never have, never would, put something out unless we felt confident about it. I mean, there's always a deadline which can make things a bit difficult, but this time we kept pushing the deadline further and further back so that the record was right.

In the past we've already been committed to touring and there wasn't even a record ready. This was a good one, because we finished touring in '88 and our manager said we could have

free rope to sit down, take our time and not feel any pressure, which left me and Mal with a clear field to be able to write at leisure, rather than have one month to come up with four or five songs.

But doesn't all this lack of pressure mean that you aren't as hungry as the early days when you had no time or money – when you just did it?
When we started we did the first album in 10 days; doing it between gigs, working through the night after we came off stage and then through the day. I suppose it was fun at the time, but there was no thought put into it. Somebody picked up a guitar and went "That's a riff" and away we'd go. There was a lot of that and a lot of magic moments came out of it. But that was youthful energy. You can't recapture that any more. Things aren't the same. This is a big band now. We can even afford our own fags. We don't have to smoke the butts any more.

The biggest change this time around is that you and Mal have written all the lyrics, Were you unhappy with what Brian was writing?
No, no. It was just that through this year Brian's been having a lot of personal problems, real shit,

and Mal and I thought it would ease the pressure on him if we wrote the words, just so he could concentrate on giving his best performance. It really helped him a lot and it gave Mal and I free rope with the writing.

In the past we've always had songs finished and then start writing lyrics. This way we'd do 10 songs and the ones that stood out were always the ones that had everything, including lyrics. We didn't end up stuck for a word, scratching around.

We've always contributed in the past anyway. We'd sit down, all three of us, me, Mal and Bon – sometimes four of us with my brother George – and we'd have this big shoot-around. We'd end up spending two days sitting on one word and

but hey, we all drank out of the same tea-cup.

I don't think he felt he was a member, though. All the time I was around Simon I only heard two words. They were "Hello" at the start of a tour and "Goodbye" at the end. I couldn't get a word from him 'cos he was very quiet. He always felt like an outsider because we'd been doing it a lot longer than he had, so maybe that was our fault.

But he always had a thing about Dio. When he first joined the band he was always talking about Dio. At the end of the day I think he got bored sitting around waiting for me and Mal to get ready to go into the studio. He just got in touch one day and said "I'm off to do this Dio thing." So we thought we'd better get someone else in and

afterwards. If he hadn't stopped... he could have gone overboard and done something drastic either to himself or someone else. I mean, if you ever got in a car with Phil it was close to the edge, that's the kind of person he was.

He kind of defined the AC/DC sound too...
He was a great drummer. You couldn't get Phil to do a drum roll and that was his charm. He'd just sit there going "Wham! Wham! Wham!"; that was his style. I think he's one of the great rock drummers.

What's he doing now?
He's in New Zealand – but not sheep farming. Sheep shagging maybe! Nah, someone told me

"This is a big band now. We can even afford our own fags. We don't have to smoke butts any more."

I'd be going "George, it's only a rock'n'roll song" – but he'd insist on getting it right.

We always gave Bon a helping angle in the past; same with Brian, because if you have a lyrical idea while you're writing the song it can save you a lot of heartache and trouble at the end of the day, scratching around and saying "How am I going to squeeze a word or two in between that racket?"

Let's talk about the change in personnel. What happened to Simon Wright? I heard all kinds of rumours, one being that he was sacked after being caught stealing gear from the band's lock-up because he was being so poorly paid.
He stayed long enough if he was being so badly paid! Financially he couldn't expect to be paid the same as the guys who'd been there for years,

that was it. It was a bit stupid on his part, but he'd moved to America and was under some outside pressure. I think he kept feeling he wasn't being recognised as a star.

Nobody's ever really quizzed you about the departure of Phil Rudd in 1983. I heard some pretty wild rumours, things like he was fired for messing around with some female in the Young clan, that he was getting increasingly out on the edge, dancing on hotel balconies 30 floors up, pissed out of his brains!
Well he liked a good time, I can tell you that much. Phil could have his crazy stages, but the biggest change I saw in him was when Bon died. He couldn't take it so well because as a band things had been that tight between us – it was pretty thick. We'd done a lot together; lived in a house together, set up all the gear together, slept with the same women – at the same time! When Bon died it hit him harder than anyone. He really thought that I in particular wouldn't be doing it any more. So when we carried on he thought that the early thing, the tightness, had gone, which wasn't the case. He was going for the high life and I think it caught up with him in the end. We did 'Flick Of The Switch' in the Bahamas and we were due to start in the States straight

he's flying choppers, he put some money into a helicopter business. He passed on a message to us through George that he was thankful that things worked out the way they did. He would have gone the way of Bon and I think he was grateful for his sanity.

Without wanting to sound too *Spinal Tap* – talking about drummers all the time – how did new man Chris Slade join the band?
Well I wanted one with hair. Nah, I think Mal saw him playing with Gary Moore and said he was a good rock drummer, so when Simon left, Chris' name came up. He sat in, we tried out and he fitted in great. He's another one who can bang 'em. He's like Phil, a bit frightening, a big guy looming over the kit. When we did the album he was just helping out because we didn't want a session drummer. Things worked out so well that we asked if he wanted to join and he was into it.

I presume Malcolm is back in the fold again, too...
Yeah, he's kicked his drink habit. He had to stop, it had just gone too far. From the age of 17 I don't think there was a day when he was sober. I never knew how he could function like that. I don't drink, but everyone else was doing it for me.

When the last album, 'Blow Up Your Video',

came out we knew we had a problem. We toured Australia and the UK and he'd held up pretty good, he'd been doing his best. But after we finished here he admitted that he couldn't make it through America. We decided to ask my nephew Stevie to do it. He did a great job. Most people thought he was Mal. They're very similar, he's got a strong personality. I was more nervous than he was. He was a big plus for us, he did a good job!

When you last toured the States – at a time when everybody was stiffing out on the live circuit – you did phenomenal business, to the point where you were selling more concert tickets than records...
That's probably true. I reckon I've signed more autographs than I've sold records. We've always been lucky on the live side. I remember in America after 'Back In Black', a lot of people said it wasn't the same, record-wise. Over there 'Back In Black' is their bible because they count numbers, but the audiences were still there long after that album. For a while we didn't even need a record to tour. People talk about 'Back in Black' as this special album, but I thought it more like a make-or-break record. It could easily have gone the other way for us after having built it all up with Bon and having a new face fronting the band. We didn't know what was going to

happen. In a lot of cases if a band has a tragedy it's very hard to pick up the pieces.

What do you think of the school of thought that says AC/DC died when Bon Scott died?
With Bon it's a real cult thing. It's weird, because when he was alive all people would say about Bon was that he was this creature straight from the gutter, no-one would take him seriously. Then after he died all of a sudden he was this great poet. Even he would have laughed at that. I find it a bit hypocritical, because as far as I was concerned he did have a great talent; as a vocalist, as a lyricist and as a person.

He could be a crafty devil sometimes too! It's like if some girl walked in the room he'd always say "She's not for you Ang, she's not your type. She's trouble!" Then at the end of the night I'd see him walking out with her! But Bon was unique. He did have a great life. Every day could be a party.

I can see that Bon would have acquitted himself well in the rough Aussie pubs when you first started. But didn't you have a real hard time from the beer swillers, what with the schoolboy uniform and all the rest of it?
Yeah I did. We used to play the roughest places – like what you'd call redneck bars in America. But

once we started playing people would stop and look and if it was loud enough and hard enough then they'd go for it. They never went for that overblown heavy metal kinda stuff over there. Deep Purple was a bit polished to them. They liked it hard and they liked it fast and they loved rock'n'roll, but they wanted you to cut the bullshit. No twiddly-twiddly, if you know what I mean. I think they liked our intensity. When I'd be rocking up and down they'd say "Well at least Angus doesn't dance like a poof!" That was important to them.

I can't resist asking how the hell you do your live performance thing? I mean, it's not human that one man can play so much and move so much and sweat so much!
I dunno how it happens. People are always asking me if when I'm up onstage I see things, but the only thing I see is my feet. It started off with me trying to keep time by tapping my foot, so I'd only look up when I was trying to sneak a look at what Mal was playing. He was better than me and knew a lot of the old R&B stuff, but I played lead because that would have interfered with his drinking. Now I don't feel comfortable unless I'm doing all that stuff. Anyway, I don't think people would want it any other way now.

VIDEO NICEY

Paul Cadden couldn't wait to be a convict at the video shoot for 'Are You Ready'. So, was he ready after all?

PRESS PLAY: Back in the early '90s when good old Auntie Beeb's Radio One didn't think rock was something of a four letter word, there was a show broadcast on Friday nights called, funnily enough, *The Friday Night Rock Show,* hosted by Tommy Vance, now VJ at VH1.

Anyhow, during a show broadcast in early March 1991, Mr Vance uttered the tantalising words "If anyone is interested in being in an AC/DC video shoot they must phone the following telephone numbers, blah, blah, blah. Places on the video shoot will be determined on a 'first come first served' basis. Phone after 9 am tomorrow." "Oh yes. I'll have some of that," I thought.

FAST FORWARD: Saturday morning.
1) Go to work.
2) Break into office to use telephone with outside line.
3) Find out that number is actually Way Ahead Records in Birmingham.
4) Ask about AC/DC video shoot and am told to pick up said tickets in person.
5) Drive like a bat out of a Ford Orion up the A45 to Brum and procure three tickets for the shoot.

STOP: Mission accomplished.

PRESS PLAY: The video shoot for 'Are You Ready' (second single from 'The Razors Edge' album) is to be held at Bray Studios in Windsor (OK, yah!)

on Monday 18th March. Not exactly the most rock'n'roll of days, is it? Still, Angus won't have a hangover, will he?

The big day soon arrives. My cousin Tony, mate Rob and my good self catch a British Rail snail train from Coventry to Birmingham and quickly arrive at The Ritzy (that's the name of a dodgy club, as if you didn't guess!) in Hurst Street. The coach is due to pick us up at 11.45 and we arrive at 10.55. We accidentally notice a nearby public house that is open, so being public-minded we enter the hostelry to consume a few quick halves, as you do!

Armed with emergency alcoholic rations we get on the waiting coach and 50 plus avid DC fans set course for Windsor. After a couple of hours we arrive at Bray, a representative of the video production unit welcomes us and informs us we'll be required to be extras, convicts on the AC/DC 'prison' set. White baseball caps and boiler suits are provided to be worn on the set. Nice!

Well and truly convicted and sentenced to a day's repeated participation in DC's video, we are indeed truly ready to rock and scream! Approximately 500 DC fans are shepherded onto the set, which consists of a stage (natch!) at one end, a gantry overhead and rows of prison doors on either side – a heavy rock prison!

The director of the video welcomes the assembled

throng to the shoot and asks us to sing along with the band on the chorus and generally make some noise. "Yes, we get the idea mate. Now piss off and get the band on stage!"

RECORD: Cue AC/DC on stage, 'Are You Ready' booming out of the sound system, DC miming like their lives depend on it, convicts jumping up and down like the floor is electrified. All t op stuff and great fun!

After the sixth or seventh run-through of the song I decide it's time for a change of view. Me, Tone and Rob have had enough of playing sheep down the front. I've noticed the band disappear through a cell door at the side of the left gantry. That's the place to be!

The plan is to move to the back of the set, up the stairs and along to the side of the stage. This is achieved with ease as we mingle with our fellow convicts. We are Masters of Disguise! We arrive at the side of the stage just in time to see the director 'Harold J. I'minlovewithmyselfmeyer' eject two convicts from the middle of the crowd for looking like Spike from the Quireboys and Axl Rose. Not wearing their caps, see? Shot continuity ruined, you see. Fuckin' rock stars, eh?

Out come DC again and again for more run-throughs of the song. During the breaks Brian seems to be taking more of an interest in one of the female prison wardens. Probably just checking if she's warm enough.

Eventually get to meet the band and after getting the obligatory autographs on boiler suit and cap I also manage to procure a highly-prized plectrum off the man himself (gold logo on one side, gold cartoon of Angus on the other, red marble effect background to boot! Nice!).

Things seem to go around and around as we keep getting asked to do this bit again and that bit again, but finally Harold J. announces that the sentence is completed for the convicts and it's time to leave. Then he changes his mind and decides to ask for just one last effort before we go. So, intro, guitar, bass, drums – "Are you ready? Are you ready? Are you ready for a good time… then get ready for the nightline." Cue screaming, shouting, more jumping up and down. Brian screams. We give it our all as the band pump it up for this one last Herculean effort. And then finally, that's it. What do they say in the movie business? It's a wrap? For us AC/DC fans there's a much simpler way of expressing it. THE END!

HERE'S SOME WE REVIEWED EARLIER...

When the back-catalogue was remastered and reissued in 1994, I had the following piece published in RAW magazine. Not the greatest piece of writing ever, but it gives you at least an idea of the way I feel about AC/DC's music.

For those of you who were but a twinkle in your leather-jacketed father's eye in the summer of '76, the year punk rock broke, you may be only dimly aware of most of the above artefacts. While AC/DC still rule at the very apex of the hard rock firmament, their history dates a good way further back than the Brian Johnson-fronted, Donington stage-stomping, remote pin pricks in an American ice rink behemoth that racks up major sales, come rain, shine or – let's be frank – middling to average albums. AC/DC haven't made a truly shit-kickin', 'ten killers, no fillers' dizbuster since 1980's seminal 'Back In Black', the first time that Brian Johnson waxed ludicrous with the band.

While the brothers Young – Angus and Malcolm – have always found it within their three chord bluster to give us some icing, more often than not since 1980 the cake has gone wayward. Which is why RAW is duty-bound to wave the flag for these re-mastered and re-released gems from the days when Angus really had to wear short pants!

The reasoning behind this mammoth undertaking is that the early releases simply didn't do justice to the DC's crunchathon leanings. Not in a woofer and tweeter-dominated '90s, no sir. The resultant sounds are thicker, more audible and generally an improvement,

though only a massive sonic leap to the particularly trained ear. Still, it's a big doff of the cap to Ted Jensen, who warmed his backside over many a night in New York's Sterling Sound studios to update the sonic warfare and possibly awaken your interest in some truly classic hard rock that may have slipped your CD player to date.

Of the nine albums available with new, improved aural attractions, there are many classic moments which highlight original vocalist Bon Scott's integral role within the DC machine. Less bombastic and blessed with more natural swing, the AC/DC of yore mixed Scott's lewd and lascivious lyrical narratives and 'Lord Charles' vocals with some of the finest high-velocity takes on Chuck Berry's back-catalogue ever recorded in the name of art. 'High Voltage' and 'Dirty Deeds Done Dirt Cheap' still reek of the sweat of many a pub gig, where the band

had to be obnoxious to gain any attention. 'Let There Be Rock', 'Powerage' and the classic single live smash'n'grab 'If You Want Blood... You Got It' all drip with beer-swilling statements of intent, while 'Highway To Hell' and the Scott-inspired 'Back In Black' show a band at the height of its powers. Frankly it's a mistake to include 'For Those About To Rock...' and 'Flick Of The Switch' in these reworkings as these albums document a decline in songwriting prowess that has yet to be fully arrested.

Picking out standouts is arduous indeed, but if you want a neat summary of each period, try 'Rock'n'Roll Singer' from 1976's 'High Voltage', 'Gone Shootin'' from 1978's 'Powerage' and the title track from 1980's 'Back In Black' for definitive musical explanations of three classic periods. If you don't really know these epochs, then you're in for a straight A treat!

Angus on Bon...
"He couldn't have recorded records and stuff if he'd been in the condition they said he was in. When we were touring there may have been six months of the year when he was as dry as a bone and if we got one night off then he was entitled to a drink. Bon was not a heavy drinker."

Chapter Ten

THE MORE THINGS CHANGE

Very little stands still in this life. Life's driving force is always motion – moving on, moving forward. The subtle shifts of daily change snowball and gather momentum, so that over the course of the years you suddenly realise just what a long way it is from where you've come to where you've reached.

1999. Amazing. It really is twenty years since I ventured into my first AC/DC gig and began a love affair with their music that has mirrored real-life affairs pretty accurately. A first burning infatuation and obsession, then a cooling-off period that may be feigned indifference and eventually a realisation that this is something that's built to last. I'm the first to admit that, hey, it's only music, man. But whether I like it or not music has shaped my life, provided me with a living for many years, brought me here, to this place. And AC/DC, however much I might be embarrassed to admit it, are a big part of that. When drunk with friends it's a rarity indeed when the conversation doesn't turn at some point to the relative merits of 'Back In Black', or the stupidity of Beano's on-stage dancing. We can slag the band off with the best of them, but the difference between *us* and *them* is that *we* do it out of affection.

THE LAST TIME I saw AC/DC live was originally very much out of affection and for nostalgia's sake. When the band last played in London, in the summer of 1996, I have to be honest and admit that I had no intention of even going to see them. I was working at a company, John Brown Publishing, on a short-term contract as Creative Director (very fancy now, me) on a new launch which would eventually become a magazine called *Bizarre*. Anyway, the phone rang in the office one day and on the end of the line was my good friend Paul 'Gooner' Elliott. A *Kerrang!* writer of many years standing with a great sense of humour and a love of irony and heavy metal in equal measures, Gooner asked me: "Doing anything tonight?" "Not particularly," I replied. "You are now. You're coming to see AC/DC with me." I laughed out loud. I'd enjoyed the band's latest album, the stupidly-titled 'Ballbreaker', probably more than any AC/DC album since 'Back In Black'. It sounded like the band of old, less stadium rock and more pub boogie. Producer Rick Rubin, a huge fan, had already worked with the group on one song, 'Big Gun', for the Schwarzeneggar movie *The Last Action Hero* back in 1993 which had to my mind captured the essence of the band better than anything they'd done since 1980. 'Big Gun' sounded like an outtake from 'Powerage' to me. 'Ballbreaker' wasn't great from start to finish, but it sounded warm and intimate and featured half a dozen good songs, as well as two exceptional ones. 'Hard As A Rock' and the title track were as good as anything AC/DC had done in years. But even this genuine step in the right direction, as I saw it, hadn't tempted me to trek out to Wembley Arena to see the group. I'd gone through all the usual excuses of the jaded rock hack. It was right over the other side of town. I'd have to drive and so wouldn't be able to have a drink – and what fun is that? Arena gigs were never as entertaining as small venues. And anyway, I'd seen it all before, hadn't I? But here was a friend on the line, offering me a ticket. I thought about it for a second. What the hell, it'd be a fun night of nostalgia. I'd go for two or three numbers, relive my lost youth and be home across the other side of town before the band had even done their encores. "You're on," I said and made the necessary arrangements.

Inside the Arena I couldn't help but be impressed by the sheer volume of people who had turned out to see the band. I'd obviously known that Wembley Arena held about 20,000 of course; I'd been there enough times. But to see such a gathering for an act that had been doing the same shtick for the best part of a quarter century? That was impressive. As I took my seat with the rest of the freeloaders at the side of the stage I looked around and couldn't believe my eyes. There were about 10 journalists from the indie magazine *Select* lined up in a row like they were all going to the cinema. I couldn't understand it. I imagined that AC/DC would have been Satan's music itself to these trendy people, the kind of numbskull, sexist nonsense that always sent right-on folk into fits of apoplexy. I went up to the editor and asked him what on earth they were all doing here? "Oh, we love AC/DC," he explained. "Always have done." "Yeah, sure you have," I thought to myself. Wonder how many albums you've got. Could the unthinkable have happened? Could AC/DC have become trendy? The thought was not a pleasant one. It made me even more determined to leave early doors.

The band finally took to the stage in the shape which was so familiar to me. Back behind the drums was Phil Rudd, to my mind the only man who could ever make AC/DC swing the way God intended them to. He'd been on a 12-year sabbatical flying helicopters or whatever it is that he does down in New Zealand. Stage right Malcolm; stage left Cliff; Brian and Angus working the rest of the area. And the sound they made from the moment they appeared? *Incredible.* An enormous tidal wave of riffs and licks that stunned me with its power. This didn't sound like another band of old men going through the motions just to collect the pay cheque, which was a thought that had been half-floating around in the back of my mind. Within seconds I'd lost all of that detached, wryly amused stance that I walked into the place with and suddenly I was right there, in the zone. There's another term

"This didn't sound like another band of old men going through the motions just to collect the paycheque"

for it, too. I was rocking hard. I was surprised, but the band were absolutely irresistible and Gooner and I were up on the seats, two blokes in their thirties acting the giddy goat and not caring who knew it. As gigs go it was an absolute cracker. Interestingly enough, the band still packed the set with old classics. Just three songs from the new album, the title track, 'Hard As A Rock' and 'Hail Caesar'. Almost nothing at all from the post 'Back In Black' '80s. Plenty of material from the Bon Scott era. If nothing else AC/DC know themselves better than some of their fans do, I suspect. I was delighted. The choice of songs in 1996 justified my theory that the band's golden era had been a full 15 to 20 years ago. After all, 20 years before this Wembley Arena gig AC/DC had been recording 'Dirty Deeds', an album that still says more about what I believe is the essence and the unique appeal of the group than anything they've recorded in the last 15 years. Hearing songs like 'Live Wire' again gave me a thrill just the same as when I'd seen the band open with the same number at The Manchester Apollo all those years ago. I stayed until the very last chord had rung out around the arena and once the hall started to clear I sat back in my seat, savouring the moment. I thought about everything that had happened to me over the years, the people I'd been close to and who I'd now left behind, university pals, girlfriends, band members. People who'd been amazingly important to me at one time or another had come and then drifted away like mist. And yet here was this group of people, most of whom I'd never even met, who were still a part

"It was 20 years ago today." Me, Louise and Elliott.

Angus on the rock'n'roll lifestyle...
"I didn't join a band to be a casualty. There's a romantic myth that you should live fast and die young, the James Dean thing. AC/DC are here to disprove all that. We're hoping to get a pension."

of my life, a big part of it, a massive part of it. The feeling was, well, bizarre, more than anything. I didn't know whether it was something I should feel elated about or something I should be deeply depressed by. I decided on the former.

I FAFFED ABOUT after the show, hanging around in a little hospitality room deep in the bowels of the building which the band members sensibly avoided like the plague. In the end I asked myself what exactly I was waiting for. It wasn't the first time I'd been in some godforsaken room in some godforsaken shed asking myself what I was doing there. And this time I couldn't even have a free beer! I said goodbye to Gooner and started the walk back to the car. The crowds had long since departed and I was left alone with my thoughts as I tramped through Wembley's bleak industrial estates.

AC/DC, eh? What a weird one. Who would have thought that a man in his thirties would still be getting so much pleasure from a man in his forties dressed as a schoolboy leaping about the place playing one-dimensional boogie rock? I laughed out loud at myself. It almost sounded perverted. Ah, life is always so full of

surprises, isn't it? If the night had taught me anything, though, it was that I would never, ever fully lose my obsession with AC/DC. Maybe it was because they first came into my life at a time when I was really open to influence, trying to discover my way in the world and my place in it. Maybe it could've been something else that hooked me just as easily as their music. Model trains? Crocheting? Philately? Who knows? As it turned out it was a rock band from Australia. That's just the luck of the draw, I suppose. Not that I was complaining. The band had brought me great pleasure, great mates and great debates. I'd never taken AC/DC studiously seriously like many fans of groups and artists do. I was never one for collecting the red vinyl version of the 'Highway To Hell' single that was only released in Canada, or whatever piece of minutiae it was. But obsession manifests itself in many different ways. Barely a day goes by when the band doesn't cross my mind, however briefly and for whatever spurious reason. That doesn't ruin my day or my life, though. I haven't had to go to meetings where I stand up in the middle of the room, tell people my name and then confess that I'm an AC/DC-oholic trying to wean myself off them. I admit that I've got a habit, but I'm telling you I can handle it. I don't think I'll ever kick it and I'm not entirely sure I'd ever want to.

I FINALLY REACHED my car, pressed the key fob to deactivate the alarm and got in. I was lucky. I was now driving a BMW, which was a very far cry from cobbling together the train fare to get to the Apollo back in 1979. I slammed the car door and it shut with a satisfying dull thud. I flipped the glove compartment down and pulled out a tape, then slid it into the cassette player as I turned the engine and heard it roar into life. Into first, handbrake off and away. The mighty toll of the bell filled the car. I turned the stereo louder. "I'm rolling thunder, pouring rain / I'm coming on like a hurricane / My lightning's flashing across the sky / You're only young but you're gonna die / Won't take no prisoners won't spare no lives / Nobody's putting up a fight / I've got my bell I'm gonna take you to hell / I'm gonna get ya Satan get ya...HELL'S BELLS." Ah, the more things change, the more they stay the same.

NOW THIS IS THE LIFE!

So what was Phil Rudd up to while he was out of the band? According to this 1991 interview, it seems he was enjoying the life of Riley. He must have *really* wanted to come back...

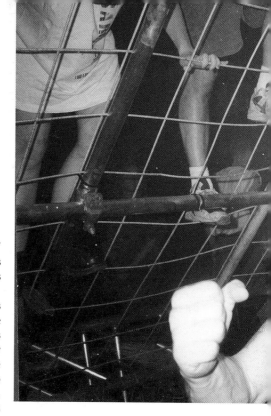

At the end of a stony road that runs right by the foot of the Kaimai range of mountains, behind kiwi plantations and herds of sheep, there lies a barn. It's not really a barn at all, though, but a fully-equipped recording studio. And here, 20 minutes by car from Tauranga, is where former AC/DC drummer Phil Rudd can be found.

After nine years of touring the world with the supergroup, Rudd took the decision to try a few other things in life. Born and raised in Tasmania, he felt drawn towards New Zealand because of the similarity in the two terrains and came to settle here. He'd always been a fan of animals, so at first he tried to breed deer in Paradise Valley, but now all he owns is a few sheep and kiwis to keep his friends and guests fed and watered. At one time he also owned a few goats, but they always kept escaping from their compound and Phil ended up selling them to a neighbour.

Phil then started the project of building Mountain Studios and while he won't say much about the cost of the exercise, he does admit that it was more than he had expected.

"We built the whole thing from scratch," he says. "We've got great sound-proofing in there because everything's built with double walls." He's right, too. Even if a guitarist is roaring away in the studio, you won't hear a thing in the control room.

With over a thousand hours of studio time clocked up over ten AC/DC albums, Phil has developed an intuitive feeling for the special needs of recording musicians. Although he didn't need

to do it, the studio floor lies on 10mm thick lambs' fleece for damping the sound and every room is incredibly spacious. The main studio measures seven by 12 metres!

The mixing desk is a 24 channel Hill Audio series 8400 with the usual array of effects and the pride of the studio are the gigantic JBL 44/35 monitors which Phil calls "absolutely awesome". Smaller JBLs stand at either end of the mixing desk. "We've tried to think of everything a musician needs to record comfortably," he says. "Comfort's important. The standards are high," he says, because he knows what's required to fulfil bands' expectations.

Designed by Keith Ballagh, the studio was built in under six weeks under the supervision of Marshall Day & Associates of Auckland. The electrics were put in by the specialist Hans Peter Frick with some help from Phil, who used to work as an electrician himself.

Although Phil has the knowledge to work as a sound engineer, in the few months that the studio has been open he's been more than happy when bands have brought their own sound people with them. "Bands of all shapes and sizes have their favourite engineers and I'm more than happy for them to bring them when they record here." Phil sees himself more in the role of a producer and he's been very pleased with the results he's had with a young Tauranga group, Hard To Handle. There's a single in the offing and they've already recorded a demo, 'Heart Of Stone'. Phil's also pleased with the recordings he's done with Ritchie Pickett.

Phil first started playing drums back in Melbourne aged 16, funding his obsession with his electrician's work. He first played with Buster Brown, Rose Tattoo singer Angry Anderson's band, and then joined up with AC/DC when they began to get established.

In the end Phil just got tired of the travelling – "It really knackers you" – and doesn't really like to talk about his days in the band, who will be visiting New Zealand for the first time in November. He's pretty modest about his musical achievements.

He ended up in New Zealand by chance. After spending a few weeks with an uncle in Hawkes Bay following the death of his mother he was due to move on to America. "But I liked New Zealand straight away, so I just kinda stayed," he explains. That was eight years ago. He met some helicopter pilots in Tauranga and decided to learn to fly himself. After earning his pilot's licence at the Rotorua Aero Club he learnt to fly a chopper with

"In the end Phil got tired of the travelling – 'it really knackers you' – and doesn't really like to talk about his days in the band."

10 QUESTIONS FOR PHIL RUDD

The drumming heartbeat of the band...

What did you do in the 12 years that you were away from AC/DC?
I got my life back! I had plenty of ideas when I left the band that I hadn't had time to put into practice before. I raced cars, flew helicopters, learnt to shoot, became a farmer and planted some crops. I lived in New Zealand which was great; nice and quiet with nobody bothering me.

So you had nothing at all to do with music?
Not quite. I built my own 24-track studio and worked with a few bands, recording and mixing. But I didn't play drums at all for six years and even since then I've only played when I wanted to, rather than when I had to. In the end I got together with a couple of close mates and started to play. We were a real 'Saturday night band' and we got a few tracks together that we

> **Angus on Phil Rudd:**
> *"Phil's got that natural swing. It's like The Stones without Charlie Watts. Take him away and it's not the same."*

could make a record with. We recorded them in my studio and gave them to a few people to listen to. They were impressed, but if we'd taken it further we would've had to go on tour and I wasn't ready for it at that point.

Did you never think about AC/DC in that time?
Not really. I didn't worry too much about what they were doing. I'd started a family, which I couldn't have done if I'd still been on the road. I had a nice life without having to be part of the circus. I'd seen the band a few years ago when they'd been in New Zealand, and we had fun. It was weird to stand out front and watch. I'd only ever done that once before, in 1975 when I'd broken my hand. I wondered what it might be like to play with them again, but they already had a great drummer in Chris Slade, so I didn't think about it any more – until Malcolm phoned me and asked if I wanted to have a bash again.

But having built up this new life it must've been a tough decision to decide to do it all again.
It was. My wife and I talked about it a lot. But at the end of the day I'm a drummer. That never left me. And I didn't want my kids growing up just hearing about what I used to be. I thought it would be good for them to see it as well as hear about it, while I still had the strength.

What did you miss most? The songs?
Well, I loved 'Powerage', and when we first started rehearsing in England we started with tunes like 'Gone Shootin'' and 'What's Next To The Moon?'. It was good. Even on tour we played older songs like 'Down Payment Blues' and 'Dog Eat Dog'. It only took five minutes to feel like I'd never been away.

Did you try to recreate the feeling of the earlier albums on 'Ballbreaker'?
Definitely. That's one of the reasons why we used Rick Rubin. We wanted to get that classic AC/DC sound back, the sound that suits us best. I'm really pleased with the results. I had the most fun I've ever had in a studio with this one.

What about changes in your drumming?
There aren't any, really. When I was younger all I wanted to do was play as fast as I could, but I've learnt since then. I like the groove – and I don't even need a click track with AC/DC.

You bring a real sense of control to the band...
You get more energy when you stick with one tempo. I don't think about making things faster, but heavier. A big hit at the right point can improve the song. The trick is the same with all the instruments. Look at the old blues players. Three notes get right to your soul whereas others can play 50 million and not touch you. That's my style. I don't do a lot but I do it right.

So it's the rhythm that matters above all?
Yes. When we play live I listen to Malcolm above everyone else. I have a stereo monitor on stage with the guitar in both channels, plenty of drums, just a little bit of the vocal and not much bass.

And your drum sound hasn't really changed over the years, has it?
No, I still like to hear the same things. That's just the way I like it.

star pilot Bruce Harvey from Taupo. Phil even used to own a few himself. The last one he had he describes as "wonderful, the best in New Zealand." But he had to sell it because it needed a full-time team to maintain it. "It was just too expensive so I sold it. It crashed not long after and all four crew members were killed."

Phil's other hobby is racing cars. He brought a Ford GT40 to New Zealand, but a collector bought it from him and shipped it to England. "I've always been crazy about cars. I had a load of them. Far too many to ever actually drive."

When he's not working in the studio or spending time with his family – partner Lisa and their two sons aged three and 22 months – then Phil likes to race his V8 in Bay Park, Manfield, Pukehohe or Taupo. He's still got ambitions to be a farmer. He's developed 10 acres and has a few sheep and some fruit trees. Well it makes a change from deer and goats. "And at least trees stand still, so you don't have to spend half your life running after them." And, surprisingly for a rock'n'roller, he likes getting up early.

"I wouldn't give up this lifestyle for anything in the world," says Phil, who does, however, admit, to having another iron in the fire. He wants to record his own solo album.

"SOMETIMES IT TAKES TWO YEARS. SOMETIMES IT TAKES SIX YEARS..."

Nikki Goff, who runs the AC/DC fan club in the UK, interviewed Angus in June of 1996 on the 'Ballbreaker' tour. Ever wondered what fans, rather than journalists, would ask Angus? Wonder no more...

Do you hang out with any other rock musicians?
Not really. Do you know any?

We saw Brian May backstage at Wembley.
Ah, but he hangs around with anybody.

He was pretty impressed by you guys
He's a nice lad, but I wouldn't play with him. I play with who I'm with and that's enough, isn't it? I'm a fan of Chuck Berry. I'm like anyone, but I like to watch. I don't want to interfere with anything. I saw Buddy Guy playing a while ago and it's great to look and see, but I don't get up with them. You know what they do best. I'd rather play with Malcolm than with anyone else, because he plays exactly the same as me.

Did you play a gig for Arnie when you did the 'Big Gun' single?
Yeah, well he was doing the dance and he wanted to know how to do it.

Was it fun working with him?
Yeah, he'd never done anything like that before. He was nervous anyway, because he'd never done it before an audience. I know he'd done

The fan meets the man.

one with Guns N'Roses, but that was... I think they had him in one studio and they were in another. I showed him what to do. I wasn't going to argue with him.

Is there any reason why 'Big Gun' isn't in the current live set?
Is there a reason we played it in the first shows?

It's just feeling a way around what's working good. We've changed it around a few times. We started off with 'Big Gun' and what else? 'Sin City'. It's a case of we feel our way along...

Do you find that your fans react differently in different countries?
Just depends. In some cities the audience is quiet, so you play and play and then they're louder. It's hard to judge. I can tell a Monday night from a Friday night because on a Friday night everyone's singing because they don't have to go to work the next day. Come Monday everyone's got the blues.

What's it like trying to record and go on the road after a five year break?
I dunno... once you're in the studio you're kind of used to it.

Was it strange getting back into recording?
No. You psych yourself up recording. You can create something new.

Over the last year that you were recording there were rumours on the Internet about delays.

"i'd rather play with Malcolm than with anyone else, because he plays exactly the same as me."

Arnie on the set of 'Big Gun'. Oscar material.

"You mean, just shaking your hairy head like that is all there is to it?"

What were the reasons behind them?
Well Rick Rubin likes doing his stuff out of LA, which is strange because he was born in New York. He kept going on and on: "I can get a better sound in LA." It was a little better.

What's it like working with him?
He's got a good approach because he doesn't sit there and say "Let's make a hit single." Some guys want you to do a filler because they say "Let's make three hit singles."

Is there anywhere in the world that you haven't played that you still want to play?
We've never played South Africa, though we do keep trying. Apart from that I don't know. We're going to go to South America. We've

played Brazil before, but we haven't played the other places.

That was the Rock In Rio festival...
Yeah, we were going to play Argentina, but there was a war. Put a stop to that, not a good move.

There were rumours that you guys have got some material for a new album...
We've always got stuff written, there's plenty of material. Every now and again you get something that falls into place. Sometimes it takes two years, sometimes it takes six years.

Everyone's hoping that it's not going to be another five years before the next album...
Same here.

Which countries do you like touring best and get the best reaction from?
It's hard to say. Touring America is easy, because a lot of the halls are the same; but here, now, is a lot better. I always used to like playing in Hammersmith, you know? The Odeon.

Have you ever thought of going back to the small venues again, just for the fans?
We've played more clubs than any other band in the world, some of them out of necessity.

Do you still use the JTM 45 amps when you play live?
Yeah, what we do is use them for out front, maybe they put them at the side or at the bottom or between the two.

And how many separate amps do you think you have?
Well, really only that. On stage I think I'm running 4 100 watt Marshalls and just some little 45s, which they mike up.

Do they have different settings?
I just leave it.

So you don't change between clean and distorted?
Nah. Haven't got the time. People use boards and all that. When I was young, about 13, people used wah wah pedals. I borrowed one off a mate. First time I used it it went 'poof,' dead! So I thought "Get rid of that."

What settings do you use on the amps?
I don't run them full. I don't have any pre-amps on them. I've got those Marshall re-issue amps and I just use them straight. All I do is get them to where they start to get distorted, at about half, turn it up a little bit, put the treble up about half, a bit more bass and stop it if it gets too much. All amps sound different. They always want to boost them up. People will say "Well it's not dirty enough." You can hear the hum coming on before you get started.

Have you ever thought of doing an official biography?
It's a strange thing to sit down and write. It's finding enough to keep up an interest.

Would you use a ghost writer then?
I mean, if you buy a book on Napoleon, that's interesting. I don't want to read a book on myself. The trouble is that there are so many books and they make so much up. You get different stories in different books. With a lot of them, I gather they just take bits from interviews here and there.

In a recent *Mojo* article Malcolm was supposed to have slagged off a band he had never heard of.
When we were in Stockholm a journo, who had previously said we could have been any band, was standing there and he told me what a great show it was. What a hypocrite!

Journalists have been a bit unfair in this country.
A lot of them are only interested in the kind of music *they* like.

You've never been popular with journalists?
It doesn't bother me what they write. The people who matter are those who buy the records. So long as they're happy. They've paid to see you. A lot of journalists get well looked after by the record company. What I don't like is when they start insulting the audience. They can say we're crap. There was one guy in Manchester who said "Isn't it sad that you've got people following you round the world?" "What's sad about that?" I said. "Where have you been?"

Did you guest on The Poor's album?
Nah, that's my nephew.

A lot of people wanted them to support you in Europe.
A lot of what they do depends on their record company. Their record company wanted them to go into the studio. They look after them. They were lucky they wanted them to tour. A lot of record companies won't allow their bands to tour with us because they think our fans are hardcore.

I saw a lot of people with Wildhearts T-shirts.
I've seen The Wildhearts more offstage than on. I like to hang about afterwards. I'm usually the last to come and the last to get out.

Do you listen to many modern bands?
None really. I didn't listen when I started because other people were into pop and I was into rock'n'roll and blues. When I went to school everybody was into Elton John.

But you were influenced by your brothers.
Yeah, well my brothers... George spent his life making pop music and taking it to a commercial audience. With us all the great songs – the 'Rosies', 'T.N.T.s', 'Let There Be Rocks' – they're all his. He put in that rawness. 'Powerage' as well. But if you talk to our record company they'll say they never heard of it.

Has touring and recording changed much over the last few years?
You've got to keep up with the technical things to do with studios, but apart from that it's just the same old rock'n'roll. We try to keep things as simple as possible because that's the kind of band we are and that's what the fans like.

Thanks for sharing!

BRI'S THE MAN

There's no doubt that a lot of AC/DC fans prefer the Bon Scott era to the Brian Johnson period. But Oliver Woch just can't agree...

To my mind, Brian Johnson doesn't get anything like the praise he deserves and there are several reasons for that. Bon was, of course, a fantastic and exciting frontman, so it was (and still is) doubly hard for Brian to establish himself. The fact that he's managed to do it at all is an achievement in itself. Another reason for Bon's popularity so many years after his death is that because he died living his life to the full, he's become a legend with AC/DC fans. You can draw parallels with James Dean here and you can see the same phenomenon with Bon. His death has only enhanced his image.

But what would have happened to AC/DC if they'd had to throw Bon out of the band after a few more years, for example for drinking too much? I know, of course, that they never would have done it, but I reckon that the fans would have held him up as less of a hero if he'd ended up going on stage after a few too many whiskies. I don't mean to dethrone Bon by saying this, because I loved him and miss him. I have the photo of his gravestone hanging on my wall. I'm only trying to make people realise how valuable Brian is to the band

'Back In Black' was a killer album, as good as 'Highway To Hell'; a bit more mature even. These two albums marked the highpoint of the band's creativity and although the following releases had the greatest commercial success, I think there was something missing. People were quick to lay the blame for that on the new singer and seemed to forget that the music was down to Malcolm and Angus and that Brian was only adding lyrics to the music he was given. Or are you seriously going to suggest that Brian was the reason why the Young brothers haven't developed the band's sound? After Bon died, the band were adamant that they weren't after a simple clone of their former singer, but a guy with his own singing style and his own character. Brian is both of those things.

Whether AC/DC would have become so big if Brian had been there from the start is another question altogether. Brian joined when the band were just about to hit the big time. Bon was definitely the personality with the bigger aura about him, something which Brian's tried to counter with more of a stage presence. He's pulled it off pretty well too, as any of the band's videos will prove.

I've reached these conclusions after remembering that Brian's been in the band for nearly 20 years compared to Bon's six! Yet Brian still hasn't had the recognition of his predecessor. The circumstances have been different for both singers. Bon had to tour the clubs to get to the top, whereas Brian came in when the band was already on the way, when the formula had been established. AC/DC was a band from the street and they've kept that feel about them all the way through. It's what made them a success. You can see that street vibe more in Bon's lyrics than in Brian's, but at the end of the day, while people rightly remember Bon for what he did with the band, let's not forget the contribution his replacement has made. It's been huge.

MADRID RIFFS...

Enrique Diaz Galvez caught the 'Ballbreaker' tour in Madrid on a magical night...

When it was announced in November of 1995 that AC/DC would be coming to play in Madrid, I just couldn't believe it. Finally, after 16 years of collecting the band's records and listening to their music, I was going to be able to see them in the flesh, fulfilling my life's ambition. The concert was to take place in July of 1996 and the following seven months seemed to go on forever, until at last the moment finally arrived.

I was going to go to Madrid with my wife Inma, but the night before the gig I couldn't sleep with the excitement of it all. On the day itself we arrived at the venue at half four in the afternoon and had to wait in a scorching 40 degree heat until the doors opened at 7.30 that evening. The atmosphere inside the bullring as it started filling up with the band's fans was incredible.

Before AC/DC took the stage The Wildhearts put on a good show, but with a punctuality that no-one expects at Spanish rock shows, the lights went down on time and the main show began. There was a massive wall at the back of the stage and within a few seconds I could scarcely believe my eyes. There was Angus, dressed as a schoolboy with his Gibson in his hands, banging out the opening chords to 'Back In Black', a song I'd heard millions of times within the four walls of my house. The crowd went wild and suddenly Angus was off, jumping onto the stage and rocking out. Brian was in great form, covering every inch of the stage and blasting out the tune with his incredible voice. As always, Angus was giving an incredible physical performance; I don't know how he manages to put on

such a show with so much energy. Malcolm was his usual solid self, pumping out the riffs in a way that to my mind is the most honest approach in rock. I can't even begin to put into words how amazing his rhythm playing is.

Phil and Cliff were great too, keeping the band sounding as solid on the stage as they do on record. The songs just kept on coming, each of them so familiar to me, and so much the soundtrack of my life. Numbers like 'The Jack', 'Dog Eat Dog', 'Hell Ain't A Bad Place To Be', 'Shoot To Thrill' and 'Highway To Hell' were nothing less than amazing. When the band played 'Shot Down In Flames' I immediately started thinking about Bon Scott and trying to imagine what the band would have sounded like with him. It's one of my greatest regrets that I never got to see AC/DC when Bon was with the group.

When 'Boogieman' was played Angus did his weird but entertaining striptease. It's a part of the show that the audience expects and a live gig wouldn't be the same without it. But the best moment of the whole concert for me was during 'Let There Be Rock', when Angus came down into the crowd and came so close to the spot where my wife and I were standing that we could even see how much he was sweating while the rest of the band laid down that incredible sound.

Little by little the end of the gig started to draw nearer, but when I looked at my watch I saw two hours had passed and I'd hardly even noticed. The last song, 'For Those About To Rock', left us more than satisfied and immediately thinking about the next time we'd be able to see the band live. On the way out we bought a poster of the band and tried to get backstage to see if we could get it signed. It was impossible to get through because of the security at the venue, which was a shame, because that really would have been the perfect end to the perfect day.

On the journey back home to my city of Cordoba I listened to one of my favourite AC/DC songs, 'Carry Me Home' on my Walkman. It seemed like the best possible end to a fantastic day.

CHEERS!

Smari Josepsson, an AC/DC fanatic from Iceland, tells the tale of meeting Angus and getting his beloved guitar signed on the 'Ballbreaker' tour...

The night of 17th June 1996 sticks in my memory like it was yesterday. I was outside the Birmingham NEC waiting eagerly to attend my fifth AC/DC show. I'd already been to Glasgow and Newcastle, where I managed to meet Brian at a hotel. I'd brought my SG with me from Iceland and I was hoping I could get it signed by the mighty man himself, Angus Young. Several other fans were kickin' back outside the venue waiting for the band to show up. The guitarist from the covers band AB/CD spotted me with the SG and gave it a little ride and we had a great chat about the band, the 'Ballbreaker' album and the UK tour, agreeing that bringing back Phil was the best thing that could have happened to the band.

I couldn't be arsed to see the Wildhearts again as they were complete shite at the previous shows, so I decided to skip them and wait for AC/DC to come rollin' in. Just a few minutes after The Wildhearts had finished their set, the Mercedes started coming and I could see Angus sitting in the front seat of one of them. I held the guitar up in the air in one hand and a pen in the other. When Angus saw the guitar he gave me a thumbs up, got out of the car and signed it for me. "To Smari, Angus Young, AC/DC '96." I was really surprised how relaxed he was because there were only a few minutes before he was supposed to hit the stage. Another fan who was present was kind enough to take a few photos of Angus signing the SG. I then grabbed it and got

inside to prepare myself for the gig, which was one of the best on the tour.

After the show I waited for a couple of hours to see if I could meet anyone from the band and to my surprise Bob Wien, the Security Manager, invited me and a few other fans who'd been standing there backstage to meet Angus and Malcolm. I figured I'd already pushed my luck getting the guitar signed, but I asked Angus if I could have a picture taken of me and him holding the guitar and he said it was no problem. A perfect end to a perfect night.

A few days later I saw the band twice in London and again I met Angus when he was leaving Wembley Arena. At the time I'd already got the photos developed and Angus signed the one of us together for me. Someone told Angus that Ginger (The Wildhearts' singer) had been giving the audience a hard time for not being into their music and Angus' reply was "Ginger? Who's Ginger?" which gave us all a right laugh.

All in all the whole tour was brilliant, I met a bunch of great people who shared a lot of good tales of our experiences with the band. And you never know – if I'm lucky I'll get the chance to fly over and do it all over again on the next tour.

20 QUESTIONS

So You Think You Know Your DC, Do You? Well Try This Quiz From The Pages Of _Daily Dirt_ For Size...

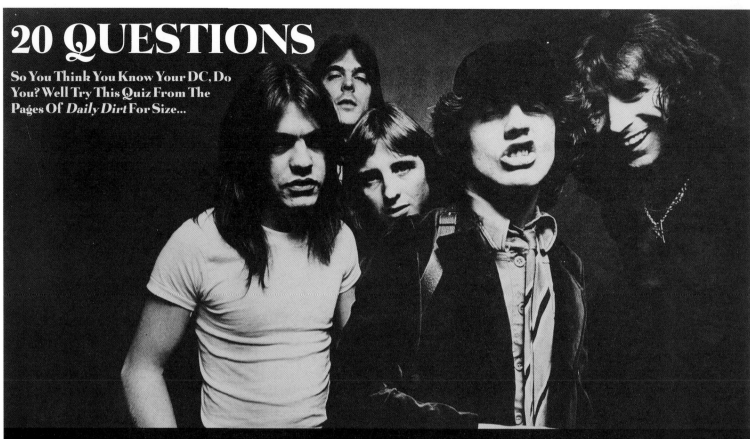

1) What was the name of AC/DC's first drummer?

2) What's Angus' middle name?

3) What did Malcolm and Angus want to call their band originally?

4) What band did Phil Rudd play drums in before joining AC/DC?

5) What Australian drummer's solo album did Angus get credited as having 'assisted' on?

6) Who played bass on the band's Australian 'High Voltage' album?

7) Where and when was the first ever AC/DC gig?

8) What's the only album where Malcolm plays some lead guitar as well as rhythm guitar?

9) What are the names of the two cover versions you can find on official AC/DC albums?

10) Who is Angus' favourite guitarist?

11) Which tracks from the 'Blow Up Your Video' sessions didn't make the album, but ended up being used as B-sides?

12) Which track from the 'Dirty Deeds Done Dirt Cheap' album wasn't recorded at Albert Studios in Sydney, and where was it actually laid down?

13) Name the town, the area, the road and the house number where Bon Scott died?

14) Where can you find Bon's grave?

15) Name the town where Cliff Williams was born?

16) On which record did Cliff Williams make his official vinyl debut with the band?

17) What make of drums does Phil Rudd play and what sticks does he use?

18) During the band's 'Ballbreaker' tour only two tracks were performed which Phil Rudd hadn't played on in the studio. Which songs were they?

19) Where did the last concert of the European leg of the 'Ballbreaker' tour take place?

20) Which song from the 'Back In Black' album was the first to be finished after Bon Scott's untimely death?

ANSWERS: 1) Colin Burgess. 2) McKinnon. 3) Third World War. 4) Buster Brown. 5) Ray Arnott's 'Rude Dudes' from 1979. 6) George Young. 7) Chequer's Club, Sydney, New Year's Eve, 1973. 8) The Australian 'High Voltage' album. 9) 'Baby Please Don't Go' and 'School days'. 10) Chuck Berry. 11) 'Down On The Borderline', 'Snake Eye' and 'Borrowed Time'. 12) 'Love At First Feel', which was recorded at Vineyard Studios in London. 13) 67 Overhill Road, East Dulwich, London. 14) Fremantle, near Perth, Australia. 15) Romford, Essex, England. 16) Live At The Atlantic Studios. 17) Sonor drums and Easton Ahead sticks. 18) 'Thunderstruck' and 'Who Made Who'. 19) Bordeaux. 20) 'You Shook Me All Night Long'.

150

AC/DC ONLINE

The Web Is The Future And DC Fans Have Made Sure The Band Is A Part Of It

Given the band's legendary suspicion of contact with the outside world, it's no surprise that they've been slow to capitalise on the possibilities of the web. Angus and Brian did go online for a chat around the time of 'Ballbreaker', but AC/DC's official presence online has been nothing to write home about. The fans, however, have been quick to see the opportunities and have been busy putting up unofficial and personal sites in honour of the band. The easiest way to cop a look at what's going on online is by checking out Thunderstruck at...

http://www.webring.org/cgi-bin/webring?ring=acdc&list

This is the last word in AC/DC webrings, with links to just about every site there is. And the beauty of the net is that things are constantly changing, so you never know just what you'll find. Here's what you can get at this one-stop DC shop right now, with comments from the people who have constructed them...

■ **The Back in Black Page**
Complete discography, history, news, picture of the week... and more!!!

■ **THUNDERSTRUCK**

■ **Shay's AC/DC Page**
My personal tribute to the greatest band in the world.

■ **AC/DC HELLS BELLS**
Contains: Bootlegs, Discography (albums/box sets/rare & unreleased/videos/singles), Downloads (sounds/videos/), links, lyrics, news, pictures, tablatures.

■ **The Un-Official AC/DC Website**
Great AC/DC site with downloads, lyrics, links etc.

■ **AC/DC's Razors' Edge**
My site contains lyrics, little known facts about the band, my reviews of all the albums and the essential AC/DC albums.

■ **The Cube**
AC/DC TABs and a little info on the band members. Also, if you choose, there is a Suicide Machines TAB page too.

■ **AC/DC Powerage Page**
The AC/DC Powerage Page has sounds, working videos, pictures and mosaics. You can also enter your own AC/DC site to win an award .

■ **AC/DC-Coverband**
The ultimate AC/DC-Coverband from Stuttgart

■ **THE AC/DC LINK PAGE**
Find AC/DC links right here. (Under construction since 07-01-1999)

■ **Parks 316**
AC/DC, Korn, Metallica

■ **FA/KE AC/DC Coverband**
FA/KE AC/DC Coverband from Fulda Germany

■ **AC/DC Thunderhouse Page**
AC/DC sounds, tabs, news, discography, band history, links and more

■ **Badboy Boogie**
The one stop resource for all your AC/DC needs.

■ **Devil Dog Style AC/DC Page**
A medium size AC/DC site, cos if you love AC/DC, then you have to LIVE AC/DC.

■ **AC/DC HIGHWAY TO HELL WEBSITE**
Dedicated to AC/DC and BON SCOTT. Focuses on AC/DC collectibles. Also features my AC/DC Tribute band – Ballbreaker. Also, certain sections pertaining to my other fave bands.

■ **PG's AC/DC Page**
Everything about AC/DC and more

■ **The Cowboys From Hell AC-DC Page!**
I have tried to make an AC-DC page that I, myself, would like to visit. I have included pictures, sounds, a chatroom, midi files, a fan list and more in this sight!

■ **My homepage**
My homepage mainly dedicated to AC/DC

■ **Rare AC/DC related MP3s**
Site with rare MP3s related to AC/DC

SNOTMAN'S AC/DC PAGE
This is a part of a two-part website devoted to the kings of heavy metal, AC/DC (the other part is devoted to Metallica). The AC/DC site is always under construction, so bear with me. As of 8th Feb 1999, the site contains group history, full discography, and lyrics for all the songs on 'High Voltage' and 'Let There Be Rock'. It is updated at least every other day,

■ **THE OFFICIAL HOMEPAGE OF AC/DC ON THE EFNET**

■ **Harv's AC/DC Pages**
A comprehensive database of AC/DC collectibles highlighting Harvey Lee's collection. Trades welcome. Also contains an AC/DC top 10 web links.

■ **Back_In_Black**
Pictures and links whenever I find them updated as often as I find something

■ **Angus Young and AC/DC**
Has information and a few pics of the best rock'n'roll group ever, AC/DC.

■ **Mike's Rock & Roll Damnation Page**
A nice little page for any AC/DC fan, that has band biogs, discography, videography, links and more coming soon.

■ **AC/DC**
For Those About To Rock...

■ **AC/DC Live Wire Site**
This site has pictures, discography and other stuff. More and more sections will be done in the future.

■ **The Thunderstruck page**

■ **Bonfire000's AC/DC Page**
This is a real kick ass AC/DC site for those lookin' for something new... It has all the needs for true AC/DC fans so come check it out.

■ **T's Mosh Pit**
Heavy Metal, Hard Rock and Classic Rock Bands. Click to see info

■ **The Ultimate AC/DC CD Discography**
A comprehensive guide to all AC/DC CDs from around the world. Can you add a CD that's not listed? (You get the credit)

■ **BKBANDITS OFFICIAL ACDC PAGE**
A site with stats links and other info on the best band of all time

■ **Ed's AC/DC Place**

■ **KEWL AC/DC Fan Page**

■ **AC/DC Talk E-mail list sign up page**

■ **ACDC Midi's at The Midi Asylum**
The AC/DC page at The Midi Asylum has all of the Midis I could find plus a commercial discography and links to other cool AC/DC sites!!

■ **-ARE YOU READY ?-**
LYRICS IN FRENCH, INTERVIEWS IN ENGLISH... A really nice page ! Don't miss it ! Soon to be totally in French and English...

■ **AC/DC Picture Page**
Lots of AC/DC pics!

■ **AC/DC, Dioses del Rock (Now in English too)**

■ **The World Heaviest Rock'N'Roll Band**
Different line-ups from 74 to 95, discography, videography, one of the most complete list of book and tour program with complete description, Bon Scott tribute page, links, info on Fan Mag and Fan club, story of the band...tons of pics !...

■ **Niteranger's AC/DC Page!**
A brand new AC/DC site featuring AC/DC links, pics, discography, etc.

■ **AC/DC LANDSLIDE GOLD**
A site for all AC/DC fans out there. Links, info, pics and much more

■ **Angus Rules!**
An AC/DC site...Has tabs, pics, and much more.

■ **Sin City**
Come have a look around. We've got lyrics, pics, member biogs, guitar tabs and lots more!!

■ **Let There Be Rock**

■ **Spike's AC/DC Page**
A basic intro to the band

■ **AC/DC**

■ **AC/DC If you want blood**

■ **AC/DC – The Jack**
Clips of every AC/DC song in WAV and RealAudio. Biogs, chat, discography, faq, pictures, links, lyrics, guitar tabs and all the latest AC/DC news.

■ **RanDog's AC/DC Art Page**
RanDog's AC/DC Art Page is a compilation of some of my graphics work, as it relates to AC/DC

■ **Sin City**

■ **Virtual Angus's Page**
AC/DC tribute band info, pics, wavs

■ **AC/DC – MetalMid**
A lot of MIDIs of AC/DC for download!!!

■ **The Bomb**
A bunch of pictures and wave and movie files. Some kick ass shit coming soon.

■ **SIN/CITY - A tribute to AC/DC**
The AC/DC Coverband SIN/CITY from Germany. The CD, Info, tour dates, contact, booking of the band, AC/DC links and more.

"I just got out my little black book the minute that you said goodbye..."

(sort of abridged from Arthur Lee and Love's cover of Bacharach and David's 'My Little Red Book')

the black book company

box 2030
pewsey
sn9 5qz
england

telephone
+ 44 (0)
7970 783652

fax
+ 44 (0)
1672 564433

email
dhende7730@aol.com

via the internet
www.blackbookco.com

The Black Book Mafia

regular guys
Dave Henderson
07970 783652
Howard Johnson
0976 916319

art guru
Keith Drummond

silent but deadly
Gary Perry
Nick Clode
0171 537 7144

accountingly
Karen Hansell
0171 537 7144

warehoused
Claire Thompson
@ Turnaround Publisher Services
0181 829 3009

So, what's the Black Book Company all about?

Well, we're interested in music. Listening. Searching for interesting unique stuff. Hearing new things. Understanding how people consume music and quite frankly the effect it has on them.

Around the time of the "Punk Rock Wars" at the end of the '70s, the media asked "Can music really change anything?". Well, we at the Black Book Company think it can. We *know* it can. And, our books intend to look at the effect that music has on the fans and the famous.

In *Touched By The Hand Of Bob* and *Get Your Jumbo Jet Out Of My Airport*, we examine the undoubted power of, respectively, Bob Dylan and AC/DC. We reveal the obsessions of fandom and the effect that these heroes have on us, you and whoever.

Each book paints a unique caricature of its subject, by analysing real life experiences, well-researched tales and the inevitable anecdotal pub-talk. Each book looks at the effect that these idols have had on the world, complete with bibliographies, chronological biographies and, of course discographies aplenty.

"Wow! A demo version of The Buzzcocks' 'Spiral Scratch' EP autographed by Howard Devoto. Now, that's what I call sexy!"

"The Black Book Company? Why, I read virtually nothing else when I need to know about music."

This is just the start...

We'll be publishing 12 books over the next three years, cross referencing each title, but possibly not the DC and Bob, using you the readers and your music-related experineces to give a more complete picture of the next projects we undertake. So, read on, look at our publishing schedule and, er, get back to us.

And, this is the team...

DAVE HENDERSON is the Creative Director for the EMAP Metro Music Group, which includes Q, Mojo, Select, Mixmag, Kerrang! and Smash Hits. He writes regularly for Q and publishes his own music magazine called Happenstance.

HOWARD JOHNSON is Associate Editor of Football 365/Music 365. He was the Creative Director for Bizarre magazine and has written for just about everyone about music and sport.

KEITH DRUMMOND is the Art Director of Q Magazine. Formerly art editor of Select, he now rules the Letraset cupboard at the UK music market's biggest selling magazine, with a readership of 750,000-plus.

GARY PERRY and NICK CLODE fix things.

our catalogue items

Touched By The Hand Of Bob
EPIPHANAL BOB DYLAN EXPERIENCES
FROM A BUICK SIX
by Dave Henderson
PUBLISHED: June 1, 1999
Paperback, heavyweight matt
finish, fully illustrated
ISBN: 1-902799-00-3

Like remembering how you heard about the assassination of
John Lennon, the world and their Walkman all have a story
about their experience with Bob Dylan. The fans - Tim, Martin,
Karl, Clare, Lambchop - and the famous - Jack Nicholson,
Roger McGuinn, Billy Bragg, Paul McCartney, Bono, Jerry
Garcia, Sheryl Crow, Elvis Costello, Cameron Crowe - all tell
the tale of being touched by the hand of Bob.

Dave Henderson delves deep into Dylanland, discovering
Fatwa-invoking fanatics, rune-juggling astrologers, hi-brow
intellectuals and a bizarre circus of followers. Touched By The
Hand Of Bob follows Dylan's miracle-strewn journey, meeting
the people who covered his songs, copied his haircut and
grabbed at the hem of his frock coat. They walk among us...

THE AUTHOR
After spending a year trying to entice Bob Dylan to attend the
Q Awards, Dave Henderson saw the blind devotion which sur
rounded Dylan's appearance at the Glastonbury Festival, he
became enthralled by the mercurial music, then by the global
effect of Dylan's very presence. While planning the 1999 Q
Awards, he dived head first into the mysterious power of Bob.

THE RADIO PROGRAMME
The book has been com
missioned as a BBC Radio 2
series and airs Autumn
1999.

Get Your Jumbo Jet Out Of My Airport
RANDOM NOTES FOR AC/DC OBSESSIVES
by Howard Johnson
PUBLISHED: June 1, 1999
Paperback, heavyweight matt finish,
fully illustrated
ISBN: 1-902799-01-1

When AC/DC vocalist Bon Scott died in
1980 few could have envisaged that 19
years later the group would still be one
of the world's most enduring hard rock
acts. But what's the real AC/DC story? And why are they still
so popular on the back of nothing more than a few boogie chords
and a schoolboy uniform?

Get Your Jumbo Jet Out Of My Airport is the first book ever to
fully document the group's massive appeal. From the obsessive owners of 500 bootlegs to the record company execs and
producers who have brought AC/DC to the world, Howard
Johnson has interviewed them all. The result is a collection of
the finest anecdotes and most revealing tales, revealing why
AC/DC remain so special, so important and so influential.
Delivering one of the most revealing pictures of the band ever,
with a wealth of previously unseen pictures, this is a work of
frankly lunatic devotion.

THE AUTHOR
Howard Johnson saw his first AC/DC gig in 1979 aged 15,
wearing shorts and school blazer. His dress sense, however,
has improved in the last 20 years and he's managed to per
suade such publications as Mojo, Q, FHM, The Daily
Telegraph, FourFourTwo, New Woman and Total Sport among
others that he can write a
bit too. Last book he
authored? British Lions
rugby captain Martin
Johnson's diary of the
incredible 1997 Tour To
South Africa. This has
very little to do with
AC/DC, of course, but we
thought you might find it
interesting anyway.

coming autumn 1999

Leaving The 20th Century
LAST WORDS ON ROCK 'N' ROLL
by Dave Henderson and Howard Johnson
ISBN 1-902799-02-X
Published: October 1, 1999
Paperback, 196-pages, fully-illustrated

Tribute albums, fond memories, conventions and super fandom reach new levels when the icon of your idealism dies. In Leaving The 20th Century, Dave Henderson and Howard Johnson have collected a moving collection of rock 'n' roll obituaries, inked by the fans, the famous and the familiar. As we head for the year 2000, Leaving The 20th Century looks at the people who built modern music and the effect their spiralling from the planet has had. From Elvis Presley, Kurt Cobain, Keith Moon, Buddy Holly, Clarence White, Tim Buckley, Jerry Garcia, Tim Hardin, Brian Jones, Freddie Mercury, Pete Ham, Sterling Morrison, Marvin Gaye, Ian Curtis, Frank Sinatra, Tupac Shakur, Joe Meek, Michael Hutchence, Nico, Sam Cooke, Randy Rhoads, John Lennon, Jeff Buckley, Richard Manuel and Sid Vicious to Tiny Tim and The Singing Nun.

Mirror ROCK STAR DIES IN CRASH

A AMERICAN rock 'n' roll singer star Eddie Cochran died yesterday after a car taking him to London Airport crashed.

Flung out as car is wrecked

The toll: 30
628 injured

CARL WILSON (1946-98)

CARL WILSON of the THE BEACH BOYS has died from complications from lung cancer. He was 51.

Wilson died on Friday evening (February 6) at an LA hospital attended by his wife Gina (daughter of Dean Martin) and his two sons. The group's publicist Alyson Dutch said Wilson was diagnosed with lung cancer last year but insisted on touring with the group while undergoing chemotherapy. At the time of his death, The Beach Boys had been lining up another US tour.

A private funeral is planned for this week, Dutch said.

Carl Wilson was the youngest member of The Beach Boys. When he was 14 and his brothers, 16-year-old Dennis and 19-year-old Brian, were asked to sing at their school, Hawthorne High. Legend has it that Carl didn't want to. To encourage him, Brian christened the band Carl & The Passions. The name would eventually be resurrected for a Beach Boys album 20 years later.

Carl's influence was felt in the quality of his harmonies – like Brian, he had perfect pitch – more than his songwriting which in the band's early days was the preserve of Brian.

As Brian Wilson's mental health deteriorated, however, Carl's input into the band grew. He contributed a number of songs to the 'Surf's Up' album and produced the 1972 LP 'Holland'.

Carl continued to tour on and off with the band until 1981 when he left to record an eponymous solo album. He returned to the band full-time after Dennis Wilson drowned in 1983. The Beach Boys last had a big hit in 1988 with 'Kokomo'.

Hank Williams (R.I.P.; 1923-

The usual celeb of good-looking corpses, funny-looking lit Actually, he took finished off the bottle finish

"I'll Never Get Out of This World Alive" Williams yowled sardonically on one of his countless hits, yet just because he knew which way he was headed, didn't mean he could stop. Country music's original bad boy was a streaking comet, who crash-landed at 29. But he's much more than a perversely picturesque disaster.

His fame has been on a slow simmer ever since. Every country singer coming up--and half the rockers--cite him as an influence for his genius in melding country, blues and pop. And he paved the way for all who followed, by writing brilliantly and from the heart on cuts like "Cold, Cold

LAL WATERSON

Lal Waterson, folk singer and songwriter, died from cancer on September 4 aged 55. She was born on February 15, 1943.

A MEMBER of Britain's foremost family of traditional singers, Lal Waterson had a plaintive voice that was one of the great glories of English folk music. She formed the Watersons with her older siblings, Norma and Michael Waterson, her cousin John Harrison and later her brother-in-law Martin Carthy. Their rich a cappella harmonies made them the most influential vocal group of the 1960s folk revival, and they were headline performers at festivals around the world. Lal Waterson went on to become an imaginative and unorthodox songwriter in her own right, and later sang and recorded with her adult children, Maria and Oliver Knight.

The Waterson family came from Hull, and music was always in the blood. But Elaine Waterson's first love was painting and she went to a school specialising in art at the age of 11. Always known as Lal, she worked for a time as a heraldic artist, but her singing career

1964 on the New Voices an- ing Steve Winwood, who later the song John Barleycorn. writing original songs in a contemporary folk style, resulting

Lal Waterson with her folk singer son Oliver Knight

KURT COBAIN

FLESH RAG

No. 490 APRIL 16, 1994 £1.40

THE DAILY TELEGRAPH

ARTS

Reaching out for heav

DEATH at Jerry Garcia so mournfully watched on his memorable Live / Dead album, don't have no mercy. 60, and at 1995 with Garcia's own death still seems to me to be the

Charles Spencer mourns the death this year of Jerry Garcia, unofficial leader of the Grateful Dead and standard-bearer of the hippie generation's

When the weird get going, Jerry Garcia celebrates his 50th birthday on August 1, 1992, by playing for Deadheads at Irvine

TRIBUTE

LAURA NYRO
1947-1997

SINGER/SONGWRITER LAURA Nyro, whose original, pioneering fusion of soul, gospel, jazz, R&B and pop created a catalog of million-selling hits for artists ranging from Three Dog Night to Barbra Streisand, died at her home in Danbury, Conn., on April 8. An intensely private woman, Nyro chose not to make public her two-year battle with ovarian cancer, which ended her life at age 49.

Debuting in 1966 as a teen prodigy, Nyro was the youngest most successful woman songwriter of her time. Her own records, while critically acclaimed, never drew a large audience, and Nyro attained her greatest fame as a songwriter for others, including Three Dog Night ("Eli's Coming"), Blood, Sweat & Tears ("And When I Die"), Barbra Streisand ("Stoney End") and the Fifth Dimension ("Wedding Bell Blues").

Nyro retired to the New England countryside in the early '70s. Following a silence, in 1976 she returned to recording with the subdued, jazz-tinged Smile. After the birth of son Gil Bianchini, in 1978, the head, feminism, ecological rights came to the fore in Mother's Spiritual and Dog and Light the Light views, Nyro was a graphical. In 1988, after from the concert stage Angeles Times, "Some one occasion to find and Singer Patti LaBelle, Nyro as the godmother Zuri, said of Nyro, "I spiritual person. She live life; she didn't see the glamour."

Earlier this year, Col retrospective, The Bea Stoned Soul Picnic. Set month is the tribute Love: The Music of Laura Place Recordings), featuring members Nyro as "a comfort" and even though she is a part of her generation really a poet for just an tions. ... I am sad that s

None of the artists tribute album knew of first clients when he was a manager, she signed with Columbia, where she recorded 1968's Eli and the Thirteenth Con

After becoming one of David Geffen's first clients when he was a manager, she signed with Columbia, where she recorded 1968's Eli and the Thirteenth Confession

news

PAGES 4, 6, 7, 8 & 9: GAVIN BUSH INJURED IN FRACAS WITH FANS, PENTHOUSE FACE PORN MAG WRIT, JOHNNY CASH HOSPITALISED, PEARL JAM ALBUM DETAILS

HUTCHENCE FOUND DEAD

MICHAEL HUTCHENCE was found dead in a hotel room in Sydney, Australia on Saturday (November 22).

...and then

Young At Heart

Dave Henderson has begun work collecting people's first, second and indeed third-hand experiences through the music of Neil Young.

He's very interested to hear from fans of Neil whose life has changed through Neil's music, who experienced a pivotal breakthrough or maybe a simple epiphanal moment. Perhaps it's you.

Were you the person listening to 'After The Goldrush' who suddenly through a hazy ambience saw God? Were you one of those people who wondered whatever happened to the sleeve of 'Harvest' that was supposed to self-destruct after a certain time?

Are you puzzled why 'On The Beach' has never been released on CD and are having a life-crisis coming to terms with it? Or were you in the parking lot at Warner Brothers, in Burbank, California, when Neil's car was blocked in and he allegedly resorted to "putting the boot in" on the blocker's motor?

Or could it be, that you were thrown out of your bedsit for playing "Arc:Weld" at sleep-prohibiting volume? Whatever your story is, Dave would like to hear it. You can contact him at The Black Book Company, Box 2030, Pewsey SN9 5QZ.

Glastonbury 2000

The in-depth story of the Glastonbury Festival told by the people who've worked on the event from day one. Exclusive interviews and anecdotes already stockpiling from the people who've played there, the thousands of on-site workers, the local Pilton community, the stars who've performed, from Radiohead and the Manics to Rolf Harris and Al Green.

If you've braved the sun, the rain or anything in between, then we'd like to hear from you at The Black Book Company, Box 2030, Pewsey SN9 5QZ.

ordering information

YOU CAN order books published by the Black Book Company direct from us, or through our website at www.blackbookco.com
(details of which are on the next page).

<u>DIRECT BY MAIL</u>
You can order copies of our titles for £13.50 each (including post and packing in the UK and within the EC).

For overseas orders, please add £1 (outside of EC but within Europe) or £3 (USA, Canada and Australia).

If you'd like to order more than one copy, please add £1 per additional copy. Please make cheques payable to the BLACK BOOK COMPANY LTD.

If you'd like to order in bulk (over five copies), then please fax your request to us at
+44 (0) 1672 564433

Or email us on
dhende7730@aol.com

<u>TITLES CURRENTLY AVAILABLE</u>
TOUCHED BY THE HAND OF BOB
by Dave Henderson
GET YOUR JUMBO JET OUT OF MY AIRPORT
by Howard Johnson

<u>WE ARE NOW ACCEPTING
ADVANCE ORDERS FOR...</u>
LEAVING THE TWENTIETH CENTURY
by Dave Henderson and Howard Johnson
(published October 1, 1999)

<u>IF YOU'D LIKE TO GET ON OUR MAILING LIST...</u>
For special offers, limited edition items and news on upcoming projects, then send your address to us by fax or email, or write to us at

THE BLACK BOOK COMPANY
BOX 2030
PEWSEY
SN9 5QZ
ENGLAND

Surf right on in for Black Book news

Find out what we're doing now, what we're doing next.

Form a direct and speedy link back to us. Get involved.

www.blackbookco.com

Find out about all kinds of Black Book Paraphernalia
Buy our books, deluxe editions, postcards, limited edition stamps direct

Find out more about our books
Bow down at
The Temple Of Bob

including book extracts, sound files of interviews, audio from the bizarre world of Dylan, fan e-mails (and lighbulb information), rare photos and links to other sites.

Go deep into
JumboJetland

Including extracts, sound files, quotes, audio of the worst DC Covers, fan e-mails (discussing the intricacies of Angus' picking), rare photos and links to other DC sites.

Read extracts from upcoming projects
LEAVING THE TWENTIETH CENTURY. BECK THREW UP. YOUNG AT HEART

Then, find out who we are by entering our connected areas
Daveworld
Where things are Strange and twangy
HoJoLand
Where Things Ain't Right
Drummond Base
Where art gets brainwashed

Online from June 1, 1999

Design of great beauty by Steve Hunt

CBS Records · 28/30 Theobalds Road · London WC1

the black book company